CONTENTS

....

INTRODUCTION

Most people are familiar with the famous figures in history, like Julius Caesar, Aristotle, Cleopatra, Henry VIII, George Washington and so on. And most people have some vague sense of the times these people lived in, like the Victorian era, ancient Rome or the Dark Ages. These are the things we learned about in school, and continue to see explored in books, documentaries and movies.

These figures and their cultures are responsible for much of the world we live in today, their influence still visible in our language, architecture, politics, religion and art. So it is fitting that such significant characters and events form the mainstay of our historical studies.

And while the great events, luminaries and movements of the past can be fascinating subjects, there are other, smaller histories that are also worth the telling, and that I've always found engrossing. For every great figure from the mists of time, there were countless others, mostly ordinary people, whose names have been long forgotten. There were also innumerable less well-known tales about famed figures that don't usually make it into the history books. Similarly there were lesser-known events of note that were greatly overshadowed by more famed or influential happenings.

And yet these fringe events often make fascinating reading in themselves. I suppose in part I've always loved exploring these minor historical figures and events as they can often have more of a resonance with insignificant mortals like myself. What I mean is, I can never fully identify with, say, Julius Caesar or Napoleon, as I've never personally ruled an empire or commanded an army. At least not yet. But it's a little easier to feel a connection with the lesser lights or events of history, most of which tales remain largely untold.

Not because they brought down kings, changed societies, created philosophies or led invasions, but because they are often startling, touching, amusing, educational or quite simply unbelievable. In other words, Genghis Khan's Mongol invasions might be extremely important historical subject matter, but wouldn't you also like to learn about the women employed to test-drive Catherine the Great's lovers, the man who survived the guillotine, the flaming camels of Mongolia or the real-life Frankenstein who went on tour 're-animating' bodies with electricity?

This is a collection of just such real-life tales loosely gathered into a handful of what you might call 'categories', although some tales could easily reside in more than one of these groupings. They may not broaden your understanding of human culture very much, but they'll most likely intrigue you, captivate you, revolt you or even make you laugh.

1

THE BIG SLEEP

....

It is something of an understatement to say that death is rife through-out history. It is so common, in fact, that there have been about one hundred billion cases of it, if you include every human who has ever lived and died up to this point. Roughly speaking, of course. Naturally, most deaths are fairly unremarkable affairs, except for the immediate families, and nowadays, most are relatively painless. Some passings have become enshrined in history's hallowed halls for the effect they produced or the drama of the event, such as Julius Caesar's stabbing in the Roman senate, Christ's crucifixion, JFK's assassination and so on. Our history books also record less dramatic famous deaths of kings, queens, politicians, generals and the like by mundane things like heart attacks, old age, beheading etc. These famed figures' fol-lowers often came to boringly generalised ends, such as 'ten thousand men perished in the battle of such and such', but as a general rule, most deaths barely even merit a statistic.

But with all the billions of cases on the books, so to speak, inevi-tably more than a few unusual deaths or consequences of death have come to pass, and below are just a handful, randomly selected, of the innumerable curious, bizarre, creepy or downright funny samples of humans meeting their maker.

Although this section is by no means chronological, we begin with one of the oldest recorded strange deaths, the victim of which also gave us a frequently used modern term. Around 620 BC, Draco, the Greek legislator of Athens, introduced a new set of written laws, said to have literally been written in blood and remarkable for their harshness – even trivial crimes were punishable by death. His name gives us the word *draconian*.

Despite the toughness of his code, he was a popular man in ancient circles. Folklore holds that after his address to the crowd in the Aeginetan theatre, the masses began to applaud enthusiastically and rain their hats and cloaks down on him in support. Unfortunately, they overdid the adulation a bit – Draco was buried under a small mountain of clothing and suffocated. But you can probably take that tale with a pinch of salt.

Remaining in the classical world but moving on a couple of centuries takes us to the Greek philosopher Heraclitus. One of history's great thinkers, he gave us such wonderful philosophical insights as, 'There is nothing permanent except change,' 'Much learning does not teach understanding,' and, 'Man is most nearly himself when he achieves the seriousness of a child at play.' Philosophy was clearly his thing.

Heraclitus.

Medicine wasn't. When he developed dropsy, a painful accumulation of fluid beneath the skin, he reputedly experimented with various cures, mostly involving cow dung. One version of the story has him burying himself in a manure pit in a cowshed, believing that the manure would draw out the excess fluid. It didn't, and he died in rather unpleasant surroundings. Another version has him smeared in dung and lying under the hot sun, essentially baking himself alive. But the most popular version of his death is the one in which he covered his entire body in dung, the stench of which attracted a pack of wild dogs who ate him alive.

By far the funniest – sorry, of course I meant *most tragic* – Classical death has to be that of Aeschylus, one of ancient Greece's greatest playwrights. With supreme irony, he is known as 'the father of the tragedy'. Much of Aeschylus's work has survived, more than can be said for the man himself when he went on a trip to Sicily in 458 BC, aged roughly sixty-five.

Roman historian Valerius Maximus wrote that the balding Aeschylus was sitting outside, enjoying the warmth of the sun, when a passing eagle mistook his shiny head for a nice rock on which to smash open the tortoise shell it had clutched between its talons. Literary giant killed by falling tortoise. Death clearly has no favourites, and no regard for dignity.

The unfortunate end of Aeschylus.

BLOODY MESS

If you're in any way squeamish, skip this bit. Botched executions are far more frequent in history than you might imagine, and are actually still a contentious issue today, especially in the US. They are frequently cited as an argument for abolishing capital punishment, and indeed they have resulted in such in certain countries or at the very least, the changing of the method of execution.

Anders 'Sjællænder' Nielsen.

Young people may be shocked to learn that France only abolished death by guillotine in 1981, and carried out its last execution by this method in 1977. Almost as shocking is that many European countries were still beheading people with an axe and block in the late nineteenth and even the twentieth century. Germany only abolished the practice in 1935 (Hitler replaced it with the guillotine). Sweden carried out its last beheading – by manual cleaver – in 1900. And in Denmark, the public execution of Anders 'Sjællænder' Nielsen in 1882 generated such a scandal and such widespread horror, that it would be a contributing factor in the abolition of capital punishment ten years later.

This execution was to take place as near as possible to where the crime (a murder) had been committed, presumably so the people most affected could see justice being carried out. Unfortunately, the executioner, one Jens Seistrup, had a nasty hangover after a night's heavy drinking. His first swing of the axe hit Nielsen's shoulder, and the man cried out in agony. His second blow cracked open Nielsen's head and the axe lodged there, yet the man was still alive. The third blow finally decapitated him.

And things became even more gruesome then. Several of the surrounding crowd rushed at the headless corpse with cupped hands in an attempt to catch the gushing blood, apparently driven by a local superstition that it could magically cure certain diseases. Whether they drank this or applied it to the skin is not recorded, which is just as well. Reports of the horrific scene caused the minister for justice to immediately bring an end to public executions and replace the axe with the guillotine. At least it was a start.

Not quite as gruesome, though not far behind, the execution by hanging of Robert Goodale in Norwich in 1885 was a horrific experience for executioner and witnesses, and quite likely the executed man. Robert Goodale was a fifteen-stone man, who'd been condemned for murdering his unfaithful wife. When executioner James Berry saw his size, he decided to shorten the rope length by a couple of feet, but not by enough. Because of Goodale's weight, his head was torn completely off his shoulders, traumatising all present.

A parting of the ways for Robert Goodale.

Goodale's horrific end was not the first or the last accidental decapitation. No less horrific was the execution of Thomas Ketchum in New Mexico in 1901. A train robber in the classic Wild West mode, Ketchum had moved up to murder before he was captured and sentenced to death.

Ketchum put on considerable weight while in custody, and this was not factored into the length of the rope used, resulting in his decapitation. The sight was greeted with horror by most present, with the exception of a photographer who recorded the entire thing for posterity and likely made a tidy profit selling the images to the press. You can still buy postcards in Clayton featuring the gruesome shots – it seems to be the town's only claim to fame.

In the interests of sexual equality, it seems fair to reference the botched execution of Eva Dugan, in Arizona in 1930. Dugan was convicted of murdering her chicken rancher employer with an axe, and the theft of his automobile and other possessions. The execution is notable for being the first of a woman in the state, and also the first with female witnesses present. Given what transpired, in retrospect they probably would have relinquished that honour.

The lever was pulled at 5am. Dugan dropped through the trapdoor, the rope severing her head. Her headless corpse crashed to the ground and her head reportedly rolled to the feet of the witnesses, five of whom (two women and three men) fainted at the horrific sight.

Following this, the gas chamber replaced the gallows, leaving Dugan with the dubious distinction of being the only woman executed by hanging in the state.

Our species has always been adept at developing new methods of capital punishment – sometimes for humane reasons, sometimes out of cruelty and sometimes as a deterrent. The famous guillotine, for example, despite its bloody reputation, was invented out of humanitarian motives.

Despite its name, it was very much *not* the invention of French doctor Joseph-Ignace Guillotin. The highly respected physician was opposed to the death penalty, but he had expressed the view that as a first step towards its abolition, a more humane method of execution should be devised, such as a mechanical device. He reputedly said, 'Now, with my machine, I cut off your head in the twinkling of an eye, and you never feel it.'

The use of the words 'my machine' resulted in the renaming of the device, which had already been invented by one Antoine Louis, another Parisian doctor. In fact, Louis's bloody contraption was known for several years as the Louisette, until Guillotin's name became associated with it.

While Guillotin was horrified to have his name associated with the decapitation device, and his family unsuccessfully petitioned the government to change the name, poor Louis had to settle for a giving his name to a term that is virtually unknown to the general public – the *angle of Louis* is the medical term for a joint between the manubrium and body of the sternum (or 'breastbone').

The first use of Louis's device was on a highwayman called Peletier on 25 April 1792, and a huge crowd gathered to witness the novel contraption. All went well, at least from the authorities' point of view, as Peletier was decapitated in the blink of an eye. Despite the massive spillage of blood, the crowd were incensed at the lack of 'entertainment', the execution having been so quick. There were chants of 'bring back the gallows!' and 'bring back the breaking wheel!' The authorities would respond in subsequent years by providing a near endless supply of victims for 'Madame Guillotine', as the device became known, and countless hours of happy diversion for the bloodthirsty crowds.

A bizarre footnote to the above: During France's Reign of Terror, there were multiple accounts of severed heads blinking, lips moving, even of heads moaning or speaking. In one famous case, the executioner raised the severed head of assassin Charlotte Corday and slapped her cheek, and the crowd were amazed to witness an apparent expression of indignation forming.

Ghoulish curiosity about severed heads' possible consciousness led to an experiment by one Dr Beaurieux in 1905. He was given permission to examine the head of an executed prisoner called Henri Languille. It is difficult to imagine a purpose for this exercise, other than morbid curiosity, but then you're probably going to continue reading this bit for the same reason ...

So, what did Dr Beaurieux witness?

Here, then, is what I was able to note immediately after the decapitation: the eyelids and lips of the guillotined man worked in irregularly rhythmic contractions for about five or six seconds. This phenomenon has been remarked by all those finding themselves in the same conditions as myself for observing what happens after the severing of the neck ...

I waited for several seconds. The spasmodic movements ceased. The face relaxed, the lids half closed on the eyeballs, leaving only the white of the conjunctiva visible, exactly as in the dying whom we have occasion to see every day in the exercise of our profession, or as in those just dead. It was then that I called in a strong, sharp voice: 'Languille!' I saw the eyelids slowly lift up, without any spasmodic contractions – I insist advisedly on

ORLÉANS 1905 — Exécution de Languille

The execution of Henri Langui le by Guillotine in 1905.

this peculiarity – but with an even movement, quite distinct and normal, such as happens in everyday life, with people awakened or torn from their thoughts.

Next Languille's eyes very definitely fixed themselves on mine and the pupils focused themselves. I was not, then, dealing with the sort of vague dull look without any expression, that can be observed any day in dying people to whom one speaks: I was dealing with undeniably living eyes which were looking at me. After several seconds, the eyelids closed again, slowly and evenly, and the head took on the same appearance as it had had before I called out.

It was at that point that I called out again and, once more, without any spasm, slowly, the eyelids lifted and undeniably living eyes fixed themselves on mine with perhaps even more penetration than the first time. Then there was a further closing of the eyelids. I attempted the effect of a third call; there was no further movement – and the eyes took on the glazed look, which they have in the dead.

The whole thing had lasted twenty-five to thirty seconds.

One method of execution was so horrific that its conception almost defies belief, given that it was used in relatively modern times. 'Blowing from a gun,' as it became known, was a method of execution used on and off since the sixteenth century, although it was more off than on, given its nature. It really came into its own with the British authorities in India in the latter half of the nineteenth century.

The execution involved securing a prisoner with the small of his back against the barrel of a cannon, although occasionally the prisoner was tied facing the weapon, with his stomach pressing against the muzzle. A blank cartridge or grapeshot was usually used, but the use of cannonballs was not uncommon. The gun was fired, and one can imagine the result. Actually, you don't have to imagine, as George Carter Stent, British officer, writer and lexicographer, left us a first-hand account:

> *The prisoner is generally tied to a gun with the upper part of the small of his back, nesting against the muzzle. When the gun is fired, his head is seen to go straight up into the air some forty or fifty feet; the arms fly off right and left, high up in the air, and fall at, perhaps, a hundred yards distance; the legs drop to the ground beneath the muzzle of the gun; and the body is literally blown away altogether, not a vestige being seen.*

The method was only used on native soldiers found guilty of desertion or mutiny, and was done in front of the massed ranks of other native soldiers, as a deterrent. Yes, it probably would have something of a deterrent effect, I would imagine.

Of course, like most methods of execution, it didn't always go according to plan. Here is a contemporary account by the pacifist American Peace Society:

> *One wretched fellow slipped from the rope by which he was tied to the guns just before the explosion, and his arm was nearly set*

on fire. While hanging in his agony under the gun, a sergeant applied a pistol to his head; and three times the cap snapped, the man each time wincing from the expected shot. At last a rifle was fired into the back of his head, and the blood poured out of the nose and mouth like water from a briskly handled pump. This was the most horrible sight of all. I have seen death in all its forms, but never anything to equal this man's end.

'Blowing from a gun'.

Let us make one last visit to the bloody pool of state-sponsored killing, notable for its incredible brutality. If you're squeamish, skip the next bit.

William the Silent, as he was known, was silenced forever in July 1584 by an assassin called Balthasar Gérard. William, also known as the Prince of Orange, led the Dutch revolt against the Catholic Spanish Hapsburgs that sparked the Dutch War of Independence. Gérard, on the other hand, was a Catholic and supporter of Philip II of Spain.

Gérard managed to break into William's palace in Delft. He waited until the nobleman passed, then sprung out and shot William with two pistols, killing him. He fled, but was captured immediately and severely beaten. Before his trial, his gaolers devised some punishments of their own. They put wet leather boots on his feet and then dried them over a fire, causing the leather to contract tightly, crushing and burning his feet. He was hanged from a post outside his cell and flogged on a daily basis.

But his pain was far from over. Tried and found guilty, the magistrates delivered a sentence that was gruesome even by the brutal standards of the age. One has to imagine them sitting down and discussing the sentence in detail before agreeing to it, with each of them tossing in increasingly barbarous and perverse elements. Balthasar Gérard was sentenced to, eh, well, let's leave it to a contemporary, French historian Seigneur de Brantome, to explain:

> The assassin of William of Orange was abandoned to what seems like an infinity of vengeance. On the first day, he was taken to the square where he found a cauldron of boiling water, in which was submerged the arm with which he had committed the crime. The next day the arm was cut off, and, since it fell at his feet, he was constantly kicking it up and down the scaffold; on the third day, red-hot pincers were applied to his breasts and the front of his arm and on the fourth day, the pincers were applied similarly on the back of his arm and on his buttocks; and thus, consecutively, this man was tortured for eighteen days. On the last day, he was put to the wheel and 'mailloti' [beaten with a wooden club]. After six hours, he was still asking for water, which was not given him. Finally the police magistrate was begged to put an end to him by strangling, so that his soul should not despair and be lost.

By some accounts, he was actually still alive even at this point, but they weren't done yet. Next up he was to be disembowelled, quartered and his heart torn from his chest and flung in his face. 'His lips were seen to move up to the moment when his heart was thrown in his face. Then,' said a looker-on, 'he gave up the ghost.'

The assassination of William the Silent.

But just to be absolutely sure, the magistrates had further decreed that his head was to be severed. They didn't believe in half measures back then.

We can look back at the horror of these events now from the comfort of our moral high ground, safe in the knowledge that modern society has moved on from such barbarities. Unfortunately, executions are still a daily part of life in many developed countries, and nightmarish scenarios like the botched executions described above are a regular occurrence in certain middle-eastern countries. In reality, humanity will only have moved on when terms like gas chamber, electric chair and beheading are as obsolete on the planet as the practice of crucifixion.

Death is no laughing matter, but given enough time and distance from the event, we can sometimes have a good giggle with a clear conscience.

Among those whose passing has raised a chuckle or two down the years was Hans Steininger in 1567. The burgomaster or chief magistrate of the Bavarian town of Braunau (more famous as the birthplace of Adolf Hitler), Steininger was already notable for having possibly the world's longest beard – almost one-and-a-half metres, or almost five

Hans Steininger.

feet. When walking about, he would be obliged to roll the thing up and pin it to his chest in a leather pouch. Long beards were very fashionable at the time, and he was clearly out to impress the ladies with the length of his.

Unfortunately, when fire bells sounded one day, Hans scrambled to his feet to flee, having forgotten to gather his beard, and crashed to the ground, snapping his neck. Hair today, gone tomorrow.

You are what you eat, goes the saying, and if that's true, then King Adolf Frederick of Sweden was a meal consisting of substantial portions of lobster, caviar, smoked herrings, saurkraut and champagne, topped off with fourteen servings of his favourite dessert: semlor, a very filling sweetened bun stuffed with cream and served in warm milk. Yum. He dropped dead soon after this dinner, entering posterity as 'the king who ate himself to death'.

The scales of justice have a strange way of balancing out on occasion, as evidenced by a courtroom drama enacted in Ohio in 1871. A man called Thomas McGehan was brought to trial for the alleged shooting dead of one Tom Myers. His defence attorney was Clement Vailandigham, a famed and controversial political figure who had headed an anti-war faction in the Democratic party and opposed the abolition of slavery.

Clement Vailandigham.

During the trial, Vailandigham decided to prove that Myers had accidentally shot himself while rising from a kneeling position and simultaneously drawing his weapon. He repeated the action with a borrowed pistol he believed to be unloaded, but the gun apparently snagged on his pocket as he rose. It discharged, shooting him in the abdomen, and he died of blood poisoning the following day. At least the demonstration proved effective, as Thomas McGehan was subsequently acquitted.

Returning to royalty, and the strange tale of Sunandha Kumariratana, the daughter of Mongkut, the King of Siam, he upon whom the famous Oscar-winning musical *The King and I* was based. Because the royal family was considered kind of divine, mere mortals like the entire population was forbidden from laying hands on them, under pain of death. Besides reducing certain earthly pleasures, such as getting a back rub, this particularly superior attitude had other drawbacks that probably hadn't been foreseen.

In 1880, fourteen years after her father's death, Sunandha and her daughter, Kannabhorn Bejaratana, were travelling to the royal palace

Princess Sunandha Kumariratana

when their boat capsized. Although it was near to shore and there were many onlookers, clearly none of them was a sufficiently devoted subject to commit suicide by rescuing the queen or her daughter, neither of whom could swim. So they just stood there, no doubt shaking their heads and 'tut-tutting' about it being such a shame, while the two royals disappeared beneath the surface. Killed by royal snobbery, you might say.

The death of Arius – the famous, some would say infamous, fourth-century theologian of Constantinople – is among the grossest in the history books, so if you're eating, stop now.

Without going into too much detail, suffice it to say that Arius had expressed views regarded by many as heretical. After he'd rowed back on his most extreme statements in 336 AD, the Holy Roman Emperor largely forgave him, and ordered Bishop Alexander of Constantinople to receive him.

But the Bishop wasn't in a forgiving mood. He prayed fervently that Arius would drop dead before he reached the Bishop's palace. And lo and behold, that's exactly what happened, and in the grossest way imaginable. Church historian Socrates of Constantinople – writing almost a century later it must be said, so to be regarded with a pinch of salt – described what happened on that fateful morning:

... going out of the imperial palace he paraded proudly through the midst of the city, attracting the notice of all the people. As he approached the place called Constantine's Forum, where the column of porphyry is erected, a terror arising from the remorse of conscience seized Arius, and with the terror a violent relaxation of the bowels: he therefore enquired whether there was a convenient place near, and being directed to the back of Constantine's Forum, he hastened thither. Soon after a faintness came over him, and

The rather gruesome death of Arius.

together with the evacuations his bowels protruded, followed by a copious hemorrhage, and the descent of the smaller intestines: moreover portions of his spleen and liver were brought off in the effusion of blood, so that he almost immediately died.

Given the obvious antipathy towards Arius (even by the historian), and the Bishop's stated wish to see Arius drop dead, one would be forgiven for smelling a rat, not to mention the unfortunate Arius's innards, even at this remove. He didn't so much evacuate his bowels as exterminate them.

Although it sounds suspiciously like an early Woody Allen movie, for quite a number of minor historical figures this was no laughing matter. Let's start with those supposedly devout celibates, the popes.

There is little recorded history regarding Pope Leo VII, especially as he only served as Pope for three years, and in that time made little impact on world or religious affairs. His mistress evidently did make something of an impact on him, however – in 939, he died of a massive heart attack while *in flagrante delicto*.

Just a few popes later came John XII, who made Leo look like an angel and a saint rolled into one. Incredibly, John was only an unprecedented eighteen when elected Pope, principally through the influence of his father. In the full flush of hormone-fuelled youth, he obviously decided that he wasn't going to waste his time on anything as trivial as God – not when he had the entire Catholic faith at his beck and call.

The holy father Pope John XII.

Most of his papal acts came about through the actions of his advisors, as it seems that John was too busy fornicating, gambling and toasting the devil. A contemporary described him as 'worthy of being the rival of Elagabalus [the decadent Roman emperor – see Chapter 8] ... a robber, a murderer, and an incestuous person, unworthy to represent Christ upon the pontifical throne ...'

John XII met his maker aged just twenty-seven, thanks entirely to his insatiable sexual appetite. Multiple versions of his end have been told. Among the most popular is that he had a massive stroke while having sex with an adulterous wife called Stefanetta. Another version is that Stefanetta's husband found the two having sex, and either beat the Pope to death with a mallet or threw him out of a high window, leaving one unholy mess in the Vatican courtyard below.

Lots of other popes before and after these two were sexually active, but we have to leap forward to the fifteenth century to find the next successor of Saint Peter to actually meet Saint Peter while enjoying some carnal distraction. This was Pope Paul II, who died in 1471. He introduced printing to the Papal States, bringing books to the masses. On the other hand, he was virulently anti-Semitic, and introduced a 'carnival' that saw Jews forced to run naked down a street in Rome for the

Another debauched pope – Paul II.

amusement of Christians. He also made it compulsory for Jews to wear a yellow handkerchief to indicate their faith, an idea that the Nazis borrowed in the 1930s and 1940s.

He also lavished vast amounts of money on purchasing jewels – an inventory after he died found a treasure horde fit for an Arabian tale. And talking of his death, the official story was that he had over-indulged in melon and had a heart attack. But he had previously been given the nickname Maria Pietissima (Our Lady of Pity), due to his propensity for crying and appearing pitiful when he wanted his own way, his effeminate manner and his propensity for dressing up in excessive finery, and some historians had little doubt he was homosexual. All of which supports the alternate version of his end – that he died while being sodomised by a pageboy.

Similarly ignominious was the passing of Félix François Faure, President of France for four years up to 1899. Of course, unlike in most western countries, it is almost *de rigueur* for male French politicians to have mistresses, although most of them tend to keep such affairs as private as possible.

Faure's mistress at the time was Marguerite 'Meg' Steinheil, a woman well known for her sexual liaisons with prominent people – including writers Emile Zola and Pierre Loti, composers Jules Massenet and Charles Gounod and diplomat and Suez canal developer Ferdinand de Lesseps. The President was her biggest catch yet.

On 16 February 1899, Marguerite paid Félix a visit in the Élysée Palace. Soon after she'd entered his private apartments, the President's aides heard frantic screams emanating from the rooms. They rushed in, to discover both in a state of undress, the President unconscious, his hand holding Marguerite's hair in a vice-like grip. His hold was so tight, they had to cut her hair to free him for treatment. But it was no use, as during their throes of passion, he had suffered a massive cerebral haemorrhage. He died later that night.

President Félix François Faure and Meg Steinheil

Madame Steinheil's position relative to the President, and the fact that he was clutching her hair, led the press and public to speculate that she'd been fellating him. This caused widespread tittering, and was the source of a few new jokes, including a nickname for Marguerite – 'la pompe funèbre' (meaning the mortician), based on a French pun on the word 'pump', also a euphemism for fellatio.

As if that wasn't enough scandal and intrigue for Marguerite, nine years later, she was arrested on charges of strangling her husband, Adolphe Steinheil, and her stepmother. The trial was a sensation, as many of Marguerite's lovers, past and present, were brought up to attest to her scandalous nature (among the most recent of these was King Sisowath of Cambodia!), causing widespread embarrassment for these society figures and much hilarity for the general public.

She was eventually acquitted, although suspicions remained and nobody else was charged with the murders. The judge described her evidence as 'a tissue of lies'. Marguerite lived to the ripe old age of ninety-five.

Britain, not to be outdone by the French, beat them to it with their own political sex and death scandal almost half a century earlier. Or so the rumour mill said at the time. Officially, Prime Minister Lord Palmerston passed away after a bout of pneumonia at the age of eighty. But rumours abounded at the time, and lingered ever since, that he actually died of a heart attack while having sex with a young maid on a billiard table.

British Prime Minister Lord Palmerston, who clearly had a strong constitution.

What diminishes this scandalous tale a little is that Lord Palmerston had long since retired from politics at that stage. What enhances it, however, is the fact that he was still able to mount both a billiard table and a young maid at the age of eighty.

Death offers no favour to the powerful and wealthy, as we've seen, although a woman called Megan Marshack was quite happy to offer favours of a certain kind to one of the richest men on the planet, Nelson Rockefeller. Rockefeller's wife at the time was Margaretta Large Fitler Murphy (I kid you not), more commonly known as 'Happy Murphy', but she must have been anything but happy at the events of 26 January 1979.

Screwed by the Grim Reaper.

The official version of the event had Rockefeller writing a book about his private art collection in the Rockefeller Centre when he suffered a major heart attack. In reality, the seventy-year-old was in the apartment of his pretty, bespectacled, blonde, twenty-six-year-old aide, Megan. The commonly held belief is that they were not discussing interest rates or political ambitions, but that Nelson had a heart attack in Megan's bed mid-orgasm.

His death famously caused *New York* magazine to remark, 'He thought he was coming, but he was going.'

2

ENOUGH TO MAKE
YOU SICK

Advancement in the medical sciences crawled along for millennia, and it is only in the past hundred years or so that serious progress has been made in treating human ailments. But even in the early twentieth century, mercury was still being used to treat such minor conditions as children's coughs; in the 1950s, companies in the US were selling the 'Z-Ray Applicator', which 'expanded the atoms in your body' and thus relieved rheumatism and arthritis in the elderly (just to be clear, there's no such thing as a 'Z-Ray'); and, most horrifyingly, lobotomies as a treatment for mental illness were still common up to the late 1960s! So perhaps we shouldn't scoff too much at the medical practices and practitioners of the distant past. Yet they often make for fascinating, if sometimes gruesome and occasionally buttock-clenching, reading.

SPIN DOCTORS

History has thrown up quite a few doctors who either prescribed the oddest of treatments, had the most unusual methods or simply needed to have their own heads examined.

Dr Robert Liston was a Scottish surgeon whose fame came primarily from his speed in performing amputations. This was in the age before anaesthesia, when lessening the agonies of the patient and minimising the risk of infection could be best served by getting the operation over as quickly as possible. Undoubtedly skilled as he was, however, Liston also became legendary in medical circles as the only man ever to perform an operation on one man and yet achieve a 300 percent mortality rate. But more of that anon.

Even those of us with the strongest stomachs and nerves can only imagine the force of will and the composure it takes first to slice into the leg or arm of a man or woman, and then to commence sawing through their bones, all while the restrained patient is fully conscious and shrieking in agony. Clearly, the sooner the limb was removed the better. Recognising this, Liston prided himself on rapid incision and sawing techniques, and could amputate a leg in two-and-a-half minutes. He is said to have carried out amputations in less than thirty seconds, but one has to assume that these were of hands or even fingers.

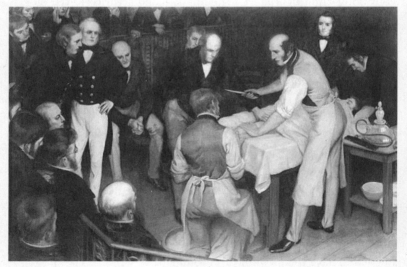

Dr Liston at work.

Liston entered the record books on 21 December 1846, becoming the first surgeon in England, and possibly even in Europe, to perform an operation using anaesthetic (ether), administered by a Dr Squire. This was a successful above-the-knee amputation on a Mr Frederick Churchill, at University College Hospital, London. He remarked afterwards to his audience

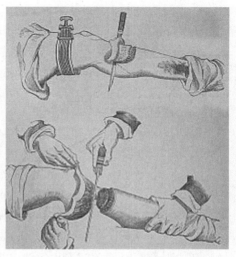

Two illustrations of Liston's surgical procedures.

of medical professionals, 'This Yankee dodge, gentlemen, beats mesmerism hollow.' More of so-called 'mesmerism' later.

Liston's term 'Yankee dodge' refers to the first operation in the world carried out using anaesthetic – performed by William TG Morton on 16 October 1846, in Massachusetts General Hospital, for which all those needing surgery on the planet can be eternally grateful.

English medical historian and surgeon Richard Gordon recounts Liston's most gruesome moment, though you have to take this tale with a pinch of salt. He once amputated a man's leg in less than three minutes, but the patient subsequently died of gangrene poisoning. Unfortunately, in his haste, Liston had also severed two fingers of a young colleague's hand, his assistant also perishing from gangrene. And lastly, his flashing scalpel slashed through the pants of another colleague, who was so alarmed at the possibility of damage to his privates, he dropped dead of a heart attack. Thus Liston achieved a triple death rate, even though there was only one patient.

Another Scot, and a contemporary of Liston, was Andrew Ure, who besides his medical practice, was also a reputable chemist, business theorist, scholar and scriptural geologist. 'What the hell is a scriptural geologist?' you might well ask. I had to look it up too. The nearest modern equivalent I could find was a creationist, and even back then, this earned Dr Ure some scorn.

That's not why he's featured in this book, though, but because of his experiments in re-animating the dead, which he revealed in 1818. Yes, you read that correctly. Bringing the dead back to life. And although *Frankenstein* was officially published that same year, Mary Shelley had started writing it a couple of years beforehand, so I can't credit Ure as a source of her inspiration.

Ure had been carrying out experiments on a hanged murderer called Matthew Clydesdale. Inserting metal rods into the body, he applied an electrical current to the phrenic nerve, which runs from the neck to the diaphragm. He startled the medical community by claiming he'd brought the corpse back to life, albeit briefly. He described the experiment thus:

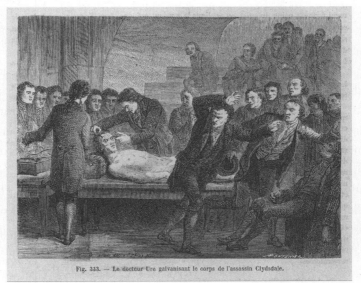

Fig. 333. — Le docteur Ure galvanisant le corps de l'assassin Clydsdale.

The body was made to perform the movements of breathing by stimulating the phrenic nerve and the diaphragm. Every muscle of the body was immediately agitated with convulsive movements resembling a violent shuddering from cold. On moving the second rod from hip to heel, the knee being previously bent, the leg was thrown out with such violence as nearly to overturn one of the assistants, who in vain tried to prevent its extension. When the supraorbital nerve was excited every muscle in his countenance was simultaneously thrown into fearful action; rage, horror, despair, anguish, and ghastly smiles, united their hideous expressions in the murderer's face.

Several of his medical spectators fled the scene in terror, and one fainted. Unfortunately, word of his experiment reached the ears of many a crackpot, and before you could say 'Lazarus', there were quacks performing on-stage, Frankenstein-like reanimations before live, morbidly curious audiences – the Victorian equivalent of going to a horror movie, although much worse.

From Scotland we take a trip across the sea to Ireland, the birthplace of James Miranda Stuart Barry (1789–1865), who from an early age longed to be a doctor. Originally from a well-known, well-to-do family in Cork, Barry thrived at school. Deciding not to study in Ireland, where he might be recognised, he applied and was admitted to Edinburgh University School of Medicine at just fourteen.

On qualifying, he garnered a fine reputation as a surgeon, campaigned against unsanitary practices and quack, often dangerous, medicines, and introduced radical and effective treatments for leprosy. As a military surgeon in the British Army, he served in India, the Crimea, Canada and South Africa, and entered the record books as the first doctor to successfully perform a Caesarean section – and this in Africa, at a time when no woman in Britain had survived the

Distinguished surgeon Dr James Barry.

procedure. He died in 1865, leaving behind a reputation as an excellent, skilled and caring, albeit a bit cantankerous, surgeon, who did much for the advancement of military hospital practice. Well, great, you may say, but why have I included this gentleman in this book?

Well, when he passed away in London, a local charwoman called Sophia Bishop was called in to prepare the body for burial. And when she lifted his nightshirt to wash him, she was shocked to discover that *he* was in fact a *she* – and a woman who had given birth at some point, as evident from stretch marks.

Barry had actually been born Margaret Ann Buckley in Cork, and came from a family who were supporters of education for women. One can only speculate that the plan to disguise her as a man in order for her to study medicine was undertaken with the consent of her parents, who would have had to support her. Studying in Edinburgh rather than Dublin was probably to avoid running into anyone who would recognise her.

In hindsight it might have been obvious – Barry was only five feet tall in his/her bare feet, and spoke with a high-pitched voice. He/she had been chided for his/her effeminate mannerisms in the army, and had reputedly challenged two people to a duel over such 'slights'. As to the pregnancy, historians believe the child was stillborn, and probably early in the pregnancy while Barry was in a more remote posting.

The decision was taken to keep James Barry's sex a secret, as such a revelation would surely have scandalised Victorian Britain. Margaret Ann Buckley's true identity was only revealed to the modern world a century after her death, granting her the very laudable honour of having been the first woman to practise medicine as a qualified doctor in British history.

Another doctor of Irish extraction was Pennsylvanian Evan O'Neill Kane, who had a fine career as a surgeon. A period of his life was spent working as a so-called 'railway surgeon', treating injured men building America's vast rail network. In the course of this, he performed more than 1,000 operations in a three-year period – about one a day. Many of the injuries he encountered were a result of crushing, and he invented several techniques and devices to aid in such surgeries. This vast experience of surgical procedures ultimately led to an event that created a big splash in the media at the time – on 15 February 1921, he performed surgery on himself!

He had actually had something of a practice run at this – a couple of years earlier, he had amputated one of his own fingers, which had become badly infected. But now he announced that he would perform his own appendectomy. It was the first recorded time that a person operated on himself. Another doctor present that day described the scene:

> *Sitting on the operating table propped up by pillows and with a nurse holding his head forward that he might see (into a mirror), he calmly cut into his abdomen, carefully dissecting the tissues and closing the blood vessels as he worked his way in.*

According to Kane, he performed the self-surgery to demonstrate the safety both of local anaesthesia for a 'major operation' and of appendectomy, as well as to experience surgery from the patient's point of view. At one point during the procedure, Kane's intestines popped out

SURGEON OPERATES ON HIMSELF

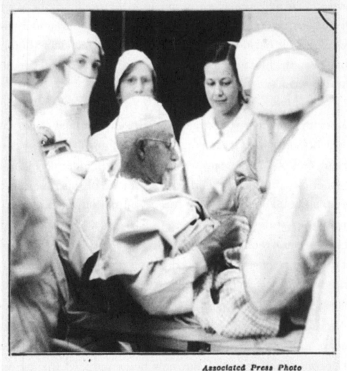

Dr. Evan O'Neill Kane, 70-year-old Kane, Pa., surgeon, is shown as he operated on himself for inguinal hernia. Ten years ago Dr. Kane astonished the medical world by removing his appendix. Occupying the unique position of both patient and attending surgeon he can shake hands with himself and say: "That was nice work, doctor." The operation was considered successful.

when he leaned too far forward, and he calmly reinserted them himself. The sixty-year-old made a full recovery, and was back working a couple of weeks later.

Kane wasn't finished self-operating either – he repaired his own inguinal hernia under local anaesthetic when he was seventy, and was back in the operating theatre working on a patient a day-and-a-half later. He died that same year, from pneumonia, and not even his own miraculous self-treatment could save him.

While O'Kane's self-surgeries were somewhat bizarre, they were at least genuine medical procedures, unlike most of those performed by John R Brinkley. He opened a clinic in the Kansas town of Milford in 1918, offering to treat male impotence by implanting goats' testicles in men's scrotums at $750 a pop. That's just short of $10,000 in today's money. This 'operation' would prove at best harmless, as the body would slowly absorb the implanted glands,

First 'Goat-Gland' Baby Blesses Kansas Home

Milford, Kan.— Picture shows Dr. John R. Brinkley, holding "Billy," one of the famous goat-gland babies. Dr. Brinkley, a surgeon, has startled the scientific world by transplanting goat glands to men and omen as a means of restoring a lost heritage. The parents of "Billy" had wanted a baby for 16 years. Dr. Brinkley persuaded the father to submit to an operation involving the transplanting of glands from a goat. This perfectly healthy and laughing baby came along to bless a home that had been childless for those many years.

but it was totally laughable as a treatment for impotence. Brinkley would assure his patients that they'd have no problems with 'a pair of those buck glands in you.'

Brinkley had studied in a dodgy medical college that favoured 'alternative' medicine, and he hadn't even finished that degree, as he'd run out of funds. His 'qualification' had been purchased from what is commonly called a 'diploma mill' – i.e. pay us some money and we'll issue you a fake but genuine-looking diploma. So he really was only a semi-qualified quack doctor.

In 1919, he had an incredibly lucky break, when the wife of his first goat-testicle patient became pregnant, although it is one hundred percent certain that Brinkley's treatment had nothing to do with it. Soon he was receiving state-wide media coverage. Patients were rolling in from all corners, despite the exorbitant cost. He earned enough money to build his own transmitter, and opened a radio station called KFKB, advertising his treatments in between the Duke Ellington and Louis Armstrong tunes.

Increasing success brought him to a nationwide audience, and the cash rolled in. Now Brinkley began to claim that his goat testicles not only imbued a man with great virility, but also cured high blood pressure, epilepsy, diabetes, senility, obesity, dementia and flatulence! At the height of his fame, Brinkley was reputedly a millionaire several times over.

The only problem was that his surgeries were worse than useless. His limited medical training, fondness for alcohol and poor hygiene standards often meant that the operations were botched, resulting in severe infection from which many people died. Eventually the lawsuits started coming in, along with accusations of charlatanism from the medical community, and he lost his broadcasting licence in 1930.

Unperturbed, he moved to Mexico and resumed his practice there, also broadcasting back into the US from across the border. But by the late 1930s, the onslaught of lawsuits had bankrupted him. To compound his troubles, he developed a blood clot in his left leg, which led to gangrene and the removal of the limb. He suffered several heart attacks, which oddly he did not attempt to treat by goat testicle implantation, and the charlatan passed away in May 1942, aged just fifty-seven. Rarely has one man fooled so many people into giving away so much money.

From the tragic and laughable, we move to the quite revolting world of Dr Stubbins Ffirth. In 1804, while still a young trainee doctor in Pennsylvania, Ffirth became obsessed with the study of yellow fever, an epidemic of which had killed ten percent of Philadelphia's population a decade earlier. He developed a theory that the disease was not contagious, and decided to prove his hypothesis by performing experiments on himself. These mostly involved trying to infect himself with the bodily fluids of victims, so if you're eating at the moment, I suggest you stop.

He first made incisions on his arms and smeared fluid that patients had orally expelled into the wounds. That's correct, he rubbed their puke into the cuts. He then advanced to applying the vomit to his eyeballs, the way you might use eyewash. As he still hadn't become infected, he decided to fry up some vomit and inhale the fumes. Lastly, he drank it undiluted. No infection resulted, so he moved on to other bodily fluids, such as blood, perspiration, saliva and urine – inhaling them, rubbing them into wounds, drinking them.

Still free of yellow fever, Stubbins Ffirth declared his theory proven. Except that it wasn't. The patients from whom he'd taken his samples had moved beyond the contagion stage. Sixty years later, a Cuban doctor called Carlos Finlay would discover that the disease was spread by mosquitoes. But you have to hand it to Ffirth for the lengths he was prepared to go to prove a theory!

Female doctors were few and far between in Victorian times (e.g. see James Barry above), and when one made a public pronouncement it usually attracted some media attention. Unfortunately, Dr Anna Hatfield of New York didn't do the cause of advancing females in medicine any good when she proclaimed, at a public meeting in December 1900, that kissing was an intoxicant more dangerous than alcohol and highly unhygienic.

> I think kissing is the worst thing a young woman can do and the amount of hugging and kissing that some girls of our best families submit to is literally a menace to our morality. I know a young man who declares that he rarely leaves a girl without kissing her goodnight. He says that they not only eagerly accede to his request, but that several have insisted upon being kissed. A ban on promiscuous osculation must be brought in at once!

This meeting of the Women's Christian Temperance Union also learned that:

> No person should kiss another without first using an antiseptic wash on the mouth to destroy bacteria. And as for the moral bacteria, that is even more dangerous.

'But I like it!' came the impetuous voice of a young woman in the audience. Cue much tittering on the night and subsequently among the media and medical community, and Dr Hatfield quietly kissed her reputation goodbye.

JUST WHAT THE DOCTOR ORDERED

Not so long ago, doctors were prescribing heroin as a cough suppressant! But that was by no means the worst 'cure' that the medical sciences have sent our way down the centuries.

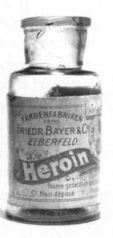

An Englishman called Charles Alder Wright was the first person to produce heroin in 1874, although he called it diamorphine, and never really went beyond initial testing on animals. A quarter of a century later, the German pharmaceutical company Bayer re-synthesised it, and marketed it as a cough suppressant. Naming it after the Greek word *heros*, because of the apparent 'heroic' effects it had on users, they sent thousands of samples to doctors, describing it as a 'non-addictive medicine'.

It seems shocking now to see a medicine bottle with the brand name 'Heroin' emblazoned across the front, but around the 1900s, pharmaceuticals were still really in their infancy. Medical professionals and the public alike would grasp anything that offered even the slightest relief.

Within months of its release, reports were coming back of people developing a tolerance for the drug, followed soon after by tales of addiction. Still, it took fifteen years before the situation was bad enough for Bayer to cease manufacture of the product. It was banned outright by the League of Nations in 1925, by which time tens of thousands of people undergoing cough medicine cold turkey around the globe.

It wasn't a good idea to be a sick baby back in Victorian days, as your mother was likely to pour all sorts of nasty things down your throat in an effort to stop you bawling. Here's a recipe for 'Godfrey's Cordial', a potion designed to help babies sleep:

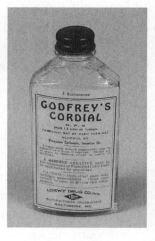

> *Heat together seven drops of water and eight drops of treacle. When cold add three fluid ounces rectified spirit, forty minims oil of sassafras, ten drops oil of aniseed, four ounces of laudanum. Mix thoroughly.*

It's hardly surprising that this made babies sleep, considering that laudanum is a derivative of opium, a highly addictive narcotic.

Another baby product, advertised as 'The Mother's Friend' and 'for teething children', bore the rather comforting name 'Mrs Winslow's Soothing Syrup'. The label shows a warm, colourful scene, featuring a mother with infant on knee. She is spooning the syrup between the innocent child's lips as her two other little girls look admiringly on.

Mrs Winslow was a real person – Charlotte N Winslow, from Maine, USA – but it was her son-in-law, Jeremiah Curtis, who marketed the product in 1849. It sold extremely well both in the US and UK, and Elgar even entitled an adagio 'Mrs Winslow's soothing syrup'. One enthusiastic mother wrote to the *New York Times* about the miracle syrup – its effect on her son was 'like magic; he soon went to sleep, and all pain and nervousness disappeared'.

Of course, it was all too good to be true. The syrup was mostly harmless, containing sodium carbonate and ammonium hydroxide, commonly used as acidity regulators. But its active ingredient, the one that essentially sent the babies on a trip, was morphine sulphate. No wonder it was marketed as 'likely to soothe any human or animal'. Amazingly, it took over sixty years before the medical community finally caught on – in 1911, the American Medical Association listed the product in a section entitled 'Baby Killers', which just about says it all. Despite the evidence of the damage it was causing in both the US and UK, the authorities in Britain didn't ban its sale until 1930!

Moving briefly away from drugs, an advertisement in 1863 featured a rather odd-looking belt contraption manufactured by Benjamin Atkinson, inventor (who incidentally also sold an opiate-based infant flatulence suppresser). This device was the 'Atkinson's Registered Rectum Supporter'. A wide

An ideal Christmas present – Atkinson's Registered Rectum Supporter.

belt encircled the waist, and two smaller straps attached to the back were pulled between the legs and attached to a buckle at the front. Halfway along these smaller straps was a plug, to be inserted into the rectum. The belt could be worn by men or women, and 'thousands of persons afflicted with prolapsed ani [anuses] could testify to its advantages'. It simply doesn't bear any further thought.

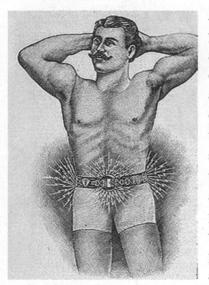

Another belt that might make you squirm, particularly if you're a man, was the 'Giant Power Heidelberg Electric Belt', marketed as a miracle cure for that other embarrassing ailment – erectile dysfunction. The belt had a series of small batteries around the waist, all connected to a ring at the front through which the penis was passed, and through which the current was also passed, electrifying the member and supposedly also the couple's sex lives. One can only imagine the agonies men suffered in these attempts to arouse their nether regions. It must have been funny to be a fly on the wall, mind.

ANIMAL MAGNETISM.—The Operator putting his Patient into a Crisis.

Franz Mesmer 'putting his Patient into a Crisis'.

Jumping back a century or so to 1780, we encounter German Franz Anton Mesmer, whose legacy includes the miracle treatment known as 'animal magnetism' and whose surname gives us the word 'mesmerise'.

Animal magnetism worked – or rather *didn't* work – like this: Apparently all animals exert a natural, invisible force ('magnetism'), and apparently this force could have magical healing effects. Practitioners of animal magnetism were called 'magnetizers'. Animal magnetism between two people allowed one to be hypnotised when the patient would be 'possessed of his senses, yet cease to be an accountable creature, yet his so-called unobstructed vision would allow him to see through objects ... even to see through the body and find the cause of illness, either in himself or in other patients'. Make sense? No? Exactly.

A French Royal Commission set up in 1784 concluded essentially that while Mesmer and his devotees did hypnotise people, very few cures could be attributed to them. Claimed 'cures' were either in people's imaginations or were hoaxes. Well, at least he didn't poison anyone.

Something we did have a cure for was scurvy. Or at least we did, and then we didn't. Then we did, and then we didn't again.

We've known about the existence of scurvy for thousands of years. Caused by a lack of vitamin C, it was the curse of sailors for millennia. It starts with sore gums, and develops into shortness of breath and aching bones. Then there's bruising on the skin, gum disease, loosening of the teeth, and a dry mouth and eyes. As it advances, the patient becomes jaundiced and suffers swelling of the limbs, numbness, fever, convulsions and eventually death.

Besides being a horrible way to go, the loss of so many men to it when on a long sailing mission often proved fatal even to those not badly afflicted with scurvy, as there simply weren't enough men left to man the ship. In the 300 years between 1500 and 1800, the death toll among sailors is estimated at around two million. The famous explorer Magellan was left with a crew of just twenty-two men in 1520. He had set out with 230, but the rest had perished from scurvy. Similarly, Vasco da Gama once lost two-thirds of his crew.

But every now and then down the centuries, someone realised that eating citrus fruits caused the symptoms to vanish. It was a miracle cure. It was further learnt that strawberries and raspberries – fruits that didn't require hot climates – also cured the disease. Kale, spinach,

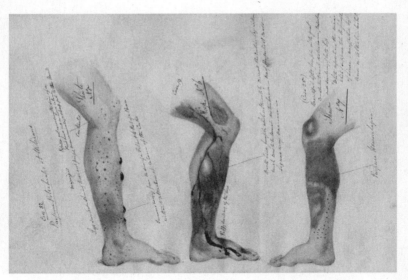

The symptoms of scurvy, as illustrated in a Royal Navy surgeon's diary.

broccoli, peas and potatoes were also seen to work. Besides the million or more who died of starvation, tens of thousands of people also died of scurvy in Ireland during the potato famine, when their main source of vitamin C was cut off.

The trouble was that nobody wrote down the cure or publicised it widely, so the cure was found, then forgotten, then found again and then forgotten again. Another problem was that citrus fruits gathered for a long journey only last so long – two weeks into a voyage, supplies might already have run out. And, despite the evidence for citrus fruits working, the scientific community rejected this as a cure, because they believed they were dealing with a disease and not simply a dietary deficiency. Error compounded error, ignorance compounded ignorance, and the lack of proper study and thorough records led to the deaths of millions.

At least scurvy was a real affliction, whereas 'female hysteria' really wasn't. One can't help but suspect that this was a male invention, a catch-all 'disease' that accounted for a virtually endless list of 'women's complaints'. These included fainting, anxiety, sleeplessness, bad temper, nervousness, fluid retention, heaviness in the abdomen, muscle spasms, shortness of breath, irritability, loss of appetite for food or sex, or conversely increased sexual desire, and also 'a tendency to cause trouble for others'. In other words, basically anything could be ascribed to female hysteria. Regarded as a serious medical complaint, especially in the eighteenth and nineteenth centuries, it also became a source of easy cash for every eager Victorian charlatan and inventor.

Treatments during the mid-nineteenth century included 'water massage', which basically involved directing a power hose into a woman's vagina. This later evolved to 'clitoral massage', usually

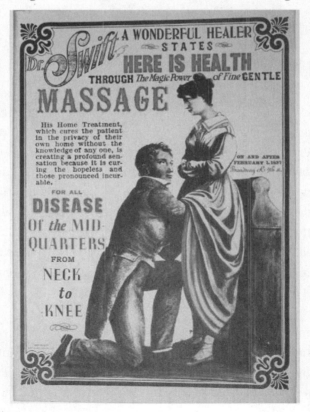

self-administered or done in the home by a physician, or in many cases performed by a charlatan passing him or herself off as a hysteria healer. Treatments such as these raised concerns in the medical community, and many doctors were also uncomfortable administering them, possibly for fear of being accused of sexual assault.

Yes, really, it's a Victorian-era, steam-powered vibrator.

The Victorian age's answer to this was to invent the vibrator. These differed from today's sex toys in many ways. Some more resembled a hair dryer, carrying as they did a large wire transformer. Others, incredibly, were steam-powered, featuring large bronze canisters, spinning wheels, knobs and tubes, with a long phallic protrusion at one end. It is frankly hard to imagine where the woman was supposed to position herself. Then there was the cheap option – a phallic object attached to a wheel, operated by cranking a handle. It looked vaguely like a rotary hand whisk. And all of this was supposed to save women physical embarrassment.

A treatment that earned glowing praise from its promoters was the use of radium to treat a variety of ailments, including arthritis, gout, neuralgias and poor circulation. Considering that radium does actually glow, this is not surprising.

Soon after the discovery of radium by Marie Curie in 1898, the medical community – and the quack community – began to look into its possibly curative properties. In those early days of research into radioactivity, its effects were little understood. This, compounded by one critically erroneous leap of deduction, brought radiation sickness into tens of thousands of homes.

The health benefits of mineral water, though not spectacular, were well documented at this time. But then the electron's discoverer, JJ Thomson, wrote an article stating that well and spring water were radioactive. This was due to the presence of small amounts of naturally occurring radon gas in the water. Unfortunately, many people leaped to the conclusion that the radon was responsible for the health benefits of spring water.

Before long, we had such contraptions as the 'Revigorator', which emerged in 1912. A large ceramic water dispenser, almost as big as a typical water cooler bottle, its walls were lined with radioactive ore. Now everyone could enjoy the health benefits of spring water at home or on the road. At least six glasses of the potentially fatal water were recommended every day. Soon your skin would be radiant. Literally.

The market for radium products soon exploded. Vita radium suppositories (guaranteed to contain REAL RADIUM, the label read) were to be inserted at night. While you slept, 'every organ will be bombarded by health-giving electric atoms'! There were also 'Radium Nutex Prophylactics', to bring that extra spark to your sex life, radium chocolate bars and radium beauty creams – you guessed it – 'for glowing skin!' There was radium boot polish, metal polish, cigarettes, soap, butter ... you name it.

Naturally, people started to get very ill soon after consuming any of the above, and eventually the first deaths were reported. But it took authorities in many countries several decades before they finally banned radioactive materials in products. The death toll from their use is unknown, as many deaths would have been ascribed to other causes. But it is not unreasonable to speculate that it was in the tens of thousands.

BITTER PILLS TO SWALLOW

If you thought that much of Victorian medicine was on shaky ground, it's just as well you didn't live in the centuries before that, when medicine was guided more by superstition than fact.

If you wished to cure your children of hyperactivity in ancient Rome, circa 77AD, Pliny the Elder's *Natural History* recommends you place some goat dung in your child's nappy. It works best for girls, apparently. You'd have to assume someone somewhere in the ancient Roman world tested this, probably trying out a bunch of other materials before settling on goat dung. The remedy clearly has the disadvantage that your child's nappy will be permanently smelly.

Pliny also has a recommendation for the much more serious condition of a fractured cranium: apply cobwebs, mixed with oil and vinegar. He tells us that cobwebs are also good for stopping 'the bleeding of wounds made in shaving'. Predating Pliny by over two centuries, Cato the Elder's *De Agri Cultura* ('On Agriculture') has a tip for those undertaking a long journey and wishing to prevent blisters – stick a sprig of wormwood up your rectum. I assume he's talking about piles, as opposed to blisters on your feet, but it's not entirely clear.

Before the Romans started giving the world the benefit of their vast medical knowledge, the Egyptians had created a genuine cure for acne, which they believed was caused by telling lies. They would rub the offending spots with sulphur, which really is a mild anti-bacterial agent.

A slightly more serious condition than a pimply nose is epilepsy, once commonly believed to be caused by possession of the body by evil spirits. In some countries, this nonsense persists. One enlightened ancient who recognised that it was just a medical condition was Hippocrates, who, in the fifth century BC, suggested that the problem originated in the brain, and was more than likely hereditary. He noted that early onset would predict worse symptoms in later life. He named it the 'great disease', which led to the term *grand mal*, a term still in use today. Unfortunately, the only available treatment at the time was exorcism!

An early depiction of a 'grand mal' seizure.

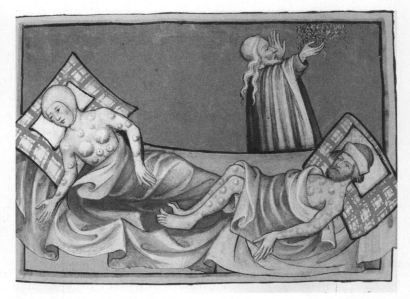

Moving forward a couple of millennia takes us to undoubtedly the greatest health crisis ever to strike mankind – the Black Death. In just seven short years, from 1346 to 1353, it was responsible for the deaths of at least seventy-five million people, and possibly as many as 200 million. We know now that it was caused by a bacteria carried by fleas in the fur of rodents, but they hadn't a clue back then and in their desperation they proposed quite a variety of potential cures.

Among the more disgusting was to regularly bathe in and drink urine from non-infected people. Worse again was a poultice made from tree resin, roots and excrement, which was applied to the open wounds caused by the plague, and most likely exacerbated the problem. There was also the traditional application of leeches of course, or you could go and live in a sewer, where the smell of human waste would 'deter the plague'. The plague-ridden sewer rats probably couldn't believe their luck.

An English physician called Thomas Vicary invented the strangest cure – he advocated shaving a live chicken's bottom and applying it to the infected area of the skin. It was often necessary to hold the chicken in place for several days. The theory was that the disease would be sucked out of you and into the unfortunate animal. If the chicken died, you were supposedly cured. Presumably most of his patients died of boredom waiting for the chicken to croak it.

Incidentally, plague doctors like Vicary are always portrayed in drawings and etchings from the time wearing a strange-looking costume – a full-length cloak covering the entire body, and headgear with a giant beak, giving them a 'birdman' appearance. The idea was to fill the beak with nice-smelling herbs and flower petals before setting off for your day's work, as protection from the fouler smells emanating from the infected masses.

Another famed English doctor from medieval times was John Arderne, who wrote a large tome entitled *The Art of Medicine*. His reputation has fared a great deal better than the likes of Vicary, thanks to his conclusions being mostly based on observation and practice, rather than pure oddball superstition, and he has been called one of the fathers of surgery.

Having said that, he also included in his work many traditional treatments and folk medicines. His cure for kidney stones was a hot plaster smeared with honey and pigeon dung. He also had a cure-all, which he claimed worked on countless ailments and which he called 'pulvis sine pari'. This translates as 'dust without equal', so it must have been good stuff. 'Sanguinis veneris' was his cure for high complexion. This was obtained by 'drawing the blood of a virgin at full moon when the moon is in Virgo and the sun in Pisces', a treatment unlikely to be granted approval by the Medical Council, but you never know.

Perhaps the less said about Arderne's illustrations the better.

Among the successful cures Arderne records in words and pictures (many of which are extremely graphic) is the case of a young man who had developed a stone the size of a bean in his penis and could not urinate. Arderne duly tied the offending member either side of the stone with string and then sliced into the middle, extracted the stone, stitched the incision, coated the penis with egg white and flour and bandaged it. And Bob's your uncle, in a few days said member was performing wonderfully. Although it brings water to the eyes to imagine the agonies of the procedure.

Oscar Wilde's father, Sir William Wilde, was a famous surgeon in Dublin in the mid-nineteenth century, and his mother, Lady Jane Wilde, was a well-known poet who wrote under the penname Speranza. Besides a famous son, they also shared an enthusiasm for folklore, including Irish folk medicine, and Lady Jane wrote a tome on the subject of medical practices of the common folk. I've listed eight of them below:

Sore throat is cured by putting the head of a live gander into the mouth of the patient and making it scream down his throat.

A love potion can be made by grinding into powder the dried liver of a black cat, mixing it with tea and pouring it from a black teapot.

To cure back sprain, the patient goes in his or her nakedness, for about ten minutes, under a waterfall.

A bunch of mint tied round the wrist is a sure remedy for disorders of the stomach.

A sick person's bed must be placed north and south, not cross ways.

The touch from the hand of a seventh son cures the bite of a mad dog.

If a person is bitten by a dog, the dog must be killed, whether mad or not, for it might become mad; then, so also would the person who had been touched by the saliva of the animal.

Clippings of the hair and nails of a child tied up in a linen cloth and placed under the cradle will cure convulsions.

Who knows, maybe they're worth a try?

LEFT TO THEIR OWN DEVICES ...

For a final foray into historical medicine, let's take a cringe-inducing look at some of the diabolical instruments doctors employed to 'cure' us of all sorts of things.

In the 1870s, a man with urinary problems might find his doctor sticking the pointy end of a *Holt's Divulsor* up his penis, and continue inserting it until only the fat end and the handle was protruding. This was used for the 'treatment of stricture by gradual distension at a single sitting ... *beyond the natural calibre of the canal.*' It doesn't bear thinking about.

The very charming *Holt's Divulsor.*

Problem with piles? Members of either sex would be instructed to bend over a table while the doctor inserted a bulbous pair of *haemorrhoid forceps* and snipped the offending growth off. If it was deep and unreachable, that was okay, as he could use a hook on a rod to yank it down first. Are your eyes watering yet? No? They soon will be.

The *double lithotome cache* has existed for at least a couple of centuries. It consisted of two sharp blades hidden within the smooth body of a long, pointed, silvery-looking instrument. Used to remove bladder stones, it was inserted by making an incision in the perineum (the space between the anus and the vulva or scrotum). At this point a small lever on the handle is pressed. The blades inside separate, like a scissors opening, and cut a hole in the bladder wall, hopefully without tearing it too much. This was all without anaesthetic, remember, so picture the patient being held in place by about six burly men.

The double *lithotome cache*.

The doctor would begin poking about with a pair of forceps, hopefully locating the bladder stone and prising it free, again hopefully not reefing the incisions any wider in the process. Then the patient was sewn up and off he or she went, albeit with a very strange gait.

But that was relatively modern medicine. Pre-nineteenth century, and pretty much back to the beginning of time, virtually all sickness was attributed to your natural 'humours' not being in balance, and believe me, this had nothing to do with your funny bone.

Re-balancing your 'humours' meant you had too much blood, urine, phlegm or some other substance in your body that had to be gotten rid of. So they'd give you something to make you pee excessively, vomit or cough up your lungs. Or, in many cases, they'd start lancing your veins with a scarification kit, releasing blood and then patching you up.

The technology had evolved by the late eighteenth century to give us the *scarificator*, which is just as scarifying as it sounds. It looks innocent enough at first glance – usually an eight-sided, fist-sized brass box with four slots on one side and a protruding lever on the other. The slotted side was placed against the flesh – usually the forearm, neck or

Humours a touch unbalanced? The *scarificator*.

temple. The lever was pulled back and then released, sending four inch-deep razors shooting into the flesh and then retracting before you'd had time to shriek some obscenity. Patients at the time believed the new bloodletting instrument was much more humane than previous devices. One can only imagine.

Incidentally, bloodletting wasn't restricted to doctors. The local barber shop was also a place to go for treatment, skilled as barbers reputedly were with sharp blades. It was from this tradition that the barber's symbol of a red and white pole originated – blood and bandages essentially.

Predating even bloodletting was the practice of brain surgery – yes, we've been fiddling around with our fellow man's grey matter since caveman days apparently. The purpose of this was either to free evil spirits, to treat conditions like epilepsy or to treat fractures. And if you wanted to get inside someone's skull in, say, ancient Rome or Greece, you needed a *trepanning drill.*

These came in all shapes and sizes, but usually took the form of either a standard brace-and-bit wood drill or a corkscrew-type mechanism. The 'bit' on the end of either type was like a hollow column with sharp teeth, and in the centre was a spike to 'anchor' the gadget to your skull while the surgeon twisted and cut through the bone. Presumably your head was held in place by some contraption to stop you thrashing about. Your brain exposed to the world, the spirits were free to fly away. A coin-sized piece of brain would be exposed for the remainder of your days, which probably wouldn't be very many.

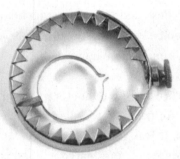

the *Spermathorrhoea Ring*.

Okay, boys, cross your legs as I introduce you to the *Spermathorrhoea Ring*, from the late nineteenth century. Strictly speaking, this wasn't a 'medical' device, but it was often supplied by a doctor to the upstanding, worried parents of a teenage boy. It was a German invention, officially designed to prevent the 'involuntary loss of semen', whatever that was. In reality, the strict Protestant society of the time wanted it to curb the immoral practice of 'spilt seed on the ground' (Genesis 38:7–9), i.e. masturbation.

It consisted of a two metal rings, the outer one of which was spiked. The penis was passed through the inner ring and the outer ring was then tightened until the spikes were just touching, but not penetrating the skin. Thus any impure thoughts leading to engorgement would be rewarded with a bunch of spikes sticking into one's organ, quickly making one abandon those lustful thoughts. Charming.

Now, before you get too smug, girls, consider the plight of your ancient female descendants in Rome who were subject to the invasion of the metal *vaginal speculum*. Nowadays the speculum is usually a smooth plastic or stainless steel device with nice

What did the bloody Romans give us? The *vaginal speculum*.

rounded corners, designed to mirror the shape of the orifice it enters. In Roman times, they were made of iron and looked like something you'd use to remove the tyre of a truck, consisting of four spikes that could be widely separated by means of a long screw and handle. Not the most comfy experience, but a virtual holiday when compared to the Spermathorrhoea contraption.

Moving up the body, we come to an area that is still a source of pain and discomfort – dental work. If you think it's bad now, a hundred years ago it was agonising, which was an improvement over previous generations, when it was pure brutality. Before the eighteenth century, rotten

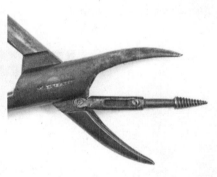

Ah, lovely, everyone's favourite medical instrument, the *dental screw forceps*.

teeth were extracted by a doctor (or a barber), without anaesthetic of course, using pliers or *dental screw forceps*, a frightening-looking plier-like tool with a menacing screw protruding from its jaws.

There are records of people experiencing 'explosions' in their mouths, possibly due to dentistry materials, or gases from decaying teeth, being ignited by a spark from a chisel – yes, a chisel. If, during your treatment, your tooth broke, the kindly dentist would reach for the much-favoured *dental chisel*. It makes your teeth curl to think about it. Then came one of dentistry's great advances – the *tooth key*. This allowed the doctor, or coiffeur, to clamp the offending tooth, then twist a handle to tortuously and excruciatingly draw it from the gum.

Lastly, let's return to the male organ, for which medical science of yore seems to have devised the most devilish gadgets. *Mercury urethral syringes* have survived from as far back as the sixteenth century, usually having been recovered from sunken ships. As a means of treating syphilis, the syringe's metal nozzle was inserted up the penis, and a large dose of mercury injected into the unfortunate organ. What effect this might have had one can only imagine.

Or perhaps it's better not to.

3

YOU CAN'T CHOOSE
YOUR FAMILY

....

The American comedian George Carlin once joked that he'd eaten in a nice family restaurant the night before – every table had an argument going. Ninety-nine percent of people can identify with this statement, but what is it that makes people who share so much DNA clash to such an extent? Familiarity perhaps? Or competitiveness?

Many of the familiar names from the history books also had brothers and sisters and nieces and nephews, people you're much less likely to have heard of. Many of these unknown siblings made a little bit of history in their own right, but were cursed (or blessed) always to have to dwell in their more famous relative's shadow.

So let's bring a handful of these blood-relations back into the light.

TO BE OR NOT TO BE
....

Late on a winter's night in 1864, a young man of twenty-one years of age was standing on a crowded platform in New Jersey, waiting to purchase a ticket for the train's sleeping car. The crowd suddenly swelled and swayed and the young man was pressed against the body of the train, which at that moment unexpectedly began to move. The man was twisted around, and found his feet suddenly suspended over the gap between the train and the platform. To his horror, he began to slip into the gap, which would surely have proven fatal.

At the last moment, a hand reached out and grasped the collar of his coat, yanking him back onto the safety of the platform. Shaken but unhurt, he turned to thank his rescuer, and was surprised to recognise the face of one of America's finest actors. His saviour was Edwin Booth, brother of the man who would, just six months later, murder President Abraham Lincoln in Ford's Theatre. The young man whose life Booth had just saved was, quite incredibly, none other than Robert Lincoln, the President's son, though Booth didn't realise that at the time. Some time later, when Edwin discovered who he had saved that night, it would be a small source of comfort to him, given the weight of shame that his younger brother had brought on his family name.

Edwin Booth had been born into an acting family in Maryland in 1833. His father, Junius, an English-born actor, was known for his bombastic style and powerful on-stage presence. As he toured with his father, Edwin slowly drifted into the profession himself, although the greatest demand on his character as a young teenager was in keeping his famously temperamental father sober. At one point in New York, when he was eighteen, he had to take his father's leading role of Richard III after Junius refused to go on stage in a fit of artistic pique.

His father died two years later, and Edwin continued with his by then blossoming acting career, touring California, Hawaii and Australia, where his performances were greeted enthusiastically. At twenty-seven, Edwin hit the big time, performing a series of Shakespearian roles in New York and Boston to rave reviews and thunderously applauding audiences.

Although a much more reserved character than Junius, he had unfortunately inherited his father's fondness for alcohol. He married an Irish-American actress called Anne Devlin, herself of some repute in the profession, and she left us an insightful account of her relationship with her husband and of theatre life at the time. Edwin loved Anne deeply, and they had a daughter together, but their marriage was brief because of Anne's tragic death from pneumonia in 1863. Edwin was in a bar getting drunk when she passed away, something for which he would never forgive himself, but at least the experience made him a more abstemious man.

Edwin Booth as Hamlet.

Edwin had two actor brothers – John Wilkes and Junius Brutus. All three did appear together on stage once, appropriately playing the roles of Mark Anthony, Cassius and Brutus. Somewhat ironically, John Wilkes played the non-assassin role of Mark Anthony.

But Edwin's star had still to rise further. Beginning in November 1864, he played Hamlet on one hundred consecutive nights, a world record at the time, his performances bringing him unheard-of acclaim from New York's critics and a reputation as 'the greatest Hamlet of the nineteenth century'.

From such highs, he was quickly thrown into a chasm of despair when, the following April, his younger brother murdered President Lincoln. The brothers had taken opposite sides in the abolitionist argument, and Edwin was aware his brother was fanatical in his opposition to the Union, but he was shocked and ashamed at what John Wilkes had done. He couldn't bring himself to face the public again for over six months (although there was no apparent hostility towards him), and he became a recluse in his home, where it was forbidden

THE ASSASSINATION OF PRESIDENT LINCOLN.
AT FORD'S THEATRE WASHINGTON D.C. APRIL 14TH 1865.

even to speak his brother's name. He returned to play Hamlet in January the following year, but his performances never again rose to the levels that had garnered such praise.

His final performance was his signature role of Hamlet, playing the youthful Dane at the age of almost sixty in New York. Later that year, he had a minor stroke and his health began to decline, until he passed away in the summer of 1893.

Tragically, today the name of Edwin Booth is commonly followed by the phrase 'brother of John Wilkes Booth, assassin of President Abraham Lincoln', and not by the epithets for which he rightly earned his own, much more honourable, place in history.

CHALK AND CHEESE

His surname is one of the most infamous in history, immediately associated with genocide and terror. This is hard on him to say the least, for if anything, Albert Goering was a man of peace and profound courage. His brother was, of course, Hermann Goering, one of the principal instigators of the 'final solution', Hitler's right-hand man, creator of the Gestapo and looter of countless priceless artworks from the homes of murdered Jews.

Actually, it is said that Hermann wasn't virulently anti-Jewish, but that he went along with the policy as a means of advancing his standing in the Nazi Party. Whatever about that, it is certainly true that his younger brother Albert was highly sympathetic to the Jews and actually despised the Nazis.

Both brothers' attitudes were likely influenced by the fact that they were, in effect, raised by Hermann von Epenstein, their godfather, a wealthy, aristocratic doctor and a Jew. In fact, rumours abounded that Albert's mother had had a fling with von Epenstein, and that Albert had been the result. This would have made Albert half-Jewish, and indeed there was a strong resemblance between the pair.

When they were growing up, the brothers were diametric opposites. Hermann was always in trouble in school, and was ultimately expelled for deliberately cutting the strings of all of the school band's instruments, and packed off to military school; Albert on the other hand was shy, soft-spoken and a bit of a loner. Hermann served as a fighter pilot in the First World War; Albert served as a communications engineer. Hermann became politically active, and was shot and wounded in Hitler's first attempt at seizing power, the Beer Hall Putsch of 1923; Albert studied mechanical engineering and kept his head down.

When Hermann went on the run following the failed 1923 coup, the pair didn't speak for over a decade. With the rise of the Nazis in Germany, Albert,

Albert Goering.

repulsed by them, moved to Vienna and began working in a film studio. He spoke publicly against the Nazis and began to help organising documents to help Jewish people escape the country.

With the 1938 annexation of Austria – the *Anschluss* – Albert worked night and day to help Jews escape the brutal regime, his attitude epitomised by a scene he came upon one day in Vienna: A bunch of Nazi thugs had happened upon a group of elderly Jewish women, and ordered them to scrub the street. Albert saw what was going on, removed his jacket and got on his knees to help the women. When the Nazi leader demanded his identification, he was horrified to realise he was dealing with the brother of Germany's second-in-command, and released the women.

As the war advanced and the death camps were established, Albert would use his connection with his brother to have certain Jews released, helping them to then flee German-controlled territory. Hermann would often become enraged at his younger brother's requests, but would usually succumb, thanks to a soft spot he had for Albert. One of the chief prosecutors at the Nuremberg war crimes trial, Richard Sonnenfeldt, said that Albert would exploit his brother's enormous ego, saying things like, 'Hermann, you're so big and so powerful, and here's a Jew who doesn't belong in a concentration camp.' Hermann would grudgingly carry out Albert's requests, to impress his younger brother with his power.

As the war dragged on, Albert was given the influential position of export director of a Skoda factory in Czechoslovakia. He frequently sent trucks to nearby concentration camps, demanding workers for his factory. The trucks would then be driven into the countryside and the prisoners released, giving them some chance at least of survival. Albert also frequently forged Hermann's name on travel documents to help Jews escape.

Inevitably, the Gestapo caught up with him. He was arrested on numerous occasions, but used his brother's influence to have himself freed, much to Hermann's growing ire. Eventually, the dossier of evidence of his freeing Jews became so thick that, in 1944, the Nazis put him under a death sentence. On the run, with a 'shoot on sight' order on his head, he appealed again to his brother for help. At the Nuremberg trials, he said, 'My brother told me then that it was the last time that he could help me ... and that he had to ask Himmler personally to smooth over the entire matter.'

Hermann was sentenced to death by hanging, but cheated the noose by taking a cyanide capsule in his cell the night before his execution. Albert was also tried, it seems on the basis of his name alone, but many people that he'd helped testified on his behalf, and he was eventually released. After the war, his name made it difficult to find work and he lived modestly, occasionally getting employment as a translator. He lived out his days in a small apartment in Munich, surviving on a Government pension, his role in rescuing hundreds of Jews largely forgotten by the world. He died in 1966, aged seventy-one.

He has thus far been denied the title of Righteous Among the Nations by the Yad Vashem Holocaust Memorial in Jerusalem, Israel's official Holocaust Institute. But there is now enormous goodwill towards Albert Goering, the antithesis of his brother, who saved hundreds of lives during humanity's darkest hour.

LA SEX POT

Her more famous brother was one of the greatest commanders and military strategists in history, ruler over an empire bound only by the Atlantic Ocean and the Mediterranean and Baltic Seas. Pauline Bonaparte, however, was known mostly as a sex maniac.

Pauline (or Paulette, as she was popularly known) was Napoleon's younger sister by eleven years, and essentially acted like a spoilt child for most of her adult life. She was a real looker, with a shapely figure and beautiful face, and she attracted endless admirers from a young age.

One of the first of these, a prominent politician called Louis-Marie Fréron, was almost thirty years her senior when he was introduced to Pauline, then aged sixteen. Fréron, known as a ladies' man, must have thought he'd hit the jackpot when he managed to seduce the voluptuous young Pauline. She fell head-over-heels in love with him, and they planned to marry. But either her mother or big brother Napoleon decided this would be a bad idea, and refused to sanction the union. Suitors continued to line up, many no doubt attracted by the flimsy, often see-through, material Pauline liked to use in her dresses.

The year after Fréron was rejected, Napoleon was working late in his office in Milan when he heard a noise from behind a screen. He discovered his young sister in a state of undress, in the arms of one of his leading officers, Charles Leclerc. A marriage was hastily arranged. Leclerc was at least in the vicinity of Pauline's age (he was eight years older), and was an accomplished officer, who would rise to the rank of General. The spring after their marriage, Pauline gave birth to a son, Dermide – not that motherly duties would in any way impede her enjoyment of the good life.

The following year, her big brother seized power, becoming First Consul of France. Pauline, by then living in Paris, probably thought she was set for a life of idling by the banks of the Seine, squandering Napoleon and her husband's vast booty. Pauline longed to be the centre of Napoleon's attention, to the point where she was bitterly jealous of his wife Josephine, and her two sisters, Elisa and Caroline. She was promiscuous to the point of recklessness, often conducting as many as three affairs at the same time. Inevitably, this caused her problems in the genital area, for which a doctor prescribed a common cure for the time – the application of leeches. Whether they worked or not is anyone's guess, but it wasn't to put a stop to Pauline's wicked ways.

Meantime, over in San Domingue (now Haiti), a black general chap called Toussaint Louverture was to throw a spanner into Pauline's plans. He'd been leading a rebellion there in the cause of independence and the abolition of slavery, and Napoleon essentially decided he wasn't having any of that. He turned to one of his most trusted generals, Pauline's husband, Leclerc.

She was furious at the idea of leaving the Paris high life, to live on some godforsaken, sun-baked, mosquito-infested island. With the huge fleet of seventy-four ships assembled in Brest, Pauline reputedly had to be carried kicking and screaming on to the flagship, l'Ocean.

But Saint Domingue wasn't half as bad as she'd expected, certainly not in terms of potential lovers. While Charles was off organising his military strategies, Pauline was plotting her own conquests, a campaign that she successfully conducted, bedding a large number of her husband's minor officers. Leclerc meanwhile was having considerable success in suppressing the rebellion, until nature intervened. Yellow fever wiped out 25,000 of his men, Leclerc himself finally succumbing in October 1802. With her husband dead, Pauline had the perfect excuse to return to Paris, which she did in the company of her son and her husband's coffin within a week of his death.

Leclerc had left her the not-insubstantial sum of 700,000 francs, but Parisian mores demanded a long period of mourning, so initially she had little chance to enjoy it and openly complained of being bored with life. When that was out of the way, her brother decided he'd have to marry her off again, and soon, before she could further scandalise the family name. Eventually, an Italian man called Camillo Borghese was chosen. This brought Pauline even more wealth, along with the use of the Borghese family's diamonds.

But it seems that Camillo held little interest for her beyond the glitter of his expensive rocks, and Pauline was soon bedding lovers anew. She became infatuated briefly with the renowned composer and violinist Niccolo Paganini, and was soon performing duets of a different kind with him in her Roman home. Her list of lovers also included many officers, actors and various other gentlemen of Italian society.

Napoleon got wind of her carry-on, and was understandably peeved:

> *Dear Sister, – I have learned with pain that you have not the good sense to conform to the manners and customs of the city of Rome; that you show contempt for the inhabitants, and that your eyes are unceasingly turned towards Paris. Although occupied with vast affairs I nevertheless desire to make known my wishes, and I hope that you will conform to them. Love your husband and his family, be amiable, accustom yourself to the usages of Rome, and put this in your head, that if you follow bad advice you will no longer be able to count upon me. You may be sure that you will find no support in Paris, and that I shall never receive you there without your husband. If you quarrel with him it will be your fault, and France will be closed to you. You will sacrifice your happiness and my esteem.*

But Pauline was insatiable in her sexual appetites, and becoming increasingly arrogant. On one occasion when attending the opera, she forced one of her hand maidens to go on her hands and knees so that she could use the back of her neck as a footstool. She bathed daily in milk and, outrageously, was carried naked to her bath by a male negro servant, a practice she defended on the basis that 'a negro is not a man'. She further scandalised Roman society by commissioning Antonio Canova, then Italy's leading sculptor, to produce a reclining nude statue of her. His hand reputedly shivered as he applied the clay to her flesh, and afterwards, when asked how she, sister of the Emperor, could have done such a thing, she replied, 'Why should I not? It was not cold, there was a fire in the studio.'

Tragedy struck in 1804, when her only son, Dermide, died aged eight, and this put a stop to her philandering for a time. She wrote to her brother:

> The blow has been so severe. Despite summoning all my courage, I find no strength to withstand it. My health is altered visibly and my husband is so alarmed he wants to take me to France, hoping that the change of air, and the pleasure of being near you, will be beneficial ...

Pauline did have one saving grace – she was incredibly loyal to her brother. There were even rumours circulating at one point that they were involved in an incestuous relationship, a fire that the British press in particular liked to stoke. Whatever the veracity of that,

Antonio Canova's statue of Pauline Bonaparte.

Pauline stood by her brother after his fall from power, unlike the rest of his family. She moved to Elba, and spent her fortune trying to ensure his life was as comfortable as could be. When Napoleon briefly returned to power, she gave him the Borghese diamonds to bolster his finances. The English were said to have seized these after Napoleon's ultimate defeat at Waterloo.

Pauline's relationship with her husband deteriorated, not surprisingly, and they were separated for years before ill health forced her to seek a reconciliation. This was briefly achieved, with the help of Pope Pius VII, three months before her death from cancer at the age of just forty-four.

Nobody could say that she hadn't lived life to the fullest, but this description by a contemporary of hers, French dramatist Antoine-Vincent Arnault, probably best sums up Pauline Bonaparte:

> No more deportment than a schoolgirl, talking inconsequentially, laughing at nothing and at everything, she contradicted the most serious people and put out her tongue at her sister-in-law when Josephine wasn't looking. She nudged my knee when I didn't pay enough attention to her rattling on and attracted to herself from time to time those ferocious glances with which her brother recalled the most intractable men to order. She had no principles and was likely to do the right thing only by caprice.

DAYLIGHT ROBBERY

A legendary figure of the Heroic Age of Antarctic Exploration, Irishman Sir Ernest Shackleton was beloved by the men under his command. He inspired the masses with his spirit of adventure, his courage and, perhaps most especially, his personal doctrine of never letting his enormous ambitions come before the safety of his men. He truly was a heroic figure, worthy of a hallowed place in history's halls.

His brother Frank, on the other hand, was a bit of a loser.

Worse still, he would be remembered only as one of the principal suspects in the theft of the Irish Crown Jewels, a robbery that remains unsolved to this day.

Sir Ernest Shackleton (second from left), a hero of the golden age of exploration.

Ernest was Frank's older brother by a couple of years. They grew up on the idyllic banks of the River Barrow in the County Kildare town of Athy in the 1870s. But when Frank was about five, his father Henry decided to give up his life as a landowner and study medicine in Dublin's Trinity College. With a medical degree under his belt, he then uprooted his family again and moved them to Sydenham in London. But the family by no means severed their bonds with Ireland.

Frank dabbled with this and that upon leaving school, first announcing that he was going to make gardening his profession, then heraldry, and then finally joining the army and going off to the Boer War. In 1903, Frank was discharged and began to enjoy the lifestyle of someone far better off than he actually was. Frank was gay, not that he advertised the fact widely – one didn't back then – and he began to indulge himself in the London social scene, making friends with many influential and powerful homosexuals, including Lord Ronald Gower, who was said to be Oscar Wilde's inspiration for *The Picture of Dorian Gray*. Gower introduced him to the Duke of Argyll, the King's brother-in-law, and, hey presto, Frank suddenly had a luxurious flat in a posh London street, without apparently having the means to buy such a property.

Through his interest in heraldry, he'd met Anglo-Irishman Sir Arthur Vickers, a wealthy genealogist and heraldic expert (who would be killed by the IRA during the Irish War of Independence).

Frank Shackleton, not a hero.

Vickers gave Frank a job on his heraldic staff in Dublin Castle, along with an invitation to share his Dublin apartment, suggesting a romantic as well as professional relationship. The location of his new employment would be quite telling down the line. Frank now began to divide his time between London and Dublin. Contemporaries of Frank describe him as 'a thinner edition of Ernest (who was a broad, handsome man) with beautiful clothes'. He was also said to be 'extremely good looking, though extremely depraved', a description that probably refers to his then-taboo homosexual practices.

Frank also found himself in possession of a small amount of land in England, on which he planned to start a rose-growing business. He also dabbled in company promotions, and various other schemes that he hoped would one day yield him riches. He never did find the pot of gold at the end of the rainbow, not in any legal way certainly, and by 1907, he was in severe financial trouble.

As it happened, besides his position as Ireland's leading heraldic expert, his good pal Sir Arthur had been charged with the responsibility of protecting the Irish Crown Jewels. These consisted of numerous diamond-, ruby- and emerald-encrusted insignia, worn on ceremonial occasions by royals visiting Dublin. The Diamond Star alone was valued at £14,000, or about £1,500,000 adjusting for a century's inflation.

The jewels were supposed to be kept in a safe housed in a specially built strong room. However, the safe wouldn't fit through the door. The jewels were stored temporarily in Sir Arthur Vicker's office until the door could be widened. As often happens in public-service matters such as this, years passed and the door widening never happened.

Sir Arthur was known frequently to get drunk in his office at night, and a popular tale was of the morning he woke not just with a hangover, but also adorned in the Crown Jewels. This prank by a member of staff should have alerted someone to the ease by which the key to the safe (in Vicker's possession) could be obtained.

On 6 July 1907, a member of staff at Dublin Castle went to fetch the Crown Jewels, in preparation for the visit of King Edward VII, four days later. To his, and apparently Sir Arthur's, horror, the safe was empty. A police investigation was mounted, and the King was said to be 'enraged' by the theft. Suspicion was immediate that it had been an inside job. There was no evidence of forced entry, no hostages, no damage to the safe – someone had simply used the key to open the door and make off with the jewels. And the only person with access to the two keys was Arthur Vickers. He and his then housemate, Frank Shackleton, fell under suspicion.

Sir Arthur vehemently denied any wrongdoing – he wasn't exactly short of money and, to be fair, it would have looked a bit obvious if he'd robbed the very safe he was entrusted with minding. He was so outraged at the suggestion, in fact, that he refused to attend when summoned to a Crown Jewel Commission the following January. He openly accused his ex-friend and cohabiter, Frank Shackleton, of the theft.

The Commission concluded that Vickers had acted negligently in his duty to protect the jewels, and that he had 'associated with a man of undesirable character' and 'introduced this man into his office'. Although not named, this was obviously a reference to Frank Shackleton, who many believed had simply taken Vickers's key from the apartment they shared, stolen into Dublin Castle and taken the jewels. Because they had not been inspected since their previous use on 17 March, St Patrick's Day, Frank Shackleton could have had several months to dispose of the jewels and distance himself from any involvement.

The jewels were never found, and nobody was ever charged with the theft. Likely as not, they were taken to pieces and resold as other objects to unsuspecting buyers.

If Shackleton did profit by that crime, the money quickly burned a hole in his pocket, as by 1910, he had debts of £85,000. He fled to Portuguese West Africa, where he worked briefly as a plantation manager, before being arrested on charges of defrauding a woman of £6,000. He was returned to London for trial, and sentenced to fifteen months' hard labour. Having tarnished the Shackleton family's reputation, upon release he changed his name to Mellor. His famous brother helped him find office work for several years.

Sometime after Ernest died prematurely in 1922, Frank moved to Chichester, where he opened an antique shop. He died in 1941, at the age of sixty-five, having apparently managed to keep his nose clean for the final years of his life.

The Shackleton boys. Same genes, same parents, same upbringing. One son a hero, one a crook. Go figure.

A LAW ONTO THEMSELVES

The young man who called himself Richard J Hart at first seemed like just another railroad hobo, one probably with Indian blood, when, early in 1919, he first walked into the tiny hamlet of Homer in Nebraska. Just north of the vast Winnebago and Omaha reservations, Hart took a liking to the place. He began to do odd jobs around town, mostly as a decorator.

Although a hard worker and clearly a bright young man, he never revealed much about where he'd come from, and it was the sort of place where nobody pushed the issue too much. He did confess to having run away to the circus when he was sixteen, where he'd acquired some sharpshooting skills, and that he'd then joined the army, fought in France and been decorated. Although later evidence would cast doubt on this tale, his gunslinger's skills were never in question.

If the townsfolk already liked the young man, they totally took him into their hearts when, during heavy rain in May 1919, he plunged into churning waters to rescue first a little girl called Margaret O'Connor, and then returned to the water to save the local grocer, Mr Winch. The grocer's nineteen-year-old daughter Kathleen duly fell in love with Hart, married him and would remain his wife for the rest of his days. Being elected town marshal was further reward. He had now truly embedded himself into the community of Homer, and left his secretive past well behind him. Or so he thought.

Almost on the day Hart had shown up in Homer, the Volstead Act was passed into law, banning the sale of alcoholic drinks and ushering in the era of Prohibition and gangsterism. Just over a year later, the Federal Government announced plans to recruit hundreds of prohibition agents to enforce the new laws. Hart applied for the role, and was accepted.

The appointment was something of a poisoned chalice – while many sections of the community lauded the actions of prohibition agents, others despised them, believing that drinking was a mostly harmless social activity. There were moonshiners aplenty in Hart's county, an area replete with vast uninhabited spaces and densely forested hillsides.

Hart had become familiar with much of the region in the previous eighteen months, and quickly began to organise raids, often based on information he'd acquired himself by going undercover as a labourer trying to buy illicit whisky. Within weeks of his appointment, he'd destroyed several stills and arrested twenty men, including, much to his horror, some law enforcement officers.

Expanding his operations, he was soon making successful raids on stills almost 100 miles from his hometown. After a string of further successes and much attention from the press ('His name alone carries terror to the heart of every criminal,' enthused one), the Bureau of Indian Affairs appointed him to tackle the problem of illicit liquor production on the Cheyenne Reservation in South Dakota, probably encouraged by the belief that he was of Indian extraction.

The image of the Prohibition agent has been fashioned by old episodes of 'The Untouchables' and modern-day shows like 'Boardwalk Empire'. These depict stern, square-jawed men in grey suits, brandishing shotguns and thrusting out badges. Richard Hart didn't remotely fit the bill. It would subsequently emerge that he had adopted his surname from silent screen actor William S Hart, the John Wayne of his day, and now he decided to model his entire persona on the movie idol. He adopted western-style clothes, with a ten-gallon hat and a pair of six-shooters, and rode into Indian territory (albeit usually in a car) with a posse of agents behind him.

He was soon wreaking havoc among the Indian moonshine community. The Indians nicknamed him 'Two-gun Hart', and the press pounced on the sobriquet, headlining his exploits with captions like 'Two-gun Hart blasts liquor ring' or 'Gangsters no match for Two-gun Hart'.

His fame spread far and wide, as repeated busts brought ever-more recognition. And eventually the romantic image of the heroic champion of the law-abiding citizen, complete with Wild West get-up, made it all the way to gangster central, Chicago. You can just imagine the surprise when the man at the very top of that illicit booze-producing empire, one Al Capone, opened his newspaper one morning to see the face of his elder brother, Vincenzo, staring back at him from beneath the rim of a cowboy hat, a sparkling sheriff's star pinned to his breast.

James Vincenzo Capone had not been born on any Indian reservation, but in a tiny village in southern Italy, his family emigrating to the US when he was still a baby. He'd reputedly been present on the day his brother Alfonse had acquired the scar that would provide his lifelong nickname. Another kid had slashed the nine-year-old Al in the face with a penknife, and Vincenzo responded by pushing the attacker through a shop window, inflicting serious wounds on the boy. He then fled Brooklyn to escape reprisal, hiding his background and, unlike his brother, following the Christian code with which they had been raised

Richard J Hart eventually learned of his brother Al's notoriety, but decided to keep shtum about his family connections. He continued his work on the Indian reservations, busting countless stills and arresting

"Two gun" R.J. Hart, with his rare collection

many men. His star did wane at one point, when he was investigated for shooting dead a fleeing subject. The scene is straight from a gangster movie – Hart is riding on the running board of a police car while a suspect flees the scene. When the driver refuses megaphone commands to stop, Hart begins firing, eventually striking the man in the back of the neck and killing him. The incident was investigated, but he escaped with a reprimand for excessive use of force.

He was also subject to many death threats, and on a couple of occasions was severely beaten up, either as revenge for an arrest or simply because he was interfering in the popular, if illicit, trade. But it seemed that Two-gun Hart was irrepressible, as the Associated Press once reported on his achievements:

> Hart has had a hand in the capture of more than 20 murderers while covering 12 reservations. In the last year he brought in three Indian killers. He has been a cowboy, soldier and police officer. A 'beat' of more than 200 square miles with supervision over more than 800 is Hart's domain. He travels by foot, in car, horseback, on snowshoes and skis. His work is different from that of his regular officers or detectives, for the criminals he captures are outdoor men, and there are few informers who aid him.

In the summer of 1927, Hart had sufficiently impressed Washington officials to be selected as a personal bodyguard for President Calvin Coolidge, during his lengthy tour through the Black Hills of Dakota.

But in 1931, it all started to go badly wrong for Two-gun Hart, when he shot another man dead and was tried for manslaughter. He was found not guilty, but the incident soured his relationship with the Bureau of Indian Affairs, and he was subsequently fired.

He couldn't have chosen a worse time to lose his job, as America was just entering the Great Depression and work was scarce. He did manage to pick up some odd jobs, but there was still a lot of resentment around towards him, and he and his family suffered badly because of it. The American Legion (of which he'd been a member) also investigated him, and announced that they could find no record of his First World War service. He continued to insist that he had served in France, and whether he did or not is a matter of debate, but it further tarnished the once great hero's record.

Vincenzo's brother Al, in 1930.

He then lost his legendary shooting ability, thanks to a cataract in his right eye that almost rendered him blind. By now desperate, he contacted his brother, Ralph 'Bottles' Capone, another bootlegging gangster and associate of the now imprisoned Al. Ralph helped Vincenzo out with cash and clothing, and even put him up for a while. He began to send Vincenzo a monthly cheque to help him and Kathleen out, their kids by now having grown up and moved away. It was an ironic and sad end for the champion of the law to end up on the receiving end of handouts from a mobster.

Vincenzo had a reunion with Al at Ralph's home in Wisconsin, but they had little contact after that. When charges were brought against Ralph for tax evasion in 1951, Vincenzo was called as a witness for the defence, and it was then that the press finally learned of the amazing secret that 'Two-gun Hart, star prohibition agent' was actually the elder brother of Al and Ralph Capone, the once emperors of Chicago gangland.

The Capones and Harts truly had been a crime family, whichever side of the law you were on.

....

Adolf Hitler's brother, Alois, was attending the Dublin Horse Show in the summer of 1909 when he met a nice gentleman called William Dowling and his pretty daughter, Bridget. They had a drink together, and Alois confided that he was a wealthy hotelier on an extended holiday around Europe. This sufficiently impressed both for his invitation to take Bridget out to be accepted, and soon the couple were courting. In truth, the only hotel Alois was associated with was Dublin's famous Shelbourne Hotel, where he worked as a kitchen porter. He was eventually forced to admit that fact, but it must have been true love, as the couple eloped to London the following year and were married, against her parents' wishes.

In mid-June the following year, they moved to Liverpool. The house they occupied would ironically be destroyed in a German air raid in 1942, but they were long gone by then, of course. Bridget seems to have become pregnant almost immediately, as on 12 March 1911, she gave birth to William Patrick Hitler.

The boy was named after her father and Ireland's patron saint, but his father turned out to be anything but saintly. He became violent towards Bridget and her son, especially after she refused to accompany him to Germany to pursue a business proposition. He then abandoned them, lost contact due to the First World War, and afterwards arranged for her to be informed that he had been killed in action. He then remarried bigamously, which deception would ultimately be discovered, and the couple would eventually divorce in 1924.

Bridget and her son meanwhile moved to London, where she found a house and took in lodgers to survive. After much pleading in letters by Alois, when William reached eighteen, his mother consented to him visiting his father in Germany in 1929. Besides renewing his relationship with his father, it also allowed him to meet his half-brother, Heinrich Hitler, the son of Alois and his second wife, Hedwig. Heinrich apparently was 'Hitler's favourite nephew', and later became an enthusiastic member of the Nazi youth and volunteered to fight on the front. He would be captured by the Red Army and die in a prison camp in 1942. After a happy family reunion of sorts. William returned home to his mother in London.

With the rise of the fascists in Germany and the UK in the 1930s, and the increasingly threatening noises emanating from Nazi Germany, William Patrick Hitler began to feel decidedly uncomfortable with his name and background. His connection to Adolf Hitler got him fired from one job, and made it difficult to find another. Now twenty-two, the young man decided to return to Germany, and make the most of Uncle Adolf's rise to power.

It worked, sort of, as Hitler used his influence to secure William a post in the Reich Credit Bank in Berlin, and later a position as a salesman in the Opel car factory (for 'used his influence' read 'scared the life out of'). As would later be revealed in a diary he kept of that time in Berlin, William even played the dangerous game of threatening to blackmail Adolf Hitler with embarrassing family revelations unless he found his nephew better and better positions.

Hitler responded by offering William a substantially elevated position on condition he become a German citizen and renounce his British citizenship. This would have allowed Hitler to prevent his departure, imprison him or even make him simply disappear without causing any diplomatic incident. But William probably suspected as much, and fled while he had the opportunity. It should be noted that his diary and early articles he wrote about Germany and his uncle indicate that he wasn't exactly averse to Nazi doctrine. But all that would soon change.

Back in Britain, he tried and failed to join the British armed forces when the war broke out, thanks naturally to his relationship with their enemy's commander in chief. So he and his mother set off for a new life in the United States. By the time he had completed a lecture tour about his time in Germany and his relationship with his uncle, the United States had entered the war. William wrote directly to President Franklin D Roosevelt, begging to be allowed to join the US military. 'I am one of many, but can render service to this great cause,' he wrote. FDR thought there might be propaganda value in the idea, and passed the letter on to FBI Director J Edgar Hoover for consideration. Any youthful courting of fascist ideals was forgiven as the folly of youth, and Hoover cleared him for military service after a thorough investigation of his background.

He didn't change his name when he went to sign up, and when he introduced himself to the recruitment officer as William Patrick Hitler, the man is reported to have said, 'Pleased to meet you Hitler, my name's Rudolph Hess.' During the war, he served with distinction as a Hospital Corpsman, was wounded in action and was awarded the Purple Heart.

After an honourable discharge in 1947, he finally decided to change his surname name and quietly disappear from history, content that he'd done his bit in the name of freedom. He became William Stuart Houston, married German-born Phyllis Jean-Jacques (who he'd met while in Berlin), and the couple settled on Long Island and had four children. William ran a small blood analysis laboratory called Brookhaven Laboratories.

William Patrick Hitler.

Despite his later anti-Nazi statements, it remains a curious fact that he gave his first-born son the middle name of Adolf, and the surname he adopted was strikingly similar to the racist, anti-Semitic author Houston Stewart Chamberlain, who had died in 1927.

William Stuart-Houston died on 14 July 1987, and was buried next to his mother Bridget, who had died in 1969, in Coram, New York.

4

STOP TAKING THE STUPID PILLS

Humanity is fond of slapping itself on the back about how we've overcome adversity of all kinds. We have conquered our basest instincts, honed our intellects to precision instruments and leapt from the caves to the exploration of space in a few thousand years. All very well, but not everything we've done would make it onto our CV if we were applying to join some interplanetary United Species organisation. In fact, every now and then, human beings are capable of perpetrating the most idiotic acts you can imagine. Presumably, these things must have seemed like a good idea at the time ...

LETTING THE CAT OUT OF THE BAG

Around the turn of the century, the CIA decided to de-classify a whole bunch of documents, mostly relating to Cold War events during the 1960s. Historians were delighted, especially as the documents shed light on some major events of that era, such as the Cuban missile crisis, the Bay of Pigs invasion and so on. But they also revealed some of the CIA's dafter plots and plans, notions that their eggheads dreamed up in the Pentagon back in those days of The Beatles and

'The Man from U.N.C.L.E.'. Actually, reading some of this stuff makes the wackier plots of that TV spy series seem quite plausible.

Perhaps the oddest was Operation Acoustic Kitty. No, that was not a spoof spy comedy like 'Get Smart'; it was a real CIA plan to use cats to carry out bugging operations in the mid-sixties. The idea was to train a bunch of cats to go where they were told. such as over the Soviet embassy wall. The thing was, these cats would have microphones implanted inside them, so the CIA would be able to overhear what those dastardly commie spies were talking about. Everyone inside the embassy would just assume it was the embassy cat, charged with no more sinister a task than tracking down mice. They would never suspect for a second that it was actually a secret CIA Spycat.

So, in 1967, veterinary surgeons were employed to implant a microphone into a cat's ear canal, and a small radio transmitter just under the skin at the base of the skull. This was connected to a very thin antenna, woven through the cat's fur to her tail.

This likely all sounded very plausible to the CIA and their bosses, as they ploughed twenty million hard-earned American tax dollars into the project. You would have to assume that none of the people involved were cat-lovers, as anyone with even a passing acquaintance with felines can tell you that trying to train a cat is about as easy as trying to poke out ear wax using a piece of cooked linguini. Whereas Rover the Labrador might fetch a stick or sit down on command, cats will simply regard you with disdain, then wander off to do their own thing. I could have explained this to the CIA for a lot less than twenty million dollars.

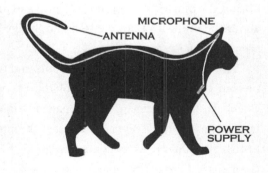

Anyway, back to Acoustic Kitty.

With their cat all wired up and recovered from its surgery, the guys decided they needed to do a test run. Two operatives, pretending to be commie spies, sat on a bench outside the Soviet Union's embassy on Wisconsin Avenue in Washington DC. The CIA boffins sat in a van nearby, surrounded by expensive equipment, headphones at the ready to eavesdrop on the men's conversation. They released the cat and directed it towards the two men. The feline, naturally, ignored its orders, decided to wander into the middle of Wisconsin Avenue and was immediately squashed by a passing taxi.

Operation Acoustic Kitty was abandoned not long afterwards, and all records pertaining it were locked away for almost thirty-five years. This was presumably because most of those involved would be dead after all that time, and would not therefore have to die of embarrassment when the story was released.

THAT SINKING FEELING

Did you know that when it was made, the movie *Titanic* was the most expensive production in history, costing just under two hundred million dollars, allowing for inflation? Astonishing, spending that amount of money on a movie, isn't it? James Cameron? No, no, no, not the one with Leonardo DiCaprio and Kate Winslet; I'm talking about the one with Hans Neilsen and Sybille Schmitz. Who the hell are they, you say?

Let's go back to the start. Not to 1912 and the middle of the Atlantic, but to 1942 and the middle of the Second World War. Joseph Goebbels, he of German war propaganda fame, decided to use the tragic story of the *Titanic* as a vessel through which to depict the British and Americans as cowardly, greed-driven capitalists and the Germans as heroic, principled men of the people. He was prepared to chuck a great deal of money at the project, despite the fact that the massive German war effort was draining the country dry of hard cash. But he thought this was an idea too good to miss, so he hired well-known film director Herbert Selpin to helm the movie.

Titanic, a disaster in every sense.

The project struck troubled waters right from the off. Selpin had recently directed another propaganda movie called *Geheimakte W.B.1*, about Wilhelm Bauer's contribution to the development of the submarine, so his nautical movie-making skills seemed perfectly appropriate. The only problem was that Selpin wasn't terribly keen on the Nazi party. Not at all.

Selpin managed to get Goebbels to free up a German liner, the *Cap Arcona*, for use on the exterior scenes, along with a large number of Kriegsmarine sailors and officers to act as unpaid extras – this despite the desperate need for sailors in the actual war effort. Incidentally, the *Cap Arcona* would ultimately succumb to a similar fate to the actual *Titanic*, but on a much larger scale. In the last days of the war, the Nazis were using the liner as a mini-concentration camp for Jewish prisoners. It was struck by RAF bombs and sank, with the loss of over 5,000 people, three times the number that died on the *Titanic*.

During production, Selpin became enraged at the behaviour of the naval officers, who he accused of being drunk most of the time and repeatedly molesting the female actors. He also made disparaging remarks about the Nazis in general, which didn't go down too well with his Nazi-sympathetic scriptwriter and soon-to-be ex-friend

SS Cap Arcona, the ocean liner used for exterior shots in the movie.

Walter Zerlett-Olfenius, who promptly reported the remarks to Goebbels. Selpin was arrested, and when he refused to retract, he was imprisoned. That night, two Gestapo officers entered his cell, murdered him and staged his apparent 'suicide'. The cast and crew were outraged, but were threatened with a similar fate if they didn't work with the treacherous scriptwriter and the new director. This was Werner Klinger, a virtual unknown, who would receive no credit for his functional work.

The plot for *Titanic* loosely went like this: White Star Line's shares are in the doldrums. The company's president, Bruce Ismay, persuades the Board to go along with a dastardly plot to make themselves even richer. They will all sell their shares and drive the price even lower, then buy them back when they are at their lowest ebb. Then, during the voyage, he will reveal that the *Titanic* can break the trans-Atlantic speed record and win the precious Blue Riband. When this sends the share price rocketing, hey, happy days for the evil western capitalists. Of course, the German First Officer tries unsuccessfully to persuade the captain to slow down, and then there is the infamous encounter with the iceberg. After they hit, the British and American cowards try to save themselves, while the German rushes about, saving women and children and poor people. The film's epilogue states: 'The deaths of 1,500 people remain un-atoned, forever a testament of Britain's endless quest for profit.'

The stars included beautiful German actress Sybille Schmitz, one of the most famous movie stars in Europe at the time. She was ultimately shunned by the Nazis because of her connections with the Jewish community. Tragically, after the war her links with Nazi Germany made her tainted goods as far as Hollywood was concerned, and she drifted into a world of drugs and alcohol, and committed suicide in 1955. Her role in *Titanic* was that of a Russian aristocrat who had recently been impoverished and was fleeing to America. Of course, she was madly in love with the German First Officer.

The heroic Leonardo diCaprio-type role fell to Hans Nielsen, who appeared in 136 movies until his death from leukaemia in 1965, aged just fifty-three. He made a couple of Hollywood appearances, usually playing a German, alongside the likes of Kirk Douglas and Christopher Lee. He was already a major star in Germany when selected for the totally fictional role of the German First Officer.

Herr Hitler himself visiting the set.

By the time Werner Klinger had finished the editing and post-production, the venture had racked up a bill of four million Reichmarks, or, if you take inflation into account, between 180 million and 190 million dollars – enough to pay the wages of 3,000 German factory workers for a year.

Goebbels watched the film, featuring people dying by the hundreds in panic and fear, with lots of screaming and explosions. He suddenly realised that it might not be so hot an idea to show this movie to people who, thanks to nightly raids by Allied bombers, were dying by the thousands in panic and fear, with lots of screaming and explosions. The movie's depictions of poor people trapped behind steel gates in steerage, begging to be released, also had uncomfortable parallels with the daily scenes of Jews being hauled off in prison vans to perish in concentration camps.

So he promptly banned from German cinemas what was at that point the most expensive movie ever made. It was released in Paris and Prague, and a few other Nazi-occupied cities, and was pretty well received, but didn't recoup even a fraction of its cost.

It effect, it sank almost without trace, with the loss of four million precious Nazi Reichmarks. On this occasion though, nobody mourned Goebbels's idiotic and disastrous maiden voyage into epic movie-making.

A still from the movie, showing a lifeboat escaping the sinking vessel.

NO KIDDING

The Paraguayan War of the late 1860s was the deadliest conflict in the history of South America, resulting in close to half a million deaths, including seventy percent of the adult males in Paraguay. Paraguay was also forced to cede large tracts of its land to its enemy – an alliance of Argentina, Brazil and Uruguay.

Near the end of the war, Paraguay was fighting a losing battle, and most people believed that ultimate defeat was merely weeks away. But Paraguay's President Francisco Solano Lopez decided that they would fight until the bitter end, despite the rapidly dwindling ranks of soldiers and resources. Depending on your point of view, he was either a champion of independence against the influence of foreign interests, or he was an ambitious and reckless leader who was prepared to risk countless lives to further his plans.

Few could argue against the fact that as the war progressed, Lopez, while obviously quite a courageous individual, became increasingly paranoid and, to be frank, a little nuts. In 1868, convinced that there was a conspiracy against him, he had hundreds of suspects rounded up, including his brothers and brother-in-law, judges, lawyers, religious leaders, cabinet ministers, senior army officers, foreign diplomats and basically anyone who

Paraguay's slightly unstable president, Francisco Solano Lopez.

looked half-crooked at him, and had them shot. That same year, when his mother admitted to him that he had been an illegitimate child (or more accurately, a complete bastard), he had her flogged and then executed.

But he reserved his strangest and creepiest behaviour for the following year, resulting in one of the most tragic events in the country's history. By August 1869, the Paraguayan army had been virtually wiped out, and only pockets of armed men survived. Still Lopez refused to surrender.

The Alliance had been pursuing the remnants of the Paraguayan army, and they finally caught up with their rearguard at Acosta Nu on 16 August. With so few men, Lopez knew they were doomed, but he came up with a plan to delay the Alliance's advance. He needed men desperately, but was willing to settle for what he believed was the next best thing – children disguised to look like adults. So he armed 3,000 children under the age of fifteen and then, bizarrely, commanded them to paint beards on their faces to make it look like the Alliance were fighting adults. He also ordered 500 old men to arm themselves for battle.

The Alliance had 20,000 men, and enough cannons to level a city. Lopez and his remaining adult army used the battle to escape, as the bearded kids stood their ground. The result was inevitable.

Child soldiers of Paraguay.

The Alliance forces overwhelmed the children and old men, killing or wounding virtually every last one of them. Their casualties amounted to less than 500.

Lopez was defeated and killed in battle the following March, bringing an end to the war. His infamous army of bearded children remains one of the most idiotic, misguided and tragic events of military history.

Today, 16 August is Paraguay's Children's Day, commemorating the courage of the children who gave their lives in a pointless, unwinnable battle.

THE MIND BOGGLES

It may have taken place over a century ago, but one would have imagined that as slavery had been abolished in the United States four decades earlier, civilised society would have moved beyond this sort of thing. But no. The following is a true account of a shockingly stupid, ill-advised and tactless stunt that was staged in St Louis and New York from 1904 to 1906.

Sometime around 1903, Ota Benga, a young member of the Mbuti tribe in what was then the Belgian Congo, left his wife and two children in his village to go hunting in the vast equatorial forests. The Mbuti were a race of indigenous pygmies who inhabited the greater River Congo basin. While Ota was away, the village was attacked and his family were brutally murdered. The attackers were the Force Publique, a militia used by King Leopold II of Belgium essentially to enslave the natives for use in the production of rubber. This atrocity was exposed by the Irish diplomat Sir Roger Casement, winning him a knighthood. (He was later stripped of his title and executed for his part in Ireland's Easter Rising of 1916.)

What happened to Ota Benga after that is uncertain. US businessman Samuel Verner made various claims about how he came to know Benga. These included tales of purchasing him from slavers for 'a bag of salt and a bolt of cloth'; of rescuing him from certain death at the hands of cannibals; or of Benga electing to go with him to escape enslavement by Belgian troops. His account of finding Ota Benga changed many times over the years, but it was generally believed that Verner had hunted down Ota Benga with the assistance of local tribesmen.

Verner was a white supremacist, born to a wealthy family in South Carolina. He was in Africa at the behest of WJ McGee, an anthropologist who wished to display 'representatives of the world's different species' at the St Louis World Fair of 1904. Verner and Ota Benga spent several weeks together as they journeyed towards the coast, picking up four more African tribesmen along the way. Although these men were effectively his property, Verner did allow them personal freedom and Ota Benga developed a liking for his captor.

Samuel Verner.

When they arrived in St Louis, Verner was ill and missed the start of the exhibition. Ota Benga and the others were put on exhibit to large crowds, who were fascinated in particular with Ota's teeth, which had been filed to points as part of a tribal ritual when he was young. People were amazed at his genial personality, considering that the newspapers had been describing him and his fellow Africans as 'savages'. One newspaper went as far as to say that Ota Benga was the 'only genuine cannibal in America,' a statement that was wildly inaccurate and offensive, and another headlined its report 'Pygamies Demand Monkey Diet!'

When Verner showed up, he revelled in the attention the exhibit was garnering, and actually encouraged the 'cannibal' myth. Verner did little to deter the eager crowds, who poked and prodded the Africans and taunted them with monkey calls. WJ McGee's so-called 'scientific anthropological exhibition' was in tatters, as the Africans had resorted to mimicking Native American dances to amuse the crowd. In a further demonstration of the horribly racist mindset of the World Fair organisers, Samuel Verner was awarded the gold medal in anthropology for his shocking display.

With the exhibition at an end, Verner returned the Africans to the Congo. He remained there for a couple of years, gathering relics of African tribal culture for sale to museums. Ota tried to reintegrate into his old way of life, and married a woman of the Batwa tribe, but sadly she was killed by a snakebite. Not having been born into her tribe, he felt he was an outsider and that he was essentially homeless. He accepted Verner's offer of a return to the US, a mistake that would cost him dearly.

Verner was by now in financial trouble. At the suggestion of the curator of the American Museum of Natural History, he took Ota to the Bronx Zoo, in an effort to exploit him for profit. Initially, Ota was allowed a free run in the zoo, and was an object of curiosity for people strolling about the place. But William Hornaday, the director, realised that he could turn the Mbuti tribesman into the zoo's biggest attraction. He encouraged the naïve Ota to spend time in the primate house, where they had fixed up a hammock for him and gave him a bow and arrows to shoot at a target. Hornaday had been right on one score – crowds of New Yorkers poured into the zoo to witness 'the human monkey', and soon the press got word of the new arrival. As the crowds grew in number, it was decided to move Ota Benga to a much larger space, and he was put inside a cage along with chimps and an orangutan called Dohang. A sign was erected that read:

The African Pygmy, Ota Benga

Age, 23 years. Height, 4 feet 11 inches.
Weight 103 pound. Brought from the Kasai River,
Congo Free State, South Central Africa,
By Dr Samuel P Verner.
Exhibited each afternoon during September

It has to be said that many New Yorkers were uncomfortable seeing the man caged with monkeys, as the New York Times reported:

... there were laughs enough in it too, but there was something about it which made the serious minded grave. Even those who laughed turned away with an expression on their faces such as one seen after a play with a sad ending.

The day after that report, a black clergyman called James H Gordon visited the Bronx Zoo, and was understandably outraged. The press reported his indignation widely:

Our race, we think, is depressed enough, without exhibiting one of us with apes. We think we are worthy of being considered human beings, with souls.

However, given the vast numbers spilling through the gates, Hornaday wasn't for turning. He defended 'the exhibit', claiming it was merely an ethnological display. He had the support of the New York Times editorial staff, who wrote:

We do not quite understand all the emotion, which others are expressing. It is absurd to make moan over the imagined humiliation and degradation Benga is suffering. The pygmies are very low in the human scale, and the suggestion that Benga should

Ota Benga.

be in a school instead of a cage ignores the high probability that
school would be a place from which he could draw no advantage
whatever. The idea that men are all much alike except as they
have had or lacked opportunities for getting an education out of
books is now far out of date.

Other prominent figures who believed in the white man's superiority
made their voices heard, among them Harvard professor of geology Louis Agassiz, and the professor of linguistics and archaeology
at the University of Pennsylvania, Daniel Brinton. A plea by Reverend
Gordon to the Mayor of New York, George Brinton McClellan, was
simply ignored. Verner defended the display saying:

If Ota Benga is in a cage, he is only there ... for his own safety ...
and to look after the animals. If there is a notice on the cage, it is
only put there to avoid answering the many questions that are
asked about him.

Verner also insisted that he was receiving no money for the exhibition. Unlikely as that was, the zoo certainly was. When reports emerged that zookeepers were accepting payments for a close-up peek into Ota's quarters, matters really started to heat up. More and more letters appeared in newspapers condemning the exhibit, especially when it was reported that Ota had to be forced into the cage, and was dragged there, kicking and biting the zookeepers.

Expressions of outrage continued to swell, from both the white and black communities. With Reverend Gordon leading the charge, the zoo and the city were threatened with a lawsuit, and with a groundswell of opinion turning in Ota Benga's favour, they finally relented. Ota was released into the Reverend Gordon's care, and was subsequently placed in an orphanage that the Reverend supervised. Later, he arranged for Ota to live with a family in Lynchburg, Virginia. He also paid to have his teeth capped, and bought him clothes that would allow him to blend into society.

But Ota Benga never settled, and he began to dream of a return to his homeland and his tribe in Africa. He had set his mind on this when the First World War broke out, dashing his hopes, as trans-Atlantic passenger shipping was suspended. In 1916, Ota Benga chipped the crowns off his teeth, reclaiming his native appearance, then built a fire in a nearby field and danced around it chanting as the sun set. That night, he stole a pistol and shot himself dead, finally joining with the spirits of his long-lost African family.

NO WIN SITUATION

The Austro-Turkish War of 1787–91, pitting the Hapsburg Empire against the Ottoman Empire, was in its second year when one of the most extraordinary battles in military history took place. Not because of any ingenious strategic battle plans, not because of the numbers of

The Ottoman army advances.

casualties, not because of the use of some new military technology, but because the two skirmishing forces were from the *same side*.

Some historians are sceptical about this event, and though three separate records of it do exist in three separate histories, all were written decades after the event. Mind you, that pretty much applies to the war in its entirety, so if doubt is to be cast on the nature of this particular battle, then doubt must also be cast on the entire four-year-long war.

One thing is certain: the Hapsburg Empire's army was a virtual Tower of Babel when it came to communication. The 100,000-strong army consisted of Poles, Czechs, Austro-Germans, French, Serbians and Croats. It had set up camp around the town of Karánsebes, in what is now Romania, on 17 September 1788, and a force of hussars was sent ahead to scout for approaching Turks. They crossed the Timis River in the dark, and soon ran into a party of Romany gypsies, who offered to sell them schnapps. The men, anticipating the possibility of death at the hands of the Turks in the days ahead, leapt at the chance and soon became quite inebriated.

A second party of infantrymen arrived, saw what had transpired and demanded their share of the schnapps. When this was refused, a brawl broke out, which became so heated that eventually someone fired a shot. Accounts say that someone also started to shout 'Turci! Turci!' (Turks! Turks!) or at least something that sounded like that, which caused widespread panic.

The infantrymen retreated back across the river, and the encamped army, having heard the shot and the commotion, became convinced that the Ottoman Empire was attacking. To make matters worse, a German officer trying to restore order started yelling 'Halt! Halt! Halt!' which was misinterpreted by non-German speakers as 'Allah! Allah!'

In the chaos and darkness, the army began to fire on their own approaching infantry. Artillery was soon booming around the vast camp, but nobody was sure who was who or where precisely the imaginary enemy was. A retreat was finally sounded, and the entire army abandoned the defence of the town. By the time they departed, 10,000 men lay dead or wounded.

Two days later, the Ottoman army marched up, scratched their heads at the sight of all the dead Austrian soldiers and the absence of any defence, and took command of Karánsebes virtually without firing a shot.

One of the theories about why it took decades to write an account of the battle is based on, well, common sense really. It was simply too embarrassing.

DRESSED TO KILL

Crinoline surely ranks as one of the stupidest fashion ideas in history, and arguably accounted for more clothing-related deaths than any other trend.

What was it? We are all familiar with images of Victorian ladies floating across the floor in their wide-bodied skirts. That is crinoline. The fashion of ladies' dresses with ridiculously large girths at the hem and ridiculously narrow girths at the waist (usually achieved with the assistance of a corset) was first conceived either by a Mademoiselle RC Millet in Paris in 1856, or by American WS Thomson around the same time. History has yet to definitively decide which one should be held accountable for this fashion atrocity.

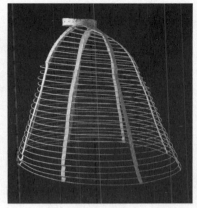

Cage crinoline.

Before their 'breakthrough' hooped-frame designs, a similar crinoline effect was achieved by making petticoats with a combination of horsehair and cotton or linen. This resulted in a very stiff and heavy fabric, often uncomfortable to wear thanks to its weight, especially in summer.

The steel-hooped cage crinoline was fashioned from thin steel struts angling out from a narrow waistband, also of steel, over which the petticoat was stitched. This design allowed for lighter fabrics than the original horsehair efforts. Other versions were made using whalebone, cane and even inflatable rubber, but the steel version was the most popular.

The fashion spread like wildfire (an unfortunate metaphor, as we will see), and soon members of the fairer sex of every social class were swishing about in their crinoline hoops. Competing hoop sizes became part of the fashion war of Victorian women, especially among the wealthy – the larger your hoops the trendier you were, or the richer. Some dresses grew to be six metres in diameter, and could only be worn when attending balls with sufficiently grandiose doors. How travel in a carriage was arranged is anyone's guess, but I imagine it required a lot of bending sideways and gentlemen averting their eyes as maids assisted the lady to maintain some modicum of dignity.

THE SAFEST WAY OF TAKING A LADY DOWN TO DINNER.

A cartoon, illustrating the daftness that fashion can lead to.

The less extravagantly proportioned crinoline dresses were also a cause of distress for many people, including working girls. Pottery factory owners, for example, despaired at the number of breakages caused by the swinging skirts. High-street shops were similarly plagued with breakages, as crockery, glass and marble ornaments, medicine bottles, preserve jars and wine decanters fell victim to the steel hoops.

More tragically, it being the era of the industrial revolution, many female factory workers were killed or horribly injured when their skirts became tangled in machinery. There are accounts of women's dresses being caught by gusts of wind, upending them. At best, this might have proven embarrassing; at worst, it resulted in fatalities, as women were blown under the wheels of vehicles or off piers while out strolling.

But by far the worst aspect of the crinoline fashion craze was the number of deaths caused by the dresses catching fire. In England alone, more than 3,000 women died in the 1860s as a result of crinoline fires. It is easy to see why – most households, rich and poor, had open coal or wood fires; given the width of the dresses at their hem, simply stepping too close to the hearth could be fatal. On top of that, the sheer circumference and area of fabric made it almost impossible to smother an entire fire with a blanket.

In 1858, the *New York Times* reported an average of three deaths per week in the city due to crinoline conflagration. In Santiago, a church fire resulted in at least 2,000 deaths, because of the flammability of the women's dresses but also because in the panic, the exits were blocked by hundreds of women trying to squeeze through the doors in wide, metal-framed dresses.

Two of the more well-known fatalities were Oscar Wilde's half-sisters, Emily and Mary. Mary was enjoying a waltz with their host, the Reverend Ralph Wilde, in his home in County Monaghan, and when she twirled by the fireplace, her dress caught fire. Emily and Ralph desperately tried to douse the flames, but then Emily's similarly flammable dress was suddenly ablaze. Reverend Ralph tried smothering them in his coat, then pushed them outside and rolled them in the snow, but it was all to no avail, and both girls perished.

Crinoline slowly declined as the new century dawned. By the 1920s and the era of the Charleston, it was all but gone, although there were attempts at reviving the fashion in the later twentieth century (truly, sometimes I wonder how humanity survives its own idiocy), including efforts from the likes of Christian Dior. Nowadays, you'll usually only find crinoline in ball gowns or wedding dresses. Of course, you might also find it in certain ladies' costumes for a Halloween fancy dress ball, but you should only wear it if you want to go dressed as a complete idiot.

5

ANIMAL CRACKERS

More than a few animals have made their mark on history, either through demonstrating abilities beyond their species' normal expectations, or because humans have employed them in unusual or sometimes downright cruel ways. Laika the Soviet space dog, Lonesome George the tortoise and Dolly the cloned sheep are obvious examples of animals who have hit the headlines, and there are lots of other beasts that have graced the pages of the past.

FIRE 'EM UP

Many eastern and north African cultures have employed elephants as weapons of war. The sight of these giants thundering towards them was often enough to scare the pants off an army. However, our tale here does not concern elephants so much as the means employed to counteract them.

In 1398, a Turco-Mongol ruler called Timur invaded northern India. Timur's stated aim was 'to lead an expedition against the infidels, to convert them to the true faith of Islam and purify the land itself from the filth, infidelity and polytheism'. Sounds kind of familiar. Anyway, advancing on Delhi, he was met by a defending army fronted by over 100 elephants with chain-mail armour and poisoned tusks.

His men were terrified at the sight of these giants facing them across the field of battle.

Timur was known as a military genius and a quick-thinking strategist – not to mention being brutal, ruthless and merciless, although that was sort of *de rigueur* for the time. He ordered his men to line up hundreds of camels facing the enemy, and to load them with as much wood and dry hay as they could bear. When the elephants began their charge towards them, he commanded the hay be set alight, and the camels prodded in the direction of the battlefield.

Timur.

The unfortunate flaming dromedaries fled, screaming in agony, towards the elephants, who were startled and terrified by the sight. Almost as one, the elephants turned tail and charged back the way they'd come, trampling hundreds of their own men and scattering the rest in panic and confusion. Timur then advanced and won an easy victory.

If you thought he'd been cruel with the camels, he augmented his reputation by butchering 100,000 of Delhi's citizens and lining the streets with their heads on poles. Lovely chap.

ON A WING AND A PRAYER

At the other end of the animal scale, the humble pigeon has often featured in history's footnotes, thanks to its message-carrying skills. And none more so than the First World War feathered friend known as Cher Ami, who was almost as famous with American kids of the time as the war's human heroes.

In 1918, several hundred men of the US 77th Infantry Division, under command of Captain Charles Whittlesey, became known as

First World War hero Cher Ami.

the 'Lost Battalion' when they were trapped behind enemy lines with no food and little ammunition. For four days, they were under fire not only from German snipers and grenades, but also from their own long-range artillery, who thought they were blowing Germans to pieces.

With the situation desperate, Captain Whittlesey released three homing pigeons. The first two were shot down immediately. The third, Cher Ami, made it past the initial German fire, but was then hit in the breast and leg and plummeted to the ground. Amazingly, Cher Ami rose again and continued on his way for the remainder of the twenty-five-mile journey, making it back to HQ in just over an hour.

His handlers were amazed that he'd been able to fly given his condition – the bottom of the leg carrying the message was gone, he was blinded in one eye and there was a huge gash on his breast. The message read, 'We are along the road parallel to 276.4. Our own artillery is dropping a barrage directly on us. For heaven's sake, stop it!'

As a result, the US Army mounted a successful rescue mission, retrieving the surviving 194 men. Cher Ami was treated for his wounds (including the fitting of a wooden leg), and became a hero and mascot of the Lost Battalion. He died the following year due to his injuries, but was immortalised thanks to a taxidermist and a nice display case in the Smithsonian Institute.

Although hippos are not particularly social animals, they do tend to hang around together, as evidenced by the blubbery crowds you'll see lolling in muddy water on wildlife programmes. They are territorial creatures, and are loathe to leave a spot once they've marked it as home sweet home. Which makes the case of Huberta the Hippo all the more strange.

Huberta, originally thought to be male and dubbed Hubert, led a seemingly contented hippo life around her watering hole in the St Lucia Estuary in South Africa's Zululand. Then, one day in late 1928, she took it into her head to go for a walk. Heading southwest, roughly following the coastline, she crossed over 200 rivers and streams, went for a dip at the popular Durban beach and had a bath in a monastery's pond. She trampled many a spring bloom as she wandered through gardens, she stomped the prized greens of a few golf courses and

she strolled down main streets of towns and villages. She slept on a railroad, holding up the train until the driver nudged her awake with the locomotive's cattle guard. Her journey naturally attracted the attention first of the local press and eventually of the international media.

Huberta arrived in the town of Port St John's and decided to set up home for a while. Her chosen spot became known as Mzimvubu River, or home of the hippopotamus.

Much to the locals' disappointment, her nomadic streak resurfaced in mid-1930, and she resumed her original trek down the coast, reaching East London by Christmas.

Thanks to her celebrity status, the Natal Provincial Council declared Huberta to be royal game, meaning no one could shoot her except a member of the British royal family. They weren't likely to be spoilsports and get themselves such bad press, so Huberta's future locked assured.

Unfortunately, a month after she'd reached East London, after a journey of an incredible 1,600 kilometres, a bunch of farmers near King William's Town shot her, bringing down a rain of national and international scorn upon their shoulders. They were arrested and tried, and claimed that they were ignorant of Huberta's celebrity and regal status. They each got a £25 fine, a light sentence considering that a sizeable proportion of the population wanted to lynch them. People do get so sentimental about animals.

No one knows why Huberta started walking. Many Zulus believed her to be the reincarnation of Shaka, one of the kingdom's greatest leaders, a belief that was reinforced when two members of the tribe threw stones at Huberta and were killed in a rockfall soon after. Others speculated that she was looking for a lost mate, or that she was fleeing after seeing her mother killed by hunters, although you'd have thought she'd have stopped fleeing such an event after a few hundred metres.

Whatever her reasons, her trek brought her a brief spell of international stardom and earned her a visit to a taxidermist. When her body was returned for display in the Amathole Museum in King William's Town in 1932, some 20,000 people turned up to welcome her. She's still there today, the museum's most famous exhibit.

SNAKES ON A SHIP

In terms of animals, the legendary Carthaginian general Hannibal is obviously most associated with elephants. But these weren't the only beasts he could turn to his advantage. Before the battle of Ager Falernus in Italy in 217 BC, Hannibal had his men secure torches to the horns of 2,000 oxen. These were lit and the animals driven in the dark towards a pass held by the Romans, tricking them into thinking that Hannibal's army was moving to attack at that point. Suffice it to say that the ruse worked, and it gave Hannibal sufficient advantage to kill over 1,000 Romans and secure victory.

Many more and far greater victories were to follow in the course of his glittering career. Leaping forward over three decades of disembowelling Romans by the tens of thousands, he also enjoyed a little-known naval victory in the east, and this one employed typically Hannibal-like originality and strategic genius.

General Hannibal in his best-known guise, commanding elephants.

Around 186 BC, he was on the run from the Romans and took refuge with Prusias I of Bithynia, a kingdom in the northwest of what is now Turkey. Like Hannibal, Prusias was no fan of Rome, and was at war with a nearby Roman ally, Eumenes II of Pergamon.

Prusias didn't have enough men to engage his enemy on land, so Hannibal counselled a sea battle, despite Prusias's navy also being inferior in numbers to that of Eumenes. Hannibal knew this was a situation he could control, especially with the masterstroke he held up his tunic sleeve.

He ordered a massive hunt for poisonous snakes. Thousands were captured alive, and loaded on board Prusias's ships in earthenware pots. As soon as the enemy's fleet came into range, Hannibal ordered the pots catapulted on to their decks.

Initially the sight of large pots raining down on them brought howls of laughter, but these were quickly replaced by screams of terror as the pots exploded and released their squirming, slithering, deadly contents. Unable to take the battle to Hannibal while count-less venomous fangs were snapping at their legs, the Pergamonians panicked and tried to flee. Hannibal attacked amid the chaos, and the enemy fleet was routed.

Prusias's gratitude lasted just a couple of years. Faced with the threat of annihilation at the hands of the ever-expanding Roman Republic, he agreed to surrender the great general. But Hannibal was determined to deny the Romans their prize, and poisoned himself in 183 BC. His final message reads: 'Let us relieve the Romans from the anxiety they have so long experienced, since they think it tries their patience too much to wait for an old man's death.' Given his antics with elephants, oxen and snakes, he could hardly blame them for being worried.

RUFFLING THE ENEMY'S FEATHERS

Perhaps the most unusual use of birds in a military confrontation occurred during the Spanish Civil War. In 1936, the war's first year, about 1,000 Nationalists were driven from their stronghold in Cordoba and had to retreat into enemy territory. They withdrew to the monastery of Santa Maria de la Cabeza, in mountainous, Republican-controlled territory.

Their comrades were desperate to supply them with food, weapons and medical supplies by airdrop, but there was an acute shortage of parachutes. Then someone hit upon the idea of replacing the parachutes with turkeys. Yes, you read that correctly.

Planes overflew the monastery, and the soldiers below were astonished to see the desperately flapping birds trying to slow their descent, having been tossed into thin air with heavy boxes attached to their backs.

Seriously, this happened.

Few succeeded in landing with anything but a splat. However, the plan worked to a degree and most of the supplies landed undamaged, thanks to the turkeys' valiant efforts to stay alive. And as for the turkeys themselves? Well, they were served up with stuffing as an added bonus for the soldiers.

The Nationalists held out for eight months, before being overwhelmed by a huge air strike combined with a ground assault involving 20,000 Republican troops. The battle also saw the end of the edible parachute.

ON THEIR HIGH HORSE

William 'Doc' Carver would later relate the life-or-death tale of his flight from bloodthirsty bandits, during which the high bridge he was crossing partially collapsed, and he and his horse plunged to the deep waters far below, dramatically escaping the desperadoes. After this hair-raising incident, he came up with the idea that would make him briefly famous.

A more mundane version told by colleagues has him riding along a bank in Medicine Creek, Nebraska, when his horse slips and they both plunge into the water far below. Dragging himself and his horse spluttering to the bank, he realises that he might just have landed on his feet in terms of making his fortune. And what is the idea that pops into his brain as he scrambles to the riverbank? Diving horses.

Doc Carver earned his sobriquet because of his early career as a dentist, or what passed for one back in the Wild West of the 1860s and 1870s. He put away his pliers in 1872 and picked up a rifle instead, soon realising that he was something of a marksman. By 1876, his skills were so good that he had become 'the man who can put a bullet through a silver quarter while the coin is flying through the air', according to the *New York Times* of the day. In 1878, he was proclaimed 'Champion Rifle Shot of the World', although there were many who would dispute his title. Yet his 'legacy' was not to be in the field of sharpshooting and his Wild West shows, which were hugely popular all over America at the time.

His encounter with the collapsing bridge/slippery bank came in 1894, when he was forty-three years old. He convinced his Wild West Show partner (his son Al) to get on board, and within months they had a sixty-foot-high tower (about the height of a modern five-storey building) and ramp built, overlooking a huge, circular pool. Carver trained several horses and riders, considering himself a bit long in the tooth to perform the act himself.

The first show was in Kansas City in August 1894. Thousands thrilled at the sight of rider atop terrified horse, which had to be repeatedly coaxed to take the plunge, though it eventually did. The enormous splash and quick reappearance of man and beast brought the crowd to their feet, and Carver knew he had a hit on his hands.

They took the show on the road, and the diving horse features became the principal attraction. Word spread far and wide about the spectacle, with pretty much nobody giving a second thought to the horses' welfare.

The craze lasted decades, and spouted imitators at home and abroad. An amusement park in Toronto featured a riderless horse plunging from a high ramp into Lake Ontario, presumably after some painful encouragement. Other shows saw horses diving into rivers, lakes and sea, saving promoters the cost of building a pool. Carver's show became a permanent fixture of Atlantic City's Steep Pier in the 1920s.

Carver's daughter-in-law, Sonora Webster, became the first female horse diver in 1924, sporting a bathing suit and adding some sex appeal to the show. This brought her a great deal of fame in her own right – she was the subject of a 1961 book, A Girl and Five Brave Horses, and a 1991 Disney movie, Wild Hearts Can't Be Broken. Sonora got to see this, as she lived until 2003, aged ninety-nine.

By 1927, Doc Carver's health was failing. This, combined with the drowning of a horse in the Pacific, caused him to go into rapid decline. He died later that year, aged seventy-six. Apparently, he dearly loved all of his horses, although repeatedly making them take a terrifying sixty-foot plunge into a small pool of water might be considered an odd way to express that love.

Incredibly, the craze for diving horses continued right up to the early 1960s, by which time animal rights activists were starting to make their voices heard. Eventually it was abandoned completely, although some idiots tried to revive it on the Atlantic City Pier as recently as 2012. Complaints and protests put a stop to it, mercifully, and no more of the noble beasts were forced to take the ridiculous plunge.

A HORSE OF A DIFFERENT COLOUR

Leaping across centuries and continents, another horsey tale from history concerns a single beast, no less fascinating than those high divers, albeit in a very different way.

William Bankes was born in Staffordshire, England, in the late sixteenth century, and trained to be a stable lad for the Earl of Essex – Robert Devereux, who would later have his head removed for trying to unseat Elizabeth I. In the course of his training, Bankes realised that he had considerable skills when it came to training horses, to put it mildly. Around 1586, when Bankes was in his early twenties, he came across a young horse and was taken by its abilities and aptitude for learning.

Sometime soon after, he purchased the horse, left his position and set off to make his fortune in London. He named the horse Marocco, after the Moroccan leather commonly used in saddles. The animal was described at the time as 'a small, muscular horse with remarkable litheness and agility; he also proved particularly intelligent and easy to educate.'

Bankes taught Marocco to do a huge variety of tricks in the years that followed, and the animal repeatedly amazed audiences by apparently counting money, bowing and curtseying, distinguishing colours, walking on two legs, playing dead and even urinating on command, which amused the less refined audiences greatly.

In one particularly popular trick, which elicited howls of laughter and produced many a red-faced girl, Bankes would order the horse to 'tell a maid from a maulkin' – in other words, to distinguish between a virgin and a married woman (or a harlot, depending on your translation of old English). This the horse would dutifully do, always picking the right girl.

Sure enough, royalty came to witness this miracle of creation. Bankes told Marocco to bow and curtsey to Queen Elizabeth, which he did. He then told the horse to do the same to Philip II of Spain (Elizabeth's arch-enemy). The horse responded by baring its teeth, rearing above Bankes and then chasing him offstage, much to Her Majesty's delight.

Bankes and Marocco's fame spread wide enough to earn him a reference in Shakespeare's *Love's Labour's Lost* – 'the dancing horse will tell you' – as well as mentions in Walter Raleigh's *The History of the World*, no less, and at least sixty contemporary histories and poems, such as this by John Bastard:

> *Bankes hath a horse of wondrous qualitie*
> *For he can fight, and pisse, and daunce, and lie,*
> *And finde your purse, and tell what coyne ye haue:*
> *But Bankes, who taught your horse to smel a knaue?*

Bankes and his horse were true stars of their times, comparable to the most popular television celebrities of modern times – more so in some ways, given that the principal media of the time was word of mouth. In fact, they became so popular that Bankes was a wealthy man by the time he was in his thirties, rich enough to build Marocco his own arena in the middle of London, which was frequently crammed with people from all walks of London society.

A tour of Shrewsbury, Oxford and Scotland proved less successful, however, as some of the local clergy and politicians began to suspect that witchcraft was afoot. Bankes returned to London, and to revive interest in the horse, he staged a publicity stunt in which Marocco climbed the 1,000-step spiral staircase to the top of the original St Paul's Cathedral, and then danced on the roof!

It seems that Bankes hadn't completely learned the lesson of that adventure in the English countryside. If you believe the account of his visit to France, after a number of shows, they were put on trial for witchcraft. The tale, likely apocryphal, is that Bankes either had the horse get on its knees to beg the presiding magistrate for mercy or else kiss a crucifix, after which they were released and returned to London.

By the early seventeenth century, Banks was employed by Henry, Prince of Wales, to manage his horses, although he still performed regularly with Marocco by all accounts. Rumours abounded at one point, including one by famed playwright Ben Jonson, that horse and master had been burned at the stake in Rome by Catholics, but there are references to Bankes being alive and operating as a vintner in 1637, some two decades after his apparent execution.

At some point, Marocco began to fade from recorded history, although he lived for decades in the oral storytelling traditions of the time. There is no existing record of how Marocco died, but he was apparently loved by Bankes as though his own child, and it is nice to think of Marocco the Wonder Horse ending his days munching on a bag of oats before falling into a quiet sleep in his London stable, happy dreams of the cheering crowds playing in his brain as he faded away.

....

Human history has its fair share of odd episodes when it comes to dealing with animals, but can anything top the fact that over the centuries, indeed up to the early twentieth century and across many advanced cultures, we have put countless animals on trial for a variety of crimes? Witnesses have been called, sentences have been pronounced (usually guilty) and thousands of animals of all sorts of species have been executed.

Among the creatures 'brought to justice' by humans are a pig and her piglets, who were accused of killing a child in Savigny, France. The trial involved a judge, defence and prosecution attorneys and multiple witnesses, and it was eventually determined that the pig was guilty. However, as her piglets were merely spattered with blood, they were exonerated. The pig was sentenced to being hanged upside down by her hind legs until dead.

TRIAL OF A SOW AND PIGS AT LAVEGNY.

Another was the famous incident of the 'monkey hangers' of Hartlepool in England. During the Napoleonic wars, a French ship was wrecked off the coast and the only survivor was the ship's pet monkey, dressed (presumably for the crew's amusement) in a tiny French uniform. The locals gathered on the beach and held an impromptu trial. Cross-examination of the creature resulted merely in agitated, terrified monkey noises. Having never seen a Frenchman before, prosecutors leaped to the rather startling conclusion that the monkey was actually a French spy. They sentenced the monkey to death and summarily hanged him on the beach. Ever since, Hartlepudlians have been nicknamed 'the monkey hangers'.

The Hartlepudlians at least had the excuse of an early-nineteenth-century education or lack of it, combined with superstition and war-time fear. The people of Erwin, Tennessee, and its environs, who lived during the modern era of the early twentieth century, can make no such defence. And compared to the monkey hangers, their act was on a jumbo-sized scale.

Mary was a five-ton Asian elephant, who performed in the Sparks World Famous Circus. She could reputedly play a musical instrument (tooting on huge horns with her trunk), stand on her head and throw footballs and baseballs. During a performance, her rider, a former janitor called Eldridge, untrained in animal handling, is believed to have poked Mary behind the ear with a sharp hook to spur her on. He clearly overdid it, as the normally placid animal seized him with her trunk and threw him against a drinks stand. Then, intentionally or not, she walked over him, breaking his neck.

Mary then calmed down and was ready to go about her business leading the elephant parade, blissfully unaware that the crowd had tried her and condemned her to death on the spot. A man arrived with a rifle and shot Mary five times. This failed to kill the animal, and did little to dampen the bloodlust of the locals.

As day turned into evening, word spread to neighbouring towns of the tragedy. The circus owners were informed of a boycott by all neighbouring districts, unless the animal was killed. And the following day, the baying – and swelling – crowd turned into a lynch mob.

The sad end of elephant Mary.

Mary was taken by train to a nearby railroad yard and chains were tied around her neck. The unfortunate beast was in considerable pain from being shot, but her situation was not about to improve. She was hoisted by the neck using a crane, to the cheers of a crowd of over 2,000 people. The chain snapped, and the elephant crashed to the ground, breaking her hip. She roared in agony, and the terrified mob fled.

A second attempt was more successful, and poor Mary finally succumbed. A vet examined her post-mortem, and determined that Mary had an infected tooth exactly where Eldridge had poked her, which simply made the idiocy of the act even more pronounced. Multiple photographs from a variety of angles exist to confirm the veracity of this outrageous tale.

NOT GIVING A RAT'S ARSE

The list of animals that have been tried and found guilty down the corridors of time includes pigs, cows, horses, mules, birds and even insects. The most common punishments included burning at the stake, hanging and beheading. But let's transport ourselves to France for a last look at one of these insane courtroom dramas, which has a fairly unique conclusion, but which is equally daft in its conception

Autun is a small town in eastern France, with a fine cathedral and some impressive Roman ruins. But an incident back in 1522 doesn't usually make it into the town's tourist brochures. Local farmers accused rats of having eaten some of the town's barley crop. The bishop formally charged the rats with the crime, and issued a summons for them to appear before the court on a particular day. He appointed a defence counsel, one Barthelemy Chassenee. This case would secure his reputation and be the starting point for a long and successful legal career (seriously, I'm not making this up).

The day of the trial came around and the farmers sat there awaiting justice. The prosecution and defence twiddled their thumbs, and the judge and the villagers grew increasingly impatient, because the rats had the temerity not to show up.

Chassenee brilliantly rose to their defence. The rats hadn't been given sufficient notice and, technically, posting the summons in the village square was insufficient, as the rats were spread over countless fields and parishes. As the original summons had also only been addressed to 'some rats of the diocese', and not, as it should have been, to every rat in the diocese, it was therefore invalid. The judge agreed, and commanded that a new summons be read out from every pulpit in the diocese every day until the date of the new trial. Not even the most retiring, reclusive of rats could fail to hear the command.

Naturally, everyone was shocked when the rats failed to appear again, which would make one wonder how humanity has progressed as far as it has. Chassenee now argued that his clients were unable in the given time to organise the complex migration over what were, to them, vast distances. The judge again deferred the trial and set a new date even further in the future. One can only assume while all this was going on that the diocese's rats were having a jolly old time feasting on all the untended barley.

When the rats failed to appear a third time, the brilliant Chassenee now argued that if his clients were being tried by the same rules as humans, then they were entitled to the same protections. As they were currently under threat of violence from all of Autun's inhabitants and their cats, his clients were unable to attend court in safety. In short, they were being intimidated. He demanded that the plaintiffs (i.e. the farmers) and their cats must all be brought before the court and threatened with severe penalties if even a single rat came to harm.

The plaintiffs threw in the towel at this point. Chassenee's brilliant legal rhetoric had finally worn them down, and the judge ruled the matter *sine die* (proceedings adjourned indefinitely), finding in favour of the rats by default.

Thus ended one of the few animal trials in history where the defendants actually got off scot free, although one might argue that the entire village were guilty of a criminally insane waste of time.

6

MURDER MOST FOULED-UP

Since ancient times, assassination has been used as a simple contrivance to achieve power, remove someone from power, right a supposed injustice, or simply get rid of someone because one takes a dislike to them. We know all about the really famous ones – Julius Caesar, Franz Ferdinand, Mahatma Gandhi, JFK and so on.

What are less well-known are some of the *failed* plots to dispatch enemies or rivals to beyond the grave. Had they succeeded, these plots would have seen our history books substantially rewritten, and perhaps even changed the world we inhabit today. Or maybe not. To be honest, who knows? Some of the conspiracies detailed below failed because they were a bit too offbeat; others because of damned bad luck, or poor timing; and others because the would-be assassins – or the plots – were quite simply insane.

AIMING HIGH

For aspiring assassins, targets don't come any bigger than the President of the United States. Of the forty-three Presidents that have been sworn into office, twenty have been the targets of assassination attempts that we know of (some of multiple attempts), and four of those (in fact, possibly six) have been successful. So before you decide to run for that office, remember that there is a forty-six percent chance that someone will try to bump you off at least once, and you have between a nine and fourteen percent chance of being killed in office. There has always been a list of candidates lining up to have a pot shot at a President.

Richard Lawrence wasn't after fame. He was after the money that was being denied him by President Andrew Jackson in January 1835. You see, Richard Lawrence was actually King Richard III of England. He had emigrated from that sceptred isle, where he still owned two large estates. Or so he believed. In case you aren't aware of this, Richard III died in 1485. He was the subject of a play by Shakespeare, and his remains were recently discovered and reinterred in Leicester Cathedral, but that's neither here nor there. Back in 1835, King Richard was still buried under a muddy Leicestershire field and not walking around Washington.

Poor Richard (Lawrence, that is) was a house painter, and in those days, manufacturers used a lot of lead in paints. As he'd been a fairly normal youth, the authorities later surmised that Lawrence's continued exposure to toxic materials, principally lead, had led to his eventual insanity.

In 1832, Lawrence's behaviour began to change dramatically. He quit his job, and announced to his family that he was going back to England to live on his 'estates'. He set off twice, each time showing up again to claim that US Government forces had prevented him from travelling. He also believed he'd read stories about himself in the press that lambasted his intentions to return to England and slighted his character. As the months passed, his delusions took on regal proportions.

President Andrew Jackson, meanwhile, was opposing the establishment of a national bank, as he believed the Bank of the United States was wildly corrupt and controlled by excessively wealthy foreigners. Richard Lawrence came to believe that he was being denied access to his fortune, and, by early 1835, had determined to do something about that 'injustice'.

Lawrence decided to take no chances. He equipped himself with two pistols, and spent several weeks observing the President's comings and goings about Washington. By now, he'd resumed his former trade of house painting, and witnesses would later recount him having conversations with imaginary people while he worked. On the day of the assassination attempt, he spent a good deal of time muttering and laughing to himself, then suddenly took off from his work saying, 'I'll be damned if I don't do it.'

On 30 January 1835, Jackson was due to attend the funeral of a congressman in the State Capitol, a fact that Lawrence had probably discovered. As the President departed after the ceremony, Lawrence emerged from behind a column in the Capitol's portico, aimed his pistol at Jackson's back at close range and pulled the trigger. The pistol misfired. The yells of fellow politicians alerted Jackson to the danger, and he swung about and commenced clobbering Lawrence with his walking cane. Among those who came to Jackson's aid was the legendary Davy Crockett, so-called 'King of the Wild Frontier', who was by then a politician.

This is where the tale gets a little odd, as before Lawrence could be subdued, he managed to pull out the second pistol and point it at the President at point blank range. Incredibly, this also misfired. When the Smithsonian Institute tested these actual pistols a century later, they both worked perfectly on the first try. The odds of both pistols failing to fire was estimated at over 100,000 to one.

Jackson was convinced that political enemies were behind the attack, but no evidence was ever produced for this. Lawrence was tried and found to be insane, and spent the rest of his life in a mental institution.

Another would-be presidential assassin who ended up in an asylum was bible scholar and poet John Schrank. Originally German, but a long-time resident of New York, Schrank had no known political affiliations. His motive for attempting to kill ex-President Theodore Roosevelt was apparently a dream he'd had, in which President William McKinley, who himself had been assassinated in 1901, rose from the grave and pointed to a portrait of Roosevelt. Roosevelt was saved by his predilection for giving really long speeches.

John Schrank was orphaned at nine, and raised by his aunt and uncle. They then died when he was a young man, leaving him distraught. He became very religious and wrote lots of poetry, spending much of his time wandering the streets of New York, lost in thought. Here's a sample of one of his efforts, called 'Be a man':

Is your country in danger
And you are called to defend
Where the battle is hottest
And death be the end
Face it and be a man.

When you fail in business
And your honor is at stake
When you bury all your dearest
And your heart would break
Face it and be a man.

Roosevelt, meanwhile, was campaigning as a member of the newly formed Progressive Party, hoping to be elected for a third term as President, contrary to the then-traditional two-term limit (the US Constitution now imposes a limit of two terms). Schrank came to believe that a third term for Roosevelt would amount to dictatorship, especially after his ghostly dream about McKinley. So, despite his fervent Catholicism, he decided it would be quite a moral act to save his country from such a fate.

It was 14 October 1912, and Roosevelt, having just dined in a Milwaukee hotel, was climbing into his car, destined for a speaking appointment. As he turned to sit, holding a copy of a speech and his glasses case in front of him, Schrank stepped from the crowd of onlookers and fired a revolver he had recently bought in New York. Unlike Richard Lawrence's weapon, this gun worked perfectly, and Roosevelt would surely have perished but for the fact that the bullet struck his glasses case and then his speech – which was fifty pages long! The bullet was sufficiently slowed by the thickness of the manuscript to prevent it doing serious harm. It penetrated the outer layers of Roosevelt's flesh but struck no organs.

Admirably, the ex-President insisted on carrying on with his evening's engagements, although mercifully for his audience, his speech was considerably shortened. Doctors treating Roosevelt in the following days decided it would be safest to leave the bullet in the ex-President's body, so he carried it around inside him as a souvenir for the rest of his days.

Schrank was determined to be insane, and spent the rest of his life in an asylum. He needn't have worried, incidentally, as Roosevelt's Progressive Party had split the Republican vote, and the Democrat Woodrow Wilson was elected by a landslide, denying Roosevelt his coveted third term. Maybe he should have given shorter speeches. Or perhaps not.

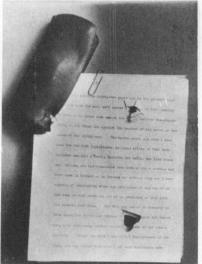

Saved by verbosity – Roosevelt's speech and glasses case.

Royals, of course, are also chart-toppers when it comes to assassination targets. And top of *that* list has to be King Zog of Albania, who reputedly survived fifty-five attempts. Zog was leader of his country for seventeen years, although in several guises: first as Prime Minister, from 1922–24; then as President, from 1925–28; and finally as Monarch, from 1928–39.

He was another chap who liked to demonstrate his resilience. Once, while PM in 1923, he had just arrived at the steps of the parliament building when sixteen-year-old Bequir Valteri shot him three times, none of the bullets doing any serious damage. Bleeding badly, tough nut Zog entered parliament, had a few quick bandages applied and delivered his speech before receiving serious treatment. Valteri was arrested and questioned about his motivations, many suspecting that one of Zog's rivals, Avni Rustemi, was behind it. Zog subsequently forgave Valteri at a private meeting – and a fortnight afterwards, Rustemi was himself assassinated.

King Zog of Albania.

Zog liked theatre and opera, and unfortunately he wore as many faces as the characters he witnessed in plays – good guy, tyrant, reformer, bandit, religious moderate, thief, and so on. He holds the title as the first Muslim king of a European nation (his royal connections were Egyptian, not European). He introduced education reforms, in an attempt to modernise his country, but he also liked to hoard the state's gold and jewellery, and resided in lavish palaces while most of the peasants endured mere subsistence and lived in nineteenth-century hovels. It was inevitable that he would make a few enemies, although he probably didn't anticipate having quite so many. He was so paranoid about being poisoned, for example, that he put his mother in charge of the royal kitchen; and so fearful of coup attempts that his four sisters were in charge of an army division each.

With all the assassination attempts, you'd imagine that Zog would do his level best to stay alive, but in fact, he smoked between 150 and 200 cigarettes a day, and indulged in frequent all-night poker parties.

Though he rarely left the safety of his palace, in 1931, he decided to visit Vienna. While there, he went to see a performance of Ruggero Leoncavallo's opera *Pagliacci*, which appropriately recounts a story of double-dealing, mistrust, betrayal and murder. As he was leaving, two exiled political opponents ran up and opened fire. Zog produced a gun from his jacket and fired back, the only known case of a European monarch doing such a thing, and this may have put the assassins off and saved his life. What's more, one of the attackers' guns misfired – yet another misfiring murder weapon. Despite Zog's quick reaction, his guard was killed and a government minister with him was injured, but the car sped off and Zog was saved, yet again.

Despite the recorded 600 blood feuds and vendettas against King Zog, and despite fifty-five assassination attempts, he eventually died of natural causes (if you can call extreme chain-smoking 'natural'), in exile in France in 1961.

England's Queen Victoria was a distant runner-up to Zog in the failed assassination attempt stakes, with eight notches in her royal sceptre.

The first came when she was just twenty-one, and four months pregnant. A man called Edward Oxford fired two shots at Victoria as her carriage passed in London. Police never definitively determined whether the guns actually had any lead balls, or merely contained gunpowder. Oxford initially claimed they were loaded, but subsequently

Edward Oxford makes an attempt on Queen Victoria's life.

denied it. His motives were never discovered, and he said later that he did it purely for notoriety. He had plenty of time to reflect on his fame – twenty-four years in an insane asylum.

Two years later came attempt number two. John Francis aimed his pistol at the Queen's carriage, but either lost his nerve or we had yet another misfiring pistol, and he fled. But Prince Albert, who was in the carriage, had seen the man, and the staggeringly unlikely story is that they decided to lure him out by going out the next day along the same route. True or not, sure enough, Francis tried again, his gun discharging this time but missing, yet deafening a policeman who intervened. He was transported to Australia for his trouble.

The day after Francis was sentenced to transportation, a hunchbacked youth called John Bean tried to kill Victoria, firing a flintlock pistol at her as she travelled to the Chapel Royal. The weapon – you guessed it – misfired, and Victoria survived. Bean's escape had the unfortunate consequence that the London police rounded up every hunchback from Paddington to Greenwich, and the city's hunchbacks were subject to attacks and abuse until Bean was finally reported caught. It transpired that his weapon had only been loaded with paper and tobacco. His little stunt earned him eighteen months' imprisonment.

Next up was unemployed Irish bricklayer William Hamilton. He tried to shoot Queen Victoria in 1849, but missed by a mile and was arrested. At first it was thought that his attempt was a political assassination, but it seems that he was probably simply looking to be imprisoned so he'd have free bed and board. He was sentenced to seven years' transportation.

The following year, an eccentric gentleman from a wealthy family, with the appropriate name of Robert Pate, bashed Queen Victoria on the pate with his cane, injuring her. Off to Tasmania he went.

In 1872, another Irishman, Arthur O'Connor, this time seemingly with a genuine political motive, ran up to the Queen, brandishing a pistol and a piece of paper. He had apparently written up an order for the release of Irish political prisoners, and intended forcing Victoria to sign. But one of her guards jumped on O'Connor, and that was that. It was later decided that O'Connor was insane, and he was sent to an asylum.

The last attempt on Victoria's life was by yet another man judged to be batty. Roderick McLean was a tramp, who had reputedly received a terse reply from Buckingham Palace about a poem he'd written. He managed to get a shot off at Windsor train station, before two Eton boys subdued him, beating him with their umbrellas. McLean's attempt was soon after the subject of a poem by Scotsman William Topaz McGonagall, widely adjudged the worst poet in history. Here's a brief flavour:

God prosper long our noble Queen,
And long may she reign!
Maclean he tried to shoot her,
But it was all in vain.
For God He turned the ball aside
Maclean aimed at her head;
And he felt very angry
Because he didn't shoot her dead.

Victoria is a good Queen,
Which all her subjects know,
And for that God has protected her
From all her deadly foes.
And she also gives the gipsies money
While at Balmoral, I've been told,
And, mind ye, seldom silver,
But very often gold.
May He be as a hedge around her,
As he's been all along,
And let her live and die in peace
Is the end of my song.

One last royally disastrous and tragic plan to kill a monarch concerned a certain Giuseppe Marco Fieschi, who wanted to rid the world of King Louis Philippe I of France in 1835. A Corsican thief and forger, Fieschi had previously been sentenced to ten years in prison, along with ongoing surveillance. He was now filled with bitterness towards French society and, in particular, the King, who symbolised everything Fieschi despised. He began to mix with other characters with political axes to grind against the monarch.

But it was the method of the would-be assassination for which Fieschi is remembered, and reviled. He conceived an 'infernal machine', which a contemporary press report described thus:

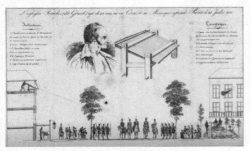

This machine consists of twenty-five gun barrels, arranged horizontally upon two cross pieces, set in a square frame. The breeches of these barrels are

Fieschi and his 'infernal machine'.

let into grooves of about half an inch in depth; the construction is rough, but solid and strong. A strong bar is fixed at the posterior extremities of the barrels to receive the shock of the recoil at the moment of explosion.

His 'infernal machine' was essentially a supergun, with twenty-five barrels that could fire simultaneously, each of which could be loaded with eight bullets and twenty buckshot lead pellets. Feischi was broke, so his co-conspirators paid for the contraption, and the assassin set about constructing his weapon in an apartment along the route the King and his three sons would take during the annual review of the Paris National Guard.

As the King's retinue passed the apartment, Feischi pulled the trigger, sending an estimated 400 metal projectiles hurtling towards their target. To describe Feischi's weapon as indiscriminate is a serious understatement. Eighteen people were killed instantly, including nine senior military officers. At least the same number were injured, some of them seriously, and there were also multiple horse fatalities. The scene was one of horrible carnage. As for the King, he received a minor graze on his forehead. To demonstrate his refusal to be intimidated, he carried on with the day's inspection. His sons were also largely unharmed.

Feischi was another victim of his supergun, as several of the barrels had exploded when he'd pulled the trigger, causing him severe head and facial injuries. He was arrested, and accounts suggest that the authorities spared no expense in treating the wounds to his head, as they intended to remove it at their own pleasure. He was tried and convicted of murder, and was guillotined the following February, along with a couple of his co-conspirators.

What survived of Feischi's supergun can still be seen in the Museum of French History in Paris. Somehow, Feischi's death mask ended up on display in Norwich Castle – if you're ever in the vicinity and fancy a look, apparently the scars from the exploding barrels are visible.

IN THE WARS

On 11 September 1926, anti-fascist operative Gino Lucetti tossed a bomb at Benito Mussolini's famous Lancia in Rome. It exploded, but not before bouncing off the windscreen, then off the running board and finally landing on the road. By the time it finally blew up, Mussolini's car was well out of danger. Lucetti was sentenced to thirty years in prison.

On 31 October the same year, fifteen-year-old Anteo Zamboni tried to shoot Mussolini while he was visiting Bologna. He fancied himself an anarchist, but was more likely influenced by puberty than anarchy. A bunch of fascist thugs immediately set upon Zamboni, beat him savagely and then lynched him. A street in Bologna is named after the youth.

In February 1931, American anarchist Michael Schirru came to Rome with the express intention of blowing up Mussolini. Bombs were later found in his hotel room. He was arrested, but not searched, and he pulled a gun and shot himself in the head. Incredibly, he survived. He was nursed back to health, stood trial and was sentenced to be shot in the back by firing squad, presumably to underline the perceived nature of his crime. This despite the fact that he never killed anyone, and never came within ten metres of Mussolini.

But the oddest attempt on Mussolini's life, and the one that came closest to succeeding, was not by an anarchist or an anti-fascist, or political conspirators of any sort. The perpetrator was a short, frail, grey-haired Irishwoman of fifty, though she looked considerably older, whose father had been the Lord Chancellor of Ireland.

Her name was Violet Gibson, and she grew up in the privileged surroundings of a large Georgian home in Dublin's Merrion Square. Her father was Edward Gibson, a prominent Irish lawyer who would serve as Lord Chancellor in the years before Irish Independence and would bear the title 1st Baron Ashbourne. Violet was plagued by ill-health all her life – including scarlet fever and pleurisy in her youth, then as an adult. Paget's Disease resulting in a mastectomy, and a botched appendectomy. She was also given to bouts of depression.

Originally a Protestant, she toyed around with various oddball religions before settling on the more conventional faith of her native country, Catholicism. This actually became an obsession, and her fixation on sacrifice in the name of God led to her spending time in a mental institution. Her Catholicism also brought her to Rome upon her release, where she lived in a convent. Yet she remained obsessed with the notion of sacrifice, initially focussing those thoughts upon herself. She managed to obtain a pistol – weapons were a lot easier to purchase in pre-war Europe – with which she attempted to kill herself in 1925, but she botched the job and somehow survived.

By the following year, she'd shifted her attention to Mussolini as the one to be sacrificed. Why she picked him in particular is anyone's guess, though she claimed later that she did it 'to glorify God'.

Early on 7 April 1926, Gibson wrapped herself in a black veil and left the convent. In one pocket she carried a gun, and in the other a rock, with which she intended to break Mussolini's windscreen. She walked to Palazzo del Littorio and waited with the adoring crowds for the fascist leader to make his scheduled appearance. She must have been pleased when he appeared on foot and began a walkabout, shaking hands and revelling in the cries of 'Viva Il Duce!'. She must have appeared the least likely assassin in history, no different to the many other black-clad elderly women you might encounter on Rome's streets in the 1920s.

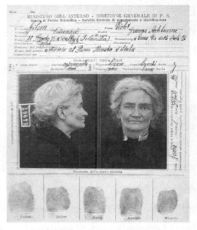

Violet Gibson's prison ID card.

With little reason to be wary of such a person, Mussolini stepped to within a metre of her, at which point Gibson pulled out the revolver and fired. 'Il Duce' for that moment became 'Il Fortunato', because his head moved back slightly in response to the appreciative crowd, and the bullet merely clipped his nose. Gibson tried to fire again, but the gun jammed – something that has foiled so many potential assassinations it seems to defy the laws of chance.

To his credit, after the initial shock, Mussolini regained his composure and assured the crowd, 'Don't be afraid. This is a mere trifle.' The crowd seized Gibson and began to beat her, but policemen wrestled her free and took her away. In the days after, Mussolini was seen sporting a large dressing on his nose.

Gibson was interrogated for days, but, after being thoroughly assessed medically, and after pleas and apologies from her family and friends, under order from Mussolini himself, she was released into the care of her sister, as she had been judged insane. She was sent to England, where she was confined to a mental institution in Northampton until her death thirty years later.

To be pipped by a nose in horse racing is failure by the smallest margin. Violet Gibson's shot was a mere nose-length away from finding its target, making hers one of the great 'what-ifs' of Second World War history.

The biggest 'what-if' of the war, of course, concerned Adolf Hitler. And we have a wealth of attempts to ponder over, any one of which might have changed the world as we know it. Claus von Stauffenberg famously came closest, his attempt the subject of many movies, most recently *Valkyrie*, starring Tom Cruise. But between his political beginnings in the early 1920s and his ultimate demise in the Berlin bunker, Hitler was the target of thirty-five attempted assassinations. These included shootings, bombings, poisonings, exposure to lethal gas and exposure to pornography. Yes, you read that correctly. Let's take a brief look at a few of the dafter or odder plots to take out Die Fuhrer.

In early 1944, a group of US airmen, armed with the belief that Hitler was puritanical in the extreme, hatched a dastardly plot to strafe the Wolf's Lair with thousands of pornographic magazines, thus driving Hitler into such a fit of rage that he would have a heart attack. Not surprisingly, their superiors rejected the men's plan as essentially crackpot, although it would undoubtedly have acted as a happy distraction to many of the thousands of German soldiers protecting Hitler.

Jumping back almost a decade, we come across the case of Heinrich Grunow, a loyal SS man who was enraged when Hitler sanctioned the execution of his colleague, and co-founder of the Nazi party, Ernst Rohm, in the Night of the Long Knives. The story goes that Grunow decided to strike while Hitler was visiting his beloved Berchtesgarten retreat in Bavaria. Using his cover as an SS guard to infiltrate the area, he waited at a spot where Hitler's chauffeur-driven car would have to slow down to take a bend. Then he opened fire, killing the back seat passenger. The story goes – and please note that this may well be apocryphal – that Hitler had decided he'd enjoy driving through the countryside that day, and had switched places with the unfortunate chauffeur. After the attack, Grunow supposedly shot himself on the spot. Or, in an alternate version of how he met his end, he was arrested and tortured by the State Police before being sent to Sachsenhausen concentration camp, where he died in March 1945.

A year before the audacious 'Valkyrie' plot, one of its masterminds, Hermann Von Tresckow, came up with a much less elaborate scheme – to kill Hitler with a couple of exploding bottles of brandy. It was March 1943, and Hitler had just made a visit to the western Russian city of Smolensk.

Another day, another assassination attempt. Herr Hitler examines the wreckage.

where von Tresckow was stationed. As Hitler was boarding the plane for the return journey, he handed one of the Fuhrer's staff a box containing two bottles of Cointreau, to be delivered to a friend in Berlin. The parcel also concealed plastic explosive and a thirty-minute fuse.

When Hitler arrived safely, von Tresckow was both stunned and terrified. What could have gone wrong? And as soon as the parcel was delivered, his plot would be uncovered. He quickly telephoned a co-conspirator in Berlin and explained what had happened. He then rang the man with the parcel and delayed its delivery on some pretext, allowing his friend time to remove the bomb. Von Tresckow survived, but only until the following year, when his next attempt failed and he committed suicide to avoid being tortured.

If you think liqueur bottles are bad, how about exploding chocolate bars and exploding tins of plums? These weren't aimed at Hitler, but at his nemesis, Winston Churchill. The Nazis' plan was to work thus: Flat slabs of explosive were stuck to a piece of canvas, which was then coated in a thin layer of chocolate. The bomb was then packaged as Peters Chocolate – a luxury item, especially in wartime.

Churchill was well known to have a sweet tooth – the evidence was there for all to see – and the Nazis somehow planned to supply the bars to the Cabinet War Office, in the hope that they would be given

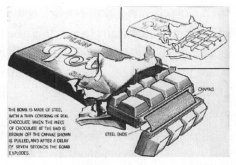

CANVAS

THE BOMB IS MADE OF STEEL WITH A THIN COVERING OF REAL CHOCOLATE. WHEN THE PIECE OF CHOCOLATE AT THE END IS BROKEN OFF THE CANVAS SHOWN IS PULLED, AND AFTER A DELAY OF SEVEN SECONDS THE BOMB EXPLODES.

STEEL ENDS

to Churchill as a treat. When a piece of the chocolate was snapped off, the tugging action would trigger the explosive, which would kill anyone within a few metres. There was a seven-second delay before the thing went off, but in theory by the time you'd scratched your head at the sight of the buried canvas, well, bang.

Fortunately, British agents uncovered the plot. A poster was commissioned illustrating the bars for the general public, in case any of them made their way onto Britain's streets.

There are no known cases of anyone being killed or injured by an exploding chocolate bar, or indeed exploding tins of plums or motor oil, thermos flasks and a variety of other common containers, all of which items were used to conceal bombs aimed at the general British public, so one has to assume the plan was abandoned and that particular can of worms was never, thankfully, opened.

LOSING THE PLOT

Finally, a collection of attempted assassinations that don't fit into any particular grouping, unless you can call 'oddball' a grouping. And what better place to start than ancient Rome, and the court of Emperor Nero.

Without going into the complicated details of the power struggles between Nero and his mother Agrippina, suffice it to say that the scheming, ruthless woman was the focus of a great deal of ill-feeling from her scheming, ruthless son. Nero decided eventually to get rid of her, but didn't want to use the usual methods, like poisoning or stabbing, as it might be too obvious that he was behind it. It seems he wanted to make it look like an accident, which makes you wonder about his sanity, given the elaborate nature of his first crackpot attempt on his mother's life.

If you've seen the comedy movie *Heaven Can Wait*, starring Warren Beatty, you might remember a scene where his character (the target of a murder plot by his wife and her lover) walks into his bedroom and casually tosses his jacket on the bed, only to see the heavily weighted ceiling of the four-poster crash down on the mattress in a cloud of dust and destruction. One might suspect that the screenwriter borrowed the idea from Nero, because that's exactly what he tried to do to his mother. He had her bed rigged so that its lead ceiling would collapse and crush her the moment she sat down. The contraption actually worked, but unfortunately for him, Agrippina wasn't on the bed at the time. One version of the tale plausibly recounts how she would have a slave warm her bed for her before she retired, and it seems this poor girl was the tragic victim.

The collapsing bed-ceiling having failed, Nero moved on to an equally elaborate and expensive plot – building a self-sinking boat. In fact, some historians combine the two attempts into one, with the collapsing bed-ceiling occurring on the self-sinking boat, but that surely would have been overkill, even for the likes of Nero.

He invited his mother to celebrate the festival of Minerva at his seaside villa in Baiae, just north of Naples. She would be honoured on board the elaborately adorned boat as part of the celebrations. Not far from the shore, the boat began to sink. Realising what was happening, she and her very loyal slave Acerronia dived into the sea and swam for shore. Acerronia reputedly saved Agrippina by crying out to Neronian conspirators on another boat that *she* was Agrippina, and pleading to them to save the mother of the Emperor. The men clubbed the courageous Acerronia to death, the distraction allowing Agrippina to swim to the safety of a passing fishing boat. (Another variation on the tale is that Acerronia selfishly pretended to be Agrippina so she would be saved, not realising a murder attempt was afoot.)

But Agrippina's reprieve was brief. Nero apparently tired of his daft, overly complex assassination plots, and finally simply sent a couple of thugs to stab her to death.

A couple of millennia later, modern man had moved well beyond disposing of his enemies by means of such ill-conceived, frankly laughable schemes. *You wish.* Well, of course, we hadn't. The target of many such hair-brained schemes was Fidel Castro, Cuba's legendary communist leader and a figure of hatred and fear in the US in the 1960s, at the height of the Cold War.

Endless hours were spent by top 'intelligence' guys in CIA HQ, brainstorming new levels of daftness in their attempts to rid the Western Hemisphere of the head of Cuba's Godless commie state. There follows a brief summary of a handful of their dastardly plots.

El Commandante, Fidel Castro.

Fidel loved scuba diving, and so a couple of the schemes were directed towards this. Fake mollusc shells, painted in bright colours, were to be positioned on the seabed near where he would dive. These, of course, were explosive devices, and as soon as he came near – boom! Another submarine scheme involved coating the inside of a strategically gifted wetsuit with the lethal tubercle bacilli bacterium.

Then there was the femme fatale approach. It was arranged for one of his mistresses, Marita Lorenz, to smuggle poisonous pills into his bedroom in a jar of cold cream, where she was to somehow administer them, possibly via a drink. Unfortunately for her, the pills dissolved in the cream. Castro somehow suspected what she was up to, and actually offered her his gun to shoot him, to which she replied, 'I can't do it, Fidel.' Ah, love.

The old James Bond movies with Sean Connery featured gadgets such as walkie-talkie wallets, shoes with poisonous spring-loaded knives, exploding lighters and dart-firing cigarette packets. The CIA guys were clearly big fans, as one of their schemes involved a ballpoint pen with a poisonous stabbing syringe in the middle, and another featured a poison-laced cigar.

The James Bond approach having failed, they shifted to more of a Groucho Marx strategy. Once again, Fidel's love of cigars was to be his downfall, but this time, when he lit the cigar it would explode, taking his head off in the process. This was actually proposed by the CIA to NYPD chief Michael J Murphy, the man in charge of security for Castro's visit to the United Nations in New York in 1967. The thinking was that a policeman could get close enough to Castro to put the cigar on his person, perhaps by slipping it into his pocket.

This plan was also abandoned for unknown reasons, but most likely because it would have made an awful mess in the UN building.

A few of the other reported 600-plus assassination schemes against the Cuban included a poisoned handkerchief, a poisoned milkshake and aerial spraying of his home with LSD, which might not kill him but would certainly have made his famous three-hour speeches a lot more interesting. Anyway, despite all attempts by the CIA, ex-Cuban exiles and God knows who else, Fidel lived to the ripe old age of ninety.

Another strange Cold War assassination plot was cooked up by none other than Joseph Stalin. This was not against an American politician, spymaster or military leader, but targeted the legendary icon of the screen, John Wayne, of whom Stalin was a huge fan. The actor was famously right wing and was well known for his anti-communist rants. Such was his popularity in the late forties and early fifties that Stalin determined to shut him up once and for all, despite his personal love of Wayne's westerns.

The story goes that the KGB despatched two agents to Hollywood, but that the FBI got wind of the plan and sent their own agents to warn Wayne. The macho actor told the Bureau to let them come for him, and not to worry about it. He came up with his own scheme, wherein he and some buddies would capture the Soviet agents, take them somewhere remote and stage a fake execution to scare them. Yes, it sounds like a Hollywood plot. But the FBI was waiting for the two Ukranian KGB agents, and the CIA later recruited them, before the world was robbed of Mr Wayne's gun-slinging talents.

John Wayne along with Gail Russell, in 1947's *Angel and the Badman.*

A second attempt to kill Wayne was made during filming of the western Hondo

in Mexico – the apocryphal account has the potential assassins foiled by Wayne himself, with the help of fellow actors. The movie star also claimed that Mao Tse-tung had tried to kill him while he was visiting US troops in Vietnam, a war he wholeheartedly supported. The sniper missed, and was subsequently caught and confessed, or so the story goes.

Undoubtedly, some of these assassination plots were in Mr Wayne's imagination and as fictional as *The Quiet Man*, but equally undoubtedly, Stalin did try to kill Wayne at least once. Nikita Khrushchev met Wayne on a visit to the United Nations in 1959, and reputedly told the star about the assassination plot: 'That was a decision of Stalin during his last five mad years. When Stalin died, I rescinded that order.' Perhaps he liked Wayne's movies even more than his predecessor.

Miles Sindercombe arguably holds the record for the most failed assassination attempts by the same person on the same target. The object of his hatred was Oliver Cromwell and, as the leader of a group of anti-Cromwellian conspirators, he tried to kill the Lord Protector no less than five times, failing miserably on each occasion.

The first attempt was in 1656. Sindercombe chose a house overlooking a London street, which they knew Cromwell would pass in his coach and from which they intended to shoot him. However, realising they had little or no chance to escape, the idea was abandoned at the last moment. Next, they decided to use a longer-range weapon and employ the marksmanship skills of one of their group, but forgot to allow for the crowds that would inevitably gather outside Westminster Abbey as Cromwell departed. Unable to get a clear shot, that plan was also abandoned.

The following attempt failed due to pure bad luck. They intended to assail Cromwell's coach as it passed through a narrow passage on its regular journey to Hampton Court, but that particular day Cromwell decided to go via a different route. The plotters were left sitting there, twiddling their thumbs. On the fourth occasion, Sindercombe decided they would simply shoot Cromwell as he strolled in Hyde Park. One of Sindercombe's men, John Cecil, waited on a horse as Cromwell approached. To his surprise, Cromwell walked over to him in a most friendly manner, and began to talk admiringly about his horse. It may have been that Cromwell's friendliness humanised him in Cecil's eyes, but for whatever reason, he couldn't bring himself to kill Cromwell.

By now deeply frustrated, Sindercombe decided on a much more indiscriminate plan – they would blow Whitehall Palace to pieces. And they actually managed to get a large explosive device of gunpowder, tar and pitch in place, in the Palace chapel, early in 1657. Perhaps because of the notion of killing so many innocent people, one of the conspirators, John Toope, sold them out to the authorities, and the bomb was disarmed.

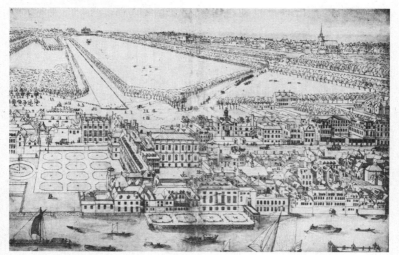

Whitehall Palace.

Sindercombe was arrested, tried and sentenced to be hanged, drawn and quartered, but his sister managed to sneak him some poison the night before his execution and he finally managed to kill someone – himself. However, not to be denied their gruesome revenge, the authorities had his body dragged through the streets behind a horse. He was buried at the foot of the gallows where he was supposed to be hanged, with a stake driven through his body, left protruding from the ground as a warning to others. Not that Miles gave two hoots at that point.

7

BYPASSED BY HISTORY

UN-REVERED

Even outside America, most English-speaking people have heard the story of Paul Revere, or at least have a vague idea of what he did. His fame originated in his legendary, romantic midnight ride to warn Colonial forces about the approach of the British Army, which led to the first battle of the American Revolutionary War, and victory  for the colonists, although the battle was really just a skirmish by normal international war standards, with roughly 120 deaths. Revere became immortalised in a poem by Henry Wadsworth Longfellow called 'Paul Revere's Ride'.

Yet there are several others who might feel somewhat peeved at the history books, as Longfellow clearly didn't want multiple heroes cluttering up his rhyming schemes. The fact is, there were many despatch riders galloping along the roads that night. One such was William Dawes, who actually accompanied Revere much of the way. Another was Samuel Prescott, who volunteered to join them and acted as their guide.

Several nights before these three set out, one Israel Bissell began an even more impressive ride to warn the colonists – his journey took four days and covered 350 miles. At one point, he had to find a new horse when his first mount dropped dead through exhaustion. At each village or house he reputedly yelled out, 'To arms, to arms, the war has begun!'

Sybil Luddington.

Perhaps the most cheated of the despatch riders was Sybil Ludington. As a woman and non-soldier, she was completely overshadowed by her male companions, and was perhaps even more worthy of a Longfellow poem than Revere. Sixteen-year-old Sybil's father was Colonel Henry Ludington, commander of the local volunteers. One week after Revere's ride, Sybil volunteered to warn the neighbour-ing towns of an impending invasion by British forces. She set out on her heroic quest, dashing off alone into the rainy darkness and covering over forty miles, twice as far as Revere had covered. If that wasn't tough enough, she had to beat off a highway robber with a stick in the middle of her journey.

All in all, she raised over 400 troops to her father's side. Although they were too late to defend the town of Danbury, in the subsequent Battle of Ridgefield they succeeded in driving the British forces back to Long Island Sound.

Among those who congratulated Sybil was a chap named George Washington. After that, unfortunately, Sybil's name generally slipped from the record books, until a statue of her was finally erected in 1961 in the village of Lake Carmel, which was along the original route she took.

GETTING THE WRONG ANGLE

The Greek mathematician and philosopher Pythagoras (470–590 BC) didn't have to do anything as dramatic as gallop through the night to achieve fame. In fact, he probably never had to leave his table, stylus and piece of papyrus.

The Pythagorean theorem is something you probably remember from school – if you don't, you obviously weren't paying attention, as it is one of the most famous of all theorems in geometry. It states that in a right-angled triangle, the square of the hypotenuse (c) (the side opposite the right angle) is equal to the sum of the squares of the other two sides (a and b). Or, expressed as an equation, $a2 + b2 = c2$. And bob's your uncle, immortality.

The only problem is, Pythagoras wasn't actually the first to come up with the theorem. Not by a long shot. Unfortunately, we don't know the name of the individual who first made this mathematical breakthrough. But we do know that the Śulba Sūtras texts from India, which predate Pythagoras by a century or two, and which provide guidelines for building sacrificial fire altars, contain Pythagorean equations. Similarly, the Chinese text known as the Zhou Bi Suan Jing, dating from around 1000 BC, contains a clear visual representation of the Pythagorean theorem. Of course, it's a little easier to say Pythagorean theorem than Zhou Bi Suan Jing-ian theorem, and on such minor variances in the spoken tongue often lie the difference between fame and obscurity ...

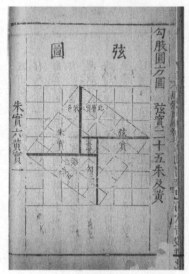

A page from the Zhou Bi Suan Jing.

THE EARTH MOVED

Another chap you might have heard about in school was the great Polish/German Renaissance mathematician and astronomer Nicolaus Copernicus. Most people will immediately think of him as the first person to suggest that the Earth revolves around the sun, and that the Earth is not at the centre of the universe. His theories led some to accuse him of heresy – the Church had arrogantly made humans the most important thing in existence, and God, naturally, would only place his greatest creation on a planet at the centre of the universe.

Aristarchus of Samos.

So Copernicus's work caused a lot of controversy, even for decades after his death in 1543. Yet his legacy survived, and history remembers him as the first to postulate a heliocentric (sun at the centre) model of the solar system.

Of course, the truth is that someone beat him to it by a year or two. Or to be more precise, by 1,700 years. His name was Aristarchus of Samos, a Greek island in the eastern Aegean Sea. This was also the birthplace of the aforementioned Pythagoras, whose own astronomical observations incidentally suggested that the Earth was a moving body. Aristarchus's written work on the subject has been lost, but luckily, that other ancient scientific genius, Archimedes, referred to Aristarchus's theory in his work 'The Sand Reckoner':

> ... the 'universe' is the name given by most astronomers to the sphere the centre of which is the centre of the Earth, while its radius is equal to the straight line between the centre of the Sun and the centre of the Earth. This is the common account as you have heard from astronomers. But Aristarchus has brought out

a book consisting of certain hypotheses, wherein it appears, as a consequence of the assumptions made, that the universe is many times greater than the 'universe' just mentioned. His hypotheses are that the fixed stars and the Sun remain unmoved, that the Earth revolves about the Sun on the circumference of a circle, the Sun lying in the middle of the orbit ...

Aristarchus clearly also realised that the universe is a very big place – way, way bigger than had previously been thought. His theory became the accepted model for several hundred years. Then it fell out of favour, mostly thanks to the second-century Greco-Egyptian scientist and geographer Claudius Ptolemy, who mistakenly returned us to the centre of the universe. Kudos is deserved by Copernicus for successfully reviving Aristarchus's theories, but not for originating them. That's not to say that Copernicus wasn't a genius in his own right, but hey, credit where credit's due.

RINGING HOLLOW

The same might be said for the inventor of a device that is among the most used on the planet. Odds are that you've used it at least once today, and more likely about ten times, although your modern version of it differs vastly from the original. It is called the telephone, and history informs us (as can most schoolchildren) that its inventor was the Scottish-born Alexander Graham Bell.

Bell did successfully lodge the first patent for a working telephone, but even that event is mired in controversy. For many people, the real inventor of the telephone was the Italian Antonio Meucci. He developed a vocal transmission device in his Staten Island home so that he could talk to his ill wife, in their bedroom on the second floor, from his lab, which was in the basement. He described it thus:

... a vibrating diaphragm and an electrified magnet with a spiral wire that wraps around it. The vibrating diaphragm alters the current of the magnet. These alterations of current, transmitted to the other end of the wire, create analogous vibrations of the receiving diaphragm and reproduce the word.

This was around 1857, pre-dating Bell's patent by nearly two decades. Unfortunately, Meucci was desperate for funding, preventing the development of the basic model into a complete working design. He did submit a patent caveat (essentially an announcement of an invention) for a 'sound telegraph' in 1871, but it was notoriously short on detail, and the caveat eventually expired because Meucci couldn't afford to renew it. So, sadly, financial hardship demoted his name to history's periphery.

The real controversy arose five years later, with Elisha Gray, another strong claimant to the throne of telephone-inventor. Gray, an engineer from Illinois, developed a practical telephone design that was strikingly similar to that featured in Bell's patent. In fact, it is so similar that there have been claims and counter-claims down the decades that Bell's attorney actually copied part of Gray's design and claimed it as his own.

On Monday, 14 February 1876, Gray's attorney submitted a patent caveat that featured a telephone using a liquid transmitter. On the same day, Bell's attorney submitted his patent application. Which one arrived first has been the subject of controversy ever since, with Gray's advocates claiming dark skulduggery was afoot.

On top of that, there are suggestions that Bell's original patent hadn't any reference to a liquid transmitter, but that when his lawyer heard about this, he altered the patent and then hand-delivered it to the patent office, insisting that it be filed immediately, leapfrogging Gray's patent caveat.

Incidentally, Bell himself appears to be without blame in all of this, as he was away in Boston at the time, unaware of the goings-on between the respective lawyers. Later biographers of all three men made duelling claims about the true inventor of the telephone, and we'll probably never know what really happened on that fateful Monday in 1876. But the upshot of it all is that Bell's patent was finally accepted, and it is his name, rather that Meucci's or Gray's, that now so easily trips off the schoolboy's tongue.

A final footnote: Elisha Gray does enjoy a much smaller niche in the inventors' hall of fame – he is credited (undisputed) with the invention of the world's first music synthesiser.

MISSING THE FAME GENE

Another scientist's name that pops easily to mind is that of Charles Darwin, who most people will instantly tell you formulated the theory of evolution through natural selection. And they'd be correct, apart from one detail – so did someone else, at precisely the same time.

Alfred Russel Wallace, a Welsh naturalist, geographer and biologist, came up with the same theory independently. He published his paper on natural selection in 1858, jointly with that of Darwin. However, his name never entered the popular consciousness in the way that Darwin's did, for a number of reasons. For a start, Darwin already had a high profile among the scientific community – had Wallace published his paper, say, ten years before he did, in all likelihood it wouldn't have been taken seriously. When the papers were jointly published, Wallace was also in the distant Malaysian islands, conducting

Illustration of a flying frog, from Wallace's *The Malay Archipelago*.

extensive scientific research. This would culminate in his signature work, *The Malay Archipelago*, detailing his eight-year exploration of the geography, geology, flora and fauna of the place where he first developed his theory of natural selection.

While Wallace was tramping around far-off jungles with a butterfly net, Darwin was back in London, publishing his own book, *On the Origin of Species*. So, by a process you might say of natural selection, the world picked Darwin for survival in the popular memory, and assigned Wallace to the cast-off gene pool.

Wallace never displayed any bitterness towards Darwin, and in fact they became friends in later life and remained so until Darwin died. Alfred Russel Wallace died in 1913, at the ripe old age of ninety. His legacy has only begun to be recognised in recent years, and a statue of him was unveiled in the grounds of London's Natural History Museum in 2013.

LAND AHOY

You've heard of Willem Janszoon, no doubt? No? Surely you must have seen a documentary or read a book about the man who discovered Australia? Oh, I see, you thought that was Captain Cook. No, afraid not.

Now, it is of course pretty arrogant for any European to claim the 'discovery' of Australia, or Brazil or North America or anywhere else where there are people for that matter. But in the sense that Captain Cook was part of the European age of exploration, then Willem Janszoon can rightly feel hard done by.

Janszoon was a Dutch navigator and employee of the Dutch East India Company, which, in 1605, sent him on a mission from Java to explore other possible trading opportunities to the east. He landed in western New Guinea a couple of months later, then wandered around the northern end of the Gulf of Carpentaria for a while, before making landfall on 26 February 1606 near the mouth of the Pennefather River in what is now northern Queensland, thus becoming the first European to set foot on the Australian continent.

Much like Columbus a century or so earlier, Janszoon wasn't quite sure what he'd hit upon, believing he'd simply landed on a southern extension of New Guinea. He and his men explored over 300 kilometres of the coast to the south. They had a number of run-ins with the natives, and it is recorded that ten of his men were killed. One presumes a number of natives died in these skirmishes also.

Eventually they came upon a tribe of more welcoming Aboriginals, called the Wik-Mungkan. Unfortunately, the crew exploited their friendliness, taking a bunch of the tribe's women for the crew's gratification. Not surprisingly, this didn't go down well and battle ensued, with multiple deaths to both groups.

At this point, Janszoon decided to call it a day. He sailed away from Australia's shore at a place now called Cape Keerweer, which is Dutch for 'turn around'. He did make a second voyage to Australia thirteen years later, this time making landfall in the north of Western Australia. In the following century, no less than six Dutchmen made voyages of discovery to every side of Australia's coastline, including Abel Tasman, who gave his name to Tasmania.

Willem Janszoon.

It was 1699 before English eyes fell on the continent, and they didn't belong to Captain James Cook. William Dampier explored large tracts of Western Australia, seventy-one years ahead of Captain Cook's voyage. Dampier was a famous explorer in his own right, who circumnavigated the globe three times and was referenced by Jonathan Swift in *Gulliver's Travels*. Interestingly, one of his crewmen was Alexander Selkirk, the castaway who provided the inspiration for Daniel Defoe's *Robinson Crusoe*. Dampier's Australian observations were referenced by the two great aforementioned naturalists, Alfred Russel Wallace and Charles Darwin. A final piece of Dampier trivia: he supplied the first written uses of the words 'avocado', 'barbeque' and 'chopsticks'.

Captain Cook can't even claim to have named Australia. The bragging rights for that are shared between Dutchman Matthew Flinders, who called the continent Terra Australis, or Southern Land, and

Janszoon's ship.

the Spaniard Pedro Fernandes de Queirós, who mistakenly thought he'd found the fabled 'great southern land' the same year as Janszoon, 1606. He had actually landed in the New Hebrides (now called Vanuatu), about 2,000 kilometres to the northeast of Australia, but he named the place 'Austrialia del Espiritu Santo' or Southern Land of the Holy Spirit, in honour of the Queen of Austria, who was the wife of the Spanish King. Between Australis and Austrialia, the name was eventually shorthanded to Australia.

Eventually, 169 after Willem Janszoon set foot on the continent, Captain Cook came along in 1770. His achievements in exploring the Pacific region and mapping those vast territories are remarkable, and he reputedly treated the natives with respect. But discover Australia, he did not. Such are the breaks, Willem.

William Dampier.

LOST IN SPACE

Another first you probably haven't a clue about is the first woman in space. Any guesses? The US astronaut Sally Ride? Not even close. When Sally blasted off into the thermosphere in June 1983, it was almost twenty years to the day after the first female space trip.

Incidentally, some of the questions asked of Sally Ride in the preceding press conference were staggeringly sexist: 'Do you weep when things go wrong on the job?' 'Will the flight affect your reproductive organs?' Of course, we've moved on from that sort of thing nowadays. Except that in 2014, a female reporter inquired of Yelena Serova, the first Russian woman cosmonaut to go to the International Space Station, if she was bringing make-up on the trip, and how she would manage her hair-do in space. The reporter was understandably given short shrift.

Which reference to Russians neatly segues into the answer to the original question. The first woman in space was Russian Valentina Vladimirovna Tereshkova, who made her historic trip on

16 June 1963. Unfortunately for Tereshkova, her name didn't quite roll off the tongue as easily as Sally Ride. On top of this, she was then part of the evil Soviet Empire, who were all baddies and nasties who wanted to blow everyone in the west to kingdom come, or so we were led to believe at the time. So Tereshkova was quietly relegated to the margins of space exploration history. Which is a pity really, as her story is quite inspiring.

The first woman in space, as depicted on a postage stamp – Valentina Vladimirovna Tereshkova.

Her father, a tractor driver, was killed during the Second World War, leaving her impoverished mother to raise three children, with the result that Tereshkova didn't receive any education until she was ten. At seventeen, she was working in a tyre factory, followed by a stint as a loom operator in a cotton mill. She educated herself through correspondence courses, and joined an Air Sports Club, becoming an accomplished amateur parachutist. At the time, Tereshkova was a believer in communism, and a member of the Young Communist League.

This, coupled with her parachuting skills, earned her a place in the cosmonaut training programme. She emerged from a field of 400 women to win the right to become the first woman in space. She made forty-eight orbits of Earth, and travelled over one million miles, easily beating the combined orbits of all the US astronauts who had previously been into space.

Her flight also marked another significant milestone – she was the first civilian in space. At the time of writing, Valentina Tereshkova is a fit eighty-year-old, and has recently volunteered her services for a one-way mission to Mars, should the opportunity arise. Perhaps she's finally had enough of the sexist questioning on this planet.

It is also worth mentioning the second woman in space, Svetlana Savitskaya, who in 1982, became the first woman to perform a spacewalk. And when she went up again in 1984, she became the first woman to make two spaceflights, making the Soviets the true pioneers of female space exploration. But the west didn't really want to admit that at the time.

The second woman in space, and the first to perform a spacewalk, Svetlana Savitskaya.

GLUED TO THE SEAT

Talking of women who were sidelined, Claudette Colvin may justifiably feel irked, to say the least, at the way that history has relegated her to the fringes. You've probably heard of Rosa Parks and the Montgomery Bus Boycott, and how on 1 December 1955, in Montgomery, Alabama, Rosa refused to surrender her bus seat to a white passenger after the white section had filled up. But heroic and monumental as Rosa's actions were that day. she was by no means the first to do this.

Actually, the first well-publicised event of a similar nature happened over a decade before that. On 6 July 1944. a black soldier called Jackie Robinson boarded a military bus in Texas, and was ordered to move to the rear of the bus by the driver. Refusing to do so, he was arrested, subjected to racist questioning, subsequently charged with multiple offences including subordination and public drunkenness, even though he was a teetotaller, and sent for court martial.

His commander, Paul L Bates, refused to perform the court martial,

Jackie Robinson.

so Robinson was transferred to a different battalion, where the court martial proceeded. Luckily, the all-white panel of officers acquitted him. Jackie went on to become a Major League baseball superstar, a significant figure in the Civil Rights Movement of the 1960s, the first black vice-president of a major US Corporation, the first black TV baseball analyst and winner of the Presidential Medal of Freedom.

Two years after Jackie Robinson made his stand, a black woman called Irene Morgan was making a journey on a Greyhound bus, which, because they travelled across state borders, were supposedly desegregated. Incredibly, states that enforced racial segregation required black passengers to move to the back of the bus as soon as the vehicle crossed the border. When her bus entered Virginia territory, Irene refused to move, prompting the driver to stop and summon the local sheriff. He duly presented her with an arrest warrant, which she tore up, then kicked him in the groin and wrestled with his deputy. You can bet the sheriff didn't see that one coming.

After various court appearances, the case attracted widespread attention. It eventually went all the way to the US Supreme Court, which made a landmark ruling that Virginian law, enforcing segregation on interstate buses, was illegal. It was a huge victory for black Americans, although a lack of enforcement meant that discrimination on buses would continue for another twenty years or more.

But perhaps the woman most denied her rightful place in the history books is the previously referenced Claudette Colvin. The fifteen-year-old high school student boarded a segregated bus in Montgomery on 2 March 1955, nine months before the Rosa Parks event. She was not looking to deliberately confront the segregation issue, and sat in the coloured section towards the back of the bus. But the rules stated that if the white section filled up, coloured people had to vacate their seats and stand.

There was a pregnant black woman sitting called Ruth Hamilton sitting next to Claudette, and when the white section filled up, the driver ordered them to surrender their seats. Ruth Hamilton refused, citing her pregnancy, and so did Claudette, at which point the driver summoned the police. They arrived, and persuaded a black man to give up his seat to Mrs Hamilton, which she accepted. Claudette Colvin, however, continued to refuse to move.

The previous day, she had written a school essay about the various humiliating, discriminatory practices to which she was subjected on a daily basis, such as not being allowed to try on shoes in a shoe shop, but having to bring a paper cut-out of her shoe size instead. Being ordered to give up her seat was the proverbial last straw, and she yelled that it was her constitutional right to sit where she was. The officers dragged her off the bus by the wrists and arrested her, and then subjected her to sexually offensive remarks in the police car.

She insisted on contesting the charges of violation of the segregation law, disturbing the peace and assault (although this last was a trumped-up charge). She lost, and appealed, and lost that case also. She was made a ward of court, and remanded to her family's custody. The NAACP (National Association for the Advancement of Coloured People) had been looking for a case to test the state's segregation laws in court, but for a variety of reasons they dithered over whether it should be Claudette – she was very young, she was regarded as hot-tempered and opinionated, she was from a very poor

Claudette Colvin.

background, she was too dark-skinned to attract widespread sympathy – and when Claudette became pregnant by an older, married man, they dropped her like a hot potato.

When Claudette heard about Rosa Parks, she thought, 'Hey, I did that months ago!' 'I was glad that an adult had finally stood up to the system, but I felt left out,' she said years later. Rosa Parks invited her to a lecture once, but according to Claudette, 'Rosa didn't give me enough time to put in for a day off.'

Claudette was completely forgotten by the history books until a reporter called Frank Sikora, writing a retrospective on the bus boycott in 1975, contacted her for an interview. Asked for her recollection of that moment on the bus in 1955, she said, 'History had me glued to the seat.'

LEADING LIGHTS

Lastly, let us shine a light on another of the great misappropriated firsts in the history of practical science. It's the sort of thing that regularly arises in pub quizzes: Who invented the light bulb? Most people write 'Thomas Edison' as the answer, and are then adjudged to have answered correctly. But whether he did or not is extremely debatable.

While Edison did obtain the first patent for a practical light bulb, in 1880, a British man called Joseph Swan invented a similar bulb independently of the American and at virtually the same time. Wishing to perfect and prolong the bulb's lifetime, Swan delayed in seeking a patent, which he was eventually granted in Britain some months after Edison. Swan immediately began installing light bulbs in British homes, and his house in Gateshead was the first in the world to be lit by a light bulb. He went one better the following year, installing electric lighting in the famous Savoy theatre, making it the first such venue in the world to be illuminated by artificial light. Swan was eventually knighted for his work.

But even before Swan and Edison, there were quite a few who could lay claim to having invented the light bulb. As far back as 1835, a Scottish inventor called James Bowman Lindsay demonstrated an electric lamp in Dundee, which allowed him to 'read a book at a distance of one and a half feet.' Lindsay didn't develop his invention further, however, as he then turned his mind towards wireless telegraphy, so we'll never know if all those early candlelit Victorian dramas could have been illuminated by Lindsay's bulbs instead.

Next up was a French-sounding English chemist called Warren de la Rue, who developed a working bulb with a platinum filament in 1840, but the cost of the platinum would have put it way out of the ordinary man's pocket, and it was dropped as impractical. He later found much greater fame in the field of astronomical photography, producing images of the moon in startling detail. Even in today's era of the ubiquitous camera, these photographs are quite impressive.

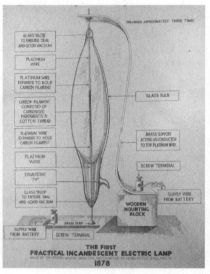

Swan's 'practical incandescent electric lamp', from 1878

If 'inventor' is defined by the person first granted the patent, then John Wellington Starr from Cincinnati has arguably the most serious claim to have invented the light bulb. Unfortunately, Starr's lamp was never developed, as he died of tuberculosis before he had a chance. He did, however, have a US patent caveat for the lamp. He also travelled to Britain to secure a patent there, where he is known to have demonstrated his carbon filament-based light bulb (both Swan and Edison would employ a carbon filament). He had two partners, but one died in the American Civil War and the other who couldn't be traced when Edison lodged his patent, so there were no surviving associates to challenge Edison's patent in court. Rotten bad luck.

Edison's carbon-filament light bulb.

French magician Jean-Eugène Robert-Houdin, from whom Houdini took his name and who was an international celebrity, also liked to dabble in practical science. Some of his dabbling magically resulted in a light bulb with a bamboo filament. That might sound quite impractical, but Edison would later develop a carbonised bamboo filament that would burn for over 1,000 hours. Houdin demonstrated his electric light in France in 1851, but never obtained a patent.

In 1874, two more strong candidates for the title of 'first' appeared on the scene. They were Canadian duo Henry Woodward and Matthew Evans. They patented a nitrogen-filled bulb with a carbon filament. This bulb worked better than anything up to that point, and held huge promise. Unfortunately, they were both effectively broke, and they sold their patent for $5,000 to ... guess who? None other than Thomas Edison, who made an obscene amount of money from his 'invention'.

Money can't buy you love, said the Beatles. But apparently it can go some way towards buying you immortality.

8

CHILD'S PLAY

....

Children's roles in our history books have largely reflected the old aphorism that they should be 'seen and not heard'. Children are usually only mentioned by reference to someone else – 'heir to the throne' or 'the Emperor's young daughter'. They are rarely heard of in their own right. But some children have earned their place on history's podium.

IT ALL ADDS UP

....

When it comes to second languages, most people struggle to mouth more than a few lines of the French, Spanish or German they learned in school. So imagine being told you had to learn those languages, along with a couple of others, like Sanskrit and ancient Persian. No problem, if you're a young Irish boy called William Rowan Hamilton.

William was born in Dublin in 1805, the fourth of nine children. His father, a solicitor, travelled a lot on business, leaving his mother, Sarah, to cope with an ever-growing brood. To help ease matters for her, at the age of three William was sent away to County Meath to live with his kindly uncle, James Hamilton, an Anglican priest and accomplished linguist.

James soon noted that the young William displayed a remarkable ability to acquire new languages. He could read English fluently before he was four, and had acquired a rudimentary grasp of Greek and Hebrew by five. Skip forward to his twelfth year and William had mastered French, German, Spanish, Italian, Sanskrit, Hindustani, Arabic, Persian, Marathi, Malay and Latin. When he was fourteen, just for fun, his father had him write a welcoming letter to a senior Persian dignitary visiting Dublin. Yet, incredibly, it was not in the field of linguistics that William Rowan Hamilton would earn his reputation, but in mathematics.

The initial turning point came when he was just eight years old. That year, 1813, the American child prodigy and mental calculator Zerah Colburn, who was nine at the time (more of him anon), was on tour in Dublin, exhibiting his talents. A mental arithmetic challenge was proposed between the pair. Colburn easily defeated Hamilton, but this in no way left him disheartened. What it did was alter his career trajectory, as after this he began to steer more and more towards the fields of mathematics and astronomy. Occasionally he managed to kill two birds with one stone, as when, a couple of years later, he used his Latin exercises as an excuse to read Euclid, the ancient Greek mathematician and so-called father of geometry.

At the age of seventeen, William discovered a previously unidenti-fied error in French mathematician

William Rowan Hamilton, 'President of the Royal Irish Academy' & 'Royal Astronomer of Ireland'.

A plaque on north Dublin's Broom Bridge commemorating Hamilton's 'flash of genius'.

Pierre-Simon Laplace's 'Méchanique Céleste'. This garnered quite a bit of attention, including that of the renowned astronomer Dr John Brinkley, President of the Royal Astronomical Society and Astronomer Royal of Ireland, who said of William: 'This young man, I do not say will be, but is, the first mathematician of his age.'

William entered Dublin's Trinity College the following year, and won virtually every prize the esteemed university had to offer. He would eventually become one of the leading mathematicians, astronomers and physicists of the age.

His achievements in later life include the discovery of quaternions, which, trust me, unless you're a maths prodigy yourself, would make your brain explode. It was while walking beneath Broom Bridge on Dublin's Royal Canal in 1843 that Hamilton was suddenly struck with a moment of inspiration. He quickly took out his penknife, and scratched the formula 'i2 = j2 = k2 = ijk = –1' into the bridge's stonework. While that might read like ancient Sanskrit to you, it was the moment in history that marked the discovery of the quaternion group. The event is commemorated with a stone plaque.

Hamilton's work proved essential to the development of modern theories of electromagnetism and quantum mechanics. He was knighted in 1835, but you can be pretty sure that even King William IV hadn't a clue what a quaternion was.

THE CALCULATOR KIDS

As mentioned, one of the reasons William Rowan Hamilton veered towards his chosen career was because of his duelling mathematics bout with Zerah Colburn. Born in Vermont in 1804, up to the age of six Zerah was thought to be mentally retarded. Then his parents reputedly heard him reciting multiplication tables. He had only started school a few weeks beforehand, and although he hadn't been taught the tables, he had overheard other children learning them.

His father began to randomly test him with questions, such as multiplying thirteen by ninety-seven. 1261, came the reply in the blink of an eye. Zerah could supply answers almost quicker than his father could formulate the questions.

When he was seven, the boy multiplied 12,225 by 1,227 in his head, and instantly produced the correct answer, which you knew of course, of 15,000,075. Soon after, his father took him on a tour of Europe, ostensibly to raise funding to further his education. It was on this adventure that he competed with Hamilton in Dublin. Scholars and mathematicians in Dublin, London, Edinburgh and Paris marvelled at his calculating abilities. At one point he was asked to calculate the number eight to the sixteenth power, and within seconds replied, 281,474,976,710,656. Perhaps his most astonishing feat was to calculate that 4,294,967,297 was not a prime number, as it is divisible by 641.

The astonishing Zerah Colburn, 'endowed by nature with the remarkable faculty of solving a great variety of arithmetical questions by the mere operation of his mind'.

Attempts to provide a formal education for Zerah, firstly in the Lycée Napoleon in Paris, and then in the West-minster School in London, both proved unsatisfactory for his father. With money in very short supply, his father then bizarrely decided to have Zerah trained as an actor. Soon after, he was granted a job in a school, bringing in some meagre earnings, which he supplemented by doing astronomical calculations for the scientist Thomas Young.

When his father died in 1824, the twenty-year-old returned to the US, unsure what to do with himself. In a mirror image of William Rowan Hamilton's career arc, Zerah, having first discovered his mathematical abilities, now realised he also had a talent for languages, although not near as startling as William's. He began teaching French, furthered his language studies in university and then, in another unusual twist in his career path, he became a wandering preacher for the Methodist Church. He finally settled into something akin to a regular life in 1835, when he was given the post of professor of languages at Vermont's Norwich University.

Beyond his astonishing calculating abilities (which mostly deserted him as he moved into adulthood), Zerah seems to have been quite a normal man, with slightly above average intelligence. Modern research has revealed that math prodigies show massive increases in blood flow to areas of the brain responsible for mathematical calculations.

Unfortunately for Zerah, and unlike William Rowan Hamilton, his childhood skills did not lead to a glittering career, and he settled for a somewhat more mundane life. In 1833, he wrote his autobiography, simply titled *Memoir of Zerah Colburn*. Sadly, he contacted tuberculosis a few years later, and died aged just thirty-four in 1839. Only a single image of him as a child exists – an illustration of an eight-year-old Zerah, holding a small bat and a shuttlecock, and besides the fact that his head looks slightly disproportionately large (perhaps the artist's way of implying genius), he looks like a normal, middle-class, Victorian-era lad. But it's very easy to imagine that as he posed for the drawing, Zerah's brain was calculating that it would take the illustrator one thousand four hundred and thirty-six seconds to complete his task.

Coincidentally, three years before Zerah died, another mathematical child prodigy was also born in Vermont, just sixty or so kilometres away to the south. His name was Truman Henry Safford, and when he first amazed his teachers with his remarkable calculating abilities, his parents were urged to display Truman's talents to the wider world. Sensibly, they refused, insisting on a conventional education in Vermont.

The calculatory feat for which Truman is most renowned occurred in 1845, when the boy was just nine. Having heard of Truman's abilities, the local priest decided to really put him to the test, with what seemed an impossible calculation to solve in one's head – the square of the number 365,365,365,365,365.

Another mathematical prodigy
– Truman Henry Safford.

This would prove impossible for most people even with pen and paper. Truman mulled over the problem for less than a minute before mouthing the number 133,491,850,208,566,925,016,658,299,941,583,225. After the adults spent a number of hours working out the answer, they were astonished to find he'd provided the correct solution.

Perhaps thanks to the decision of Truman's parents not to display their son as an object of curiosity, as had Zerah's, Truman had quite a successful career. He married and had children, and lived a relatively normal life. He studied astronomy in university, and ultimately became a director of Hopkins Observatory in Massachusetts, where he worked until his death in 1901. A portrait of him hangs in the observatory to this day. Incidentally, like Zerah, his calculating talents largely deserted him as he grew older.

THE BOY FIEND OF BOSTON

Innocence is a word we often associate with childhood, but many have that innocence stolen from them at an early age through neglect, abuse,

Jesse Pomeroy, boy fiend.

poverty and a variety of other factors. One such was Massachusetts schoolboy Jesse Pomeroy, born on 29 November 1859 to father Thomas J and mother Ruth Ann. He had a rough time as a child and was bullied in school, thanks to an unidentified condition that left his right eye almost completely white. This gave him a somewhat unsettling appearance, helping to make him fit more snugly into the media's later description of him as the 'boy fiend'.

His father was a labourer in the Boston Naval Yard, an alcoholic and a brute of a man. He couldn't bear to look at his son, and regularly thrashed a naked Jesse with a leather belt. One beating was so extreme that his mother threatened her husband with a kitchen knife if he didn't stop. He did, and he departed and never returned. As he grew older, Jesse started to ape his father's behaviour, bullying children who were smaller or younger than himself.

His mother knew that the bullying and beatings had a negative effect on her son – although bright, he was reclusive and quiet, and had gotten into trouble for stealing and skipping school. She was disturbed when she returned home from work one day to discover that he'd twisted the heads off her canaries. But she hoped his behaviour would improve now that his abusive father had left. Unfortunately, the damage had been done.

Not long after Jesse's twelfth birthday, a four-year-old boy called Billy Paine went missing. He was found alive soon after, but Boston recoiled in collective horror at reports that the child had been found naked, hanging by his wrists, his back covered in welts from a whipping. This occurred in Jesse's neighbourhood, Chelsea, then a predominantly industrial area close to Boston's waterfront. The toddler related how an older boy had lured him there, ripped his clothes off and then beaten him with a rope.

Over the next few months, there were more reports of horrific abductions and torture of children from other areas beyond Chelsea. Several of the brutal crimes were committed in the Somerville area, nowadays a highly developed Boston suburb with fine period homes and tree-lined sidewalks. It is difficult to imagine the horrors committed there back in 1871, when the population of the area was just under 1,000. Then there was a lot of isolated farmland and woodland, which made it the abductor's favourite spot.

Most of the children were under ten. They were each tied up and stripped, beaten and tortured with pins and knives. Several were almost blinded. The survivors all reported their abductor to be an older boy, who took intense pleasure in his sadistic acts, often dancing about, laughing as his victims writhed in agony. Public outrage swelled, and a reward of $1,000 was offered for information leading to his capture. Juveniles who had displayed violent behaviour were rounded up by the dozen and paraded before the victims, who each shook their heads. Seven boys had been abducted by now, and the fiend was still out there.

One person who believed she recognised the boy's description was Ruth Ann Pomeroy. She decided to flee to the south of the river in July of that year, where she opened a dress shop. Tragically, the abductions also moved to the same area, as on 17 August, seven-year-old called George Platt was taken, brutally flogged, stabbed with needles and horribly bitten in the face and buttocks.

Attacks became more frequent, and in many ways more brutal. In the next few weeks, three more boys were kidnapped and horribly tortured and sometimes mutilated. At least they were always left alive, but it seemed that murder could not be far from the mind of the attacker. One of the victims even described the assailant as 'a big bad boy with an eye like a milky' (a 'milky' was a white marble). Another victim was taken by police into countless classrooms, including Jesse's, but failed to identify him.

Boston parents and children were living in terror. Children normally permitted the run of the streets were never allowed out alone. They were accompanied to and from school and kept under close supervision. Parents were terrified to let their kids out of their sight, even for a moment. Teachers lectured classes never to go off with a strange boy – even if he offered candy or some other temptation. Schoolyards were patrolled like prisons.

By pure coincidence, Jesse Pomeroy was walking by a Boston police station when a policeman emerged with one of the victims, who identified Jesse as his attacker. He was subsequently identified by several others and indicted. It seemed the 'boy torturer' had finally been found. At his trial, his mother claimed her son was a good boy, dutiful and obedient and respectful. But the evidence against her son was overwhelming. He was found guilty, and sent to a 'house of reformation' for an indefinite period, which he probably considered a light sentence, considering that half of Boston wanted him hanged.

In confinement, Jesse was the so-called 'model inmate'. He didn't trouble any other boys, and applied himself to studies, earning him the respect of the administration, who patted themselves on the back for having so quickly reformed the 'fiend of Boston'. From a twenty-first-century perspective, it seems astonishing that when his mother applied for protective parole a year-and-a-half into the sentence, it was granted. The 'rehabilitated' Jesse, now fourteen, would be kept busy working in his mother's shop, Mrs Pomeroy assured the court.

On 18 March 1874, ten-year-old Katie Curran vanished after going to buy a school notebook. Jesse was never really considered a suspect, as his previous victims had all been boys. When asked about the missing girl, Jesse suggested that her father, an Irish Catholic immigrant, had sent the girl to a convent without telling her mother. Police continued their search, but no trace of Katie could be found.

$500 REWARD!

Mayor's Office, City Hall, April 1st, 1874.

In accordance with an order of the City Council, a reward of Five Hundred Dollars is hereby offered for the detection and conviction of the person or persons who on the 18th ultimo abducted from Broadway, South Boston,

KATIE MARY CURRAN,

aged about 10 years, the daughter of John and Mary Curran, residing in South Boston.

SAMUEL C. COBB, Mayor.

A month later, two boys were playing on some scrubland when they made the horrific discovery of the body of another missing child – four-year-old Horace Millen. He was almost naked, he was partially

castrated and his head was almost severed. Suspicion did now fall on Jesse, especially when plaster casts of footprints found near the body matched Jesse's shoes. He refused to admit the murder, but after relentless questioning, and having been forced to view Horace's mutilated body, he reputedly broke down and said, 'Put me away so I can't do such things.'

While he was awaiting trial, Mrs Pomeroy sold her shop – Jesse's notoriety had destroyed her business. When workmen were later converting the building into a grocery store, they uncovered the badly decomposed body of Katie Curran. Jesse would later confess to her murder as well, saying:

> I told her there was a store downstairs ... I followed her, put my left arm about her neck, my hand over her mouth, and with my knife in my right hand cut her throat. I then dragged her behind the water closet ... and put some stones and ashes on the body.

He later recanted his confessions to both murders, but it made little difference. He was tried for the killing of Horace Millen, and found guilty of first degree murder. Hanging was the mandatory sentence, but after almost two years of deliberation about the morality of hanging a youth, his sentence was commuted to solitary confinement for life. He was sent to Charlestown State Prison, and made repeated escape attempts. His period of forty-one years of solitary confinement was only exceeded by that of the famous 'Birdman of Alcatraz', Robert Stroud.

His mother visited him every month until she died. He was eventually transferred to Bridgewater State Prison Farm in 1929, and died there a few years later at the age of seventy-two, having spent fifty-nine years in confinement.

Pomeroy's crimes are considered among the most brutal ever carried out – by an adult or child – in American criminal history. And at the time of his trial, speculation was rife as to how many other strays and missing children from around Boston in the 1860s and 1870s might have been down to Jesse Pomeroy, the boy fiend. It seems we'll never know for sure.

BANG, YOU'RE DEAD

Although not nearly as horrific as Jesse Pomeroy's crimes, Carl Newton Mahan did outdo him in one respect – he was only six when he killed his eight-year-old friend Cecil Van Hoose, and he would become the youngest person ever tried for murder in the US.

It was 18 May 1929, and the two boys were playing on wasteland in Kentucky when they found a piece of scrap metal that could be sold to a dealer. They argued over it, and Cecil hit Carl with the metal. Carl promptly ran home, got his father's shotgun, returned and shot his friend.

He was arrested and sent for trial, during which he was required to stand in the witness box and testify about what had happened. But he spent most of the trial napping on the defence team's table or curled up on his mother's lap, looking rather bewildered.

The jury took thirty minutes to find him guilty of the lesser charge of manslaughter and astonishingly, even for the time, the judge sentenced the toddler to fifteen years in reform school. The courtroom collectively gasped, but the judge temporarily released the child to the protective custody of his parents, probably conscious that sending a very small child to a prison cell wasn't going to impress too many people.

A huge public debate followed, with hardliners claiming the sentence wasn't hard enough, but with the majority of people insisting the verdict and sentence were an outrage – how could a six-year-old have any real understanding of what he'd done? The case made national headlines and one newspaper ran a large picture of Carl in his courtroom suit, ironically captioned 'Convict!' His parents received huge amounts of supportive mail from all over America.

The case was referred to Kentucky's attorney general. One month after Carl was sentenced, he announced that, having reviewed the case, Carl should never have been tried before a jury, and ruled that he should remain with his parents. And suddenly, that was that. The law had gotten itself pinned against a wall – and escaped by slipping out the back door.

YOUNG BLOOD

....

The law had no such qualms about administering sentences on children a few hundred years before that. In King's Lynn, England, back in 1708, the authorities reputedly hanged eleven-year-old Michael Hammond and his seven-year-old sister Ann. Their crime? Stealing a loaf of bread. Folklore holds that thunder and lightning sprung up immediately after the executions, and that the hangman, Anthony Smyth, died a couple of weeks later, but you are free to raise your eyebrows sharply about that bit.

Equally horrific is the tale of the youngest boy ever hanged in Britain. At the time, in 1629, the age of criminal responsibility was seven. (Currently England and Wales maintain that age at ten, whereas it ranges from twelve to fifteen in most other European countries. In most US states it is fourteen.)

Back in the early seventeenth century, they did things differently, and the law moved with incredible swiftness. One is tempted to be envious of the speed of the legal process back then, but of course it often resulted in outrageous miscarriages of justice or excessive sentences. On 23 February 1629, in Abingdon, England, an eight-year-old boy, one John Dean, was indicted, arraigned and found guilty all in the same day for the crime of arson. The judge, Mr Justice Whitelock, found evidence of 'malice, revenge and cunning', and decided therefore against the usual commutation of the sentence for children to transportation. John Dean was 'hanged accordingly'.

We always make allowances for people's brutality in antiquity, but even our modern tolerance has its limits, and they are tested by the case of little Tsarevich Ivan Dmitriyevich. He was born in 1611, the son of 'False' Dimitry II of Russia and his wife Marina, making him a claimant to the Tsardom of Russia. After his father's death, his mother

Tsarevich Ivan Dmitriyevich, born into trouble, and his mother,
by artist Leon Yan Wyczolkowski.

married Ivan Zarutsky, who adopted the child, believing that when the infant became Tsar, he would be in effect left holding the reins of power. But when Tsar Michael I was elected, the tide turned against Marina, her husband and her 'pretender' son.

They went into hiding, but were caught by Cossacks in 1614. To remove any threat to the Tsardom of Michael, Zarutsky was executed by impaling, Marina was imprisoned and Ivan, aged three years and six months, horrifically even at this remove, was publicly hanged in Moscow. Marina died in prison a few months later. It just doesn't bear thinking about.

The youngest person ever executed in the US was twelve-year-old Hannah Ocuish, an impoverished, uneducated Pequot Indian girl. In 1786, she was found guilty of murdering six-year-old Eunice Bolles, the daughter of a prosperous farmer. Hannah had an intellectual disability, and in all likelihood had no real understanding of the gravity of her crime – Eunice had reported her for stealing strawberries some weeks earlier, and the older child had killed Eunice in revenge. The fact that she was an Indian very likely influenced the court in handing down a death sentence. At her trial the judge said:

... the sparing of you, on account of your age, would be of dangerous consequences to the public, by holding up an idea that children might commit such atrocious acts with impunity.

While Hannah was the youngest person executed in the US, the youngest person *sentenced* to death was James Arcene, who – surprise, surprise – was another Indian child, this time a Cherokee. His crime was undoubtedly brutal – at just ten, in 1872, he and a Cherokee man called Parchmeal shot a Swedish man called William Feigel multiple times, and crushed his skull with a rock. The sum total of their reward was the twenty-five cents the Swede was carrying.

They were both captured thirteen years later, tried and subsequently hanged, despite Arcene's plea that he had been only a child at the time of the killing.

One usually thinks of the execution of children as a grisly remnant of the distant past. Shockingly, it was with us in the western world until pretty recently – after a racially biased trial, South Carolina executed an African American boy called George Stinney in 1944, for the murder of two young girls. He was fourteen years old at the time. Seventy years later, he was cleared of the crime.

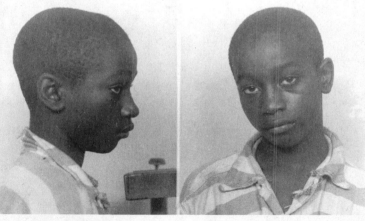

Fourteen-year-old George Stinney, executed for a crime he didn't commit.

TOY SOLDIER

Horror and death also played a part in the life of Momčilo Gavrić, although in a very different way. Barely a week into the First World War, soldiers of the Austro-Hungarian army marched into his village in Serbia, set his house on fire and murdered his parents, three sisters, four brothers and grandmother. By chance, Momčilo had been sent away for the day, and so he survived.

Orphaned and homeless, the eight-year-old set off across country until he happened upon the 6th Artillery Division of the Serbian Army. Aware of what had happened, their commander took the boy in and assigned him a caretaker soldier. Momčilo revealed the position of the soldiers who'd killed his family, and several of the Serbians (Momčilo included) returned by stealth to the spot and took their revenge, wiping them out with hand grenades.

Momčilo was given a small carbine, and taught how to use it. Later that month, the unit took part in the Battle of Cer, and Momčilo was subsequently promoted to the rank of *kaplar*, or corporal, for 'consistently displaying courage, strength and determination in the face of adversity'.

He was also provided with a uniform, making him officially the youngest soldier to participate in the First World War. In between battles, his soldier minder took the time to give him a basic education in reading, writing and maths. After two years of combat, Momčilo was injured in the Battle of Kajmakcalan. During his hospital recuperation, he completed four grades of elementary education, then promptly returned to his unit.

In late 1916, Field Marshall Živojin Mišić was touring the lines and was amazed to see a ten-year-old boy in the trenches. Upon hearing about the boy's service over the past two-and-a-half years, he promptly promoted Momčilo to *podnarednik*, or lance sergeant.

When the war ended, he was helped to travel to England by a British war charity. He completed his education, returned home at fifteen, studied to become a graphic designer, married and had children, and lived to the fine age of eighty-six. He is remembered by a number of memorials in Belgrade, Loznica and the island of Corfu, where he had also served during the war.

PUER FERUS

No such memorials were raised to honour Elagabalus, unless he raised them himself. His name will not be heard in the company of Augustus, Hadrian or Marcus Aurelius. Mostly thanks to his own youthful excesses and shocking decadence, he has been relegated to the very lowest pages of the Roman Empire's annals.

The media often revel in tales of the spoilt sons and daughters of immensely rich families, who live lives of extraordinary opulence, boasting multiple sexual partners, parading about in ridiculous sports cars, snorting cocaine and squandering millions on parties, clothing and gambling. Repulsive as these characters might be, they are seriously fourth division when compared with the Roman Emperor from

Emperor Elagabalus.

the years 218–222 AD, Elagabalus. Never mind sports cars – imagine handing a naughty, spoilt, spotty fourteen-year-old effective control over the greatest empire in world history.

Without going into too much detail on how he came to be proclaimed Emperor, suffice it to say that his scheming mother and grandmother had crucially won the army's support, by falsely presenting Elagabalus as the son of the recently deceased Emperor, Caracalla, who had been beloved by the men.

However, it soon became apparent that the fourteen-year-old was no Caracalla. He had been born in Syria, and there became a devotee of the Syrian sun god, Elagabal, from which his name derives. He soon outraged all of Rome by elevating Elagabal to the position of highest god, building a temple to him on the Palatine hill and displacing Jupiter.

His grandmother arranged a marriage for her teenage son to a noblewoman, Julia Cornelia Paula. It is uncertain if the marriage was ever consummated, as Elagabalus was widely believed to be homosexual and frequently referred to his chariot driver, Hierocles, as his husband. He is said to have liked to play the part of a prostitute in the palace, standing naked in the doorway of a corridor, offering his favours to men who passed by, and is even believed to have done the same in Roman taverns and brothels.

Aged fifteen, he decided to divorce Julia, and metaphorically shake the very foundations of Rome by taking a Vestal Virgin as his bride.

It is believed that this was a means of symbolically marrying his sun god to the Roman goddess Vesta. The chastity of the Vestals was considered fundamental to the security of the entire empire. They were considered incorruptible, chaste and pure of thought, and any interference in that would bring about the ultimate ruination of Rome. The punishment for a Vestal losing her virginity was to be stripped, scourged, dragged though the Forum and then buried alive – excessive even by Roman standards.

The marriage outraged Rome and earned the people's hatred, and his grandmother quickly realised the mistake, arranged a divorce and a new marriage to another noblewoman, Annia Faustina. But within months, he'd decided that he really wanted his first wife back, so he ditched Annia and remarried Julia.

While all of this marrying and divorcing was going on, Elagabalus was satiating his homosexual urges with his charioteer and 'husband', and with multiple male prostitutes. Roman historian Cassius Dio recounts some of his role-playing antics in brothels:

> He had numerous agents who sought out those who could best please him by their foulness. He would collect money from his patrons and give himself airs over his gains; he would also dispute with his associates in this shameful occupation, claiming that he had more lovers than they and took in more money.

Elagabalus reputedly offered physicians large sums of money if they could figure out how to perform a sex change. They never worked it out, so Elagabalus settled for having his body plucked of all bodily hair, wearing make-up and walking around in women's clothing. Meanwhile, he took another wife – number five, who he also ignored sexually.

His grandmother now realised just how badly things were going. The army, the people, the senate and the religious community despised her grandson. It was only a matter of time before he met his end. So she decided to hasten that by setting up her grandson by another daughter to be emperor. She made arrangements with the Praetorian Guard, and when Elagabalus and his mother went on what they believed was an inspection, they were set upon and beheaded. He was eighteen at the time. His death brought to an end a life, according to the great historian Edward Gibbon, 'abandoned to the grossest pleasures and ungoverned fury'.

The triumph of Elagabalus, illustrated by Auguste Leroux in 1902.

9

STATE OF THE ART

Art has been around for at least 40,000 years, so it was bound to throw up a few odd tales along the way. And accompanying art on its journey through history has been the art critic. Now, due to the very subjective nature of art appreciation, the art critic has probably found him or herself mocked more than any other form of critic. Mind you, they've often only themselves to blame, as we'll see.

WITHOUT A SHADOW OF DOUBT

In 1924, critics heaped praise on Russian artist Pavel Jerdanowitch, founder of the new disumbrationist school of art. Pavel was actually an American writer and renowned academic called Paul Jordan-Smith. His wife, an amateur artist, had her paintings slated by local critics, apparently because they weren't 'modernist' enough. Just for fun, he got out some old paint tubes and brushes. In a few minutes, he bashed out a crude image of a native female in a jungle, brandishing a banana above her head. Everyone in his family had a good laugh at it, and that was the end of the matter. Eh, no.

A friend noticed the painting (which, for a chuckle, he'd titled 'Yes, we have no bananas', and which was being used to cover up an empty fireplace), and said that it resembled a Gauguin. Intrigued at the idea of putting one over on the snotty art critics, Jordan entered the painting in New York's 1925 Exhibition of the Independents at the Waldorf-Astoria. He renamed it 'Exaltation', and slapped a ridiculous price on it.

Sure enough, the critics lauded the 'great work', and Jordan subsequently invented a background for himself – Moscow-born, but raised in Chicago, before moving to the South Seas for health reasons. He said he was the founder of 'disumbrationism', which was basically a made-up word that meant 'painting without shadows'.

Jerdanowitch's reputation soared over the next couple of years, and he was invited to submit more works for very reputable exhibitions. Writing in the highly regarded *Revue du Vrai et du Beau*, respected critic Comte Chabrier enthused thus:

> *Pavel Jerdanowitch is not satisfied to follow the beaten paths of art. He prefers to discover new lands, explore the heights, and peer into the abysses. His spirit delights in intoxication, and he is a prey to aesthetic agonies, which are not experienced without suffering.*

'Pavel' no doubt had a few laughs about that one. He had lots of fun producing a string of hilarious 'masterpieces', which he bashed out in minutes and then invented his 'inspiration' later. One of them features a woman apparently kneeling in supplication to a tall phallus, around which a snake has wrapped itself.

He finally got tired of the joke in 1927, and admitted it to a reporter. Disumbrationism quietly slipped into the shadows that were absent from its works, as did countless red-faced critics, although a few of the

cheekier ones claimed that they were actually right, and that Jordan-Smith was an artistic genius who just didn't realise it.

And who knows? Maybe he was.

'Adoration' by Pavel Jerdanowitch.

APING THE GREATS

It wasn't the first time, nor would it be the last, that art critics got egg on their faces. In 1964, the little-known French artist Pierre Brassau had four paintings exhibited at a gallery in Goteborg, Sweden. Critics showered praise on the avant-garde works, with one in particular, Rolf Anderberg of the prestigious *Goteborgs-Posten* newspaper, enthusing thus:

> Brassau paints with powerful strokes, but also with clear determination. His brush strokes twist with furious fastidiousness. Pierre is an artist who performs with the delicacy of a ballet dancer.

Yeah, right.

You see, the problem was that Pierre Brassau was a chimpanzee in Borås Djurpark Zoo. Åke Axelsson, a journalist at a Swedish tabloid newspaper, reckoned that a lot of so-called 'avant-garde' art was a big pile of hogwash. He persuaded a young zookeeper to give a chimp called Peter some paper, paints and a brush, and hey presto! Works of art! When Axelsson revealed what he'd done, Rolf Anderberg claimed haughtily that 'Brassau's work was still the best in the exhibition'. Although one can just imagine him curling up in a dark corner and wishing he was on Mars.

Genius of the avant-garde, painter Pierre Brassau.

Another painting chimp was Congo, given drawing materials by zoologist and artist Desmond Morris in 1956. Congo started banging out paintings faster than he could digest bananas – he had 400 works to his name by the age of four. Morris didn't try to fool any art critics with the prolific Congo's work, but it's said that Picasso was given one as a gift and kept it on his studio wall, which probably gave him a giggle every time a visitor made an admiring remark about it.

Congo's crowning (albeit posthumous) achievement came in 2005, when several paintings were offered for sale at the famous Bonham's auction house, alongside works by Renoir and Warhol. Congo's works brought in a tidy £25,000, while Auguste's and Andy's efforts failed to sell.

Like many great artists, poor Congo died young, in 1964 at the age of just ten, denying the world who knows what great works – reclining nude chimp? Orangutan with a pearl earring? The garden of monkey delights?

CLEVER DICKS

You don't need to be an art expert to identify the fruit sprouting from the branches of the tree in the recently uncovered Massa Marittima mural in Tuscany. The tiny town briefly made international headlines at the turn of the century, when the large mural was uncovered on a wall in an ancient bathhouse. The thirteenth-century work shows a group of women standing under a tree, eagles swooping above their heads, the branches of the tree replete with erect penises and testicles.

A couple of the women are actually tearing the hair off each other in a row over one of the substantial penises, and another appears to be trying to poke her own penis (or rather one of the tree's penises) free from the branches with a stick. Yet another woman is apparently

being sodomised by one of the penises, and seems quite content with the goings on to her rear – though this is less obvious to the casual viewer, the experts will direct your attention to the woman in red, bottom left.

The mural has been the subject of much debate, not surprisingly, and has been labelled as pornographic and obscene, also not surprisingly. It's been called 'The Fertility Tree', as this seems the most obvious interpretation, the phallus being a common symbol of fertility in Italy since Roman times. However, some believe it is an early record of witchcraft – apparently, witches used to like to collect male organs (presumably from dead males, as live ones might object), and hide them in birds' nests, for reasons probably best left unexplored.

On the subject of penises, you might have noticed that Greek sculptures of nude males usually depict them with very small, often tiny, members. Now, when one thinks of male beauty in the ancient Greek context, one imagines Adonis-like figures that would make any girl swoon. And while

A shining example of Greek manhood.

the rest of Adonis's body may be up to scratch, it won't escape your notice that his member is often no more than a few centimetres long, not to mention narrow. And that he's lacking any pubic hair. He certainly wouldn't make the pages of *Playgirl* magazine. So what's behind this dearth of manhood?

Well, in ancient Greece, one of the most common and acceptable relationships was between a man and a boy. So one of the most revered forms of beauty was that of the pre-pubescent male. Young lads reaching puberty often did their damnedest to retain their boyish looks – shaving off their pubic hair and maintaining a small figure – to attract the attentions of a wealthy male suitor.

This image of the beautiful young boy became the standard representation of male beauty. Large penises were considered crude and animal-like, and were associated with barbarians. As the great Greek playwright Aristophanes satirised it in his work *Clouds*, the ideal man had 'a shining breast, a bright skin, big shoulders, a minute tongue, a big rump and a small penis'. All of which was a little unfortunate for Greek ladies. But then, modern sensibilities insist that size doesn't matter. Perhaps they felt the same. Or perhaps not.

BIG IS BEAUTIFUL

The depiction of nudes in art throughout the centuries shows us how beauty has been seen differently over the eons. In ancient times, as mentioned, males were depicted as muscular and strong, and women's bodies were not too far from what would be considered beautiful by today's standards. But somewhere around the middle ages, it became popular to show women not as svelte beauties with gracefully curving figures, but as plump or outright chubby, with swollen bottoms, love handles, flabby bellies and folds of flesh so prominent you could warm yours hands inside them. Take a look at Rubens' 'Three Graces' or 'The Hermit and the Sleeping Angelica', or his seriously plump goddess of love in 'Venus at the Mirror'. Then check out Titian's 'Venus and the Organist' or Francesco Hayez's 'Venus playing with two doves'.

And the reason for this feast of excess flesh? Well, beauty was closely associated with status in society. If you were like one of today's matchstick supermodels, it would be assumed you were a poor ignorant wench who couldn't afford to feed herself. Rolls of fat were a clear sign that you were well looked after – you had plenty of food, and you could spend the best part of the day sitting around on your backside.

Not every artist agreed that women should be depicted thus, which is just as well, as otherwise the shell on which Botticelli's Venus stands might have gone straight to the bottom.

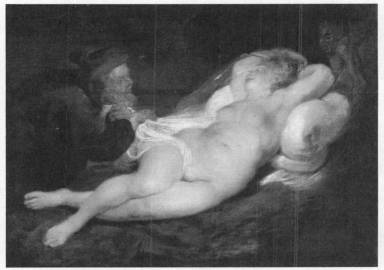

Rubens' voluptuous masterpiece 'The Hermit and Sleeping Angelica'.

But how did Michelangelo, arguably the greatest artist of them all, depict women? Well, to be blunt, he didn't really, even though his works are replete with female characters. Whether it was because he was gay and preferred to work with male nudes, or because of a shortage of women ready to shed their clothes in those prudish times, the master used male models for his female characters, often removing their genitals and sometimes adding breasts, not terribly convincingly it has to be said. A brief perusal of his females reveals them to be muscular, with male-shaped hips and male jaw-lines.

A particularly striking example may be seen on the Last Judgement wall in the Sistine Chapel. In the top left-hand quarter is a 'female' in a green dress with a blue band beneath her breasts, her arm reaching down protectively to her daughter, who is in an orange dress. The mother has muscles and a body of which the Terminator would be proud, and a decidedly square jaw line. But Michelangelo really goes

for bust with his added-on breasts, which look like silicone implants, and have an unnaturally large gap between them. The woman's terrified daughter also appears more like a cross-dressing son, who has clearly spent the previous six months lifting weights in the local gym. Evidently, the great Michelangelo was not the master of all things artistic.

Of course, nobody's perfect, and this also applies to fourth-century theologian, priest and translator Saint Jerome. He was tasked with translating the ancient Hebrew text of the bible into Latin. And a fine job he did. With one exception. The word 'karan' is now believed to mean 'bathed in light' or 'emitting rays'. This was how the ancient text described Moses's head after descending Mount Sinai with the Ten Commandments from God. Unfortunately Jerome translated 'karan' as 'horns', so we got:

> And when Moses came down from Sinai, he held the two tables of the testimony, and he knew not that his face was horned from the conversation of the Lord.

The upshot? For centuries after, poor old Moses appears in paintings, sculptures, stained glass, book illustrations, woodcarvings, you name it, as a devil-like, bearded man, with horns of various sizes protruding from his head. These artists include the aforementioned Michelangelo.

FIT FOR A KING

Returning briefly to plump women, one of art's most famous nudes is 'Portrait of Marie-Louise O'Murphy', by Francois Boucher. It is quite a rare thing for so much to be known about a model, especially about one who posed in the buff, but Marie-Louise is the exception.

Of obvious Irish ancestry, the model's mother and father weren't exactly model parents. Before she was born, her father Daniel was imprisoned in the Bastille for trying to blackmail a court official with secret political papers he'd stolen. He was released after almost two years, fortunately with his insides still on the inside and his head still on his shoulders. He was, however, banished from Paris, and so moved to Rouen. Clearly having missed intimate relations with his wife, he didn't waste any time remedying that, and almost exactly nine months after gaining his freedom, Marie-Louise was born.

Her mother, Margaret, was no paragon of virtue either, having previously been arrested for prostitution and theft. Several of her daughters would pursue careers as 'ladies of the world', as they were then described, often conducting their business by following the French army on campaign.

When Marie-Louise was thirteen, she was staying with her actress sister, a 'friend' of the famed womaniser and adventurer Casanova, who wrote that he found Marie-Louise 'a pretty, ragged, dirty, little creature', but considered her incredibly beautiful when he saw her naked. How he came to see her naked was not related, but one can guess.

'... a pretty, ragged, dirty, little creature': Marie-Louise O'Murphy, as painted by Francois Boucher.

He was so taken that he commissioned the renowned French artist François Boucher to paint her. Given Casanova's reputation, Boucher was an obvious choice, known for the sensualism of his work. Sure enough, he painted Marie-Louise lying naked, face down on a sofa, with her legs parted in an undeniably erotic pose.

While it might be shocking to us nowadays to depict a fourteen-year-old girl in such a way, it was common for girls as young as twelve to marry in the eighteenth century, so Marie-Louise was well past the age of what was considered decent.

Not long after, King Louis XV of France saw the painting, and quickly became besotted with the model. He asked to see the real thing, and so Marie-Louise was whisked off to Versailles, where she was presented to the lecherous, middle-aged monarch. Louis, who had countless mistresses and at least eleven illegitimate children, added her to his boudoir, and would father two children by her. It was written at the time that, 'The King had a new mistress who belongs to a family of prostitutes and thieves.'

She lasted two years as the King's mistress, but was kicked out when, in a bad miscalculation, she tried to unseat the King's long-time official mistress (an official court position in France), Madame de Pompadour. But she could console herself with a pension of 12,000 francs, an awful lot of money back then. She also managed to keep her head during the reign of terror, despite being imprisoned briefly, and was subsequently give a second pension of 2,000 francs by King Charles X after the Bourbon Restoration.

She lived to what was then the very ripe old age of seventy-seven, and died in Paris in 1814. Not bad for a girl from a family of thieves and prostitutes.

SHOCK, HORROR

If a fuss was kicked up about the overt sexuality of the painting of Marie-Louise O'Murphy, or Boucher's more outrageous 'Leda and the Swan', imagine the scandal created when the great Renaissance painter Titian produced his 'Venus of Urbino'. This shows a reclining nude Venus with one hand holding a bunch of flowers while the other, well, more than covers her modesty – in fact, the tips of her fingers seem to have vanished between her legs. The 'obscenity' of a woman touching herself in such a fashion shocked sixteenth-, seventeenth-, eighteenth- and even nineteenth-century sensibilities – Mark Twain described the painting as 'the foulest, the vilest, the obscenest picture the world possesses', although he may have been satirising prudes who held this view. Still, if you can produce something that shocks four centuries of society, you know you're on a sure winner.

Nineteenth-century British artist John Everett Millais managed to avoid scandalising his prudish Victorian contemporaries, but it wasn't for lack of trying. His 1849 painting 'Isabella' depicts a scene from a fourteenth-century Italian novel – the heroine wishes to marry Lorenzo, but her wealthy, nasty brothers plot to murder Lorenzo and marry her off to a nobleman.

In Millais's work, the main characters are seen sitting around a table, dining. One of the snarling brothers is struggling to crack a walnut, while

kicking out at a dog at his sister's feet, while she chats to Lorenzo. What nobody spotted for a century-and-a-half is the shadow on the

A detail from 'Isabella' by John Everett Millais.

tablecloth beside the angry brother, which is unmistakably phallic and has no clear source. Along the side of this shadow penis is a whitish blob of salt from a tipped saltcellar, and you don't need much imagination to fill in the symbolism of that. Apparently the nutcracker is also phallic.

What this tells us about the scene is anyone's guess. Lust? Power? Incest? Whatever else it tells us, some Victorian artists certainly weren't afraid to stick two fingers (or two phallic symbols) up to the mores of their day.

ART TO DIE FOR

Returning briefly to the subject of models, Russian-born American artist Elizabeth Shoumatoff earned her place in the artistic hall of fame not because her work was so stunning – although she was a very accomplished portrait artist – but because of a single unfinished 1945 painting she did of President Franklin D Roosevelt. Shoumatoff was in the middle of a sitting with the President when he proclaimed, 'I have a terrific pain in the back of my head.' He then collapsed unconscious with a cerebral haemorrhage, and died a couple of hours later. Shoumatoff had literally captured the final conscious moment of the president on canvas.

PRICELESS TALES

While bad luck played a major part in Shoumatoff's portrait, the opposite can be said of another unfinished portrait. This painting, of an unknown man, was purchased by Father Jamie MacLeod in an antique shop in Cheshire, England. He hung the painting on the wall of the Ecumenical Retreat House he runs in the town of Whaley Bridge. A few years later, he took it to the BBC's 'Antiques Road Show', where it was identified as a lost Van Dyck, the famous Flemish Baroque artist. The painting was estimated to be worth about £400,000, no doubt answering a lot of Father Jamie's prayers.

Similar good fortune fell on the family of a French engineer who bought a chest for £100 in 1970. It had a nice oriental look about it, and the man, who lived in London, decided to use it as a TV stand. He eventually took it home to the Loire Valley, where he then used it as a drinks cabinet.

Unfortunately, he died without ever realising the fortune his drinks were sitting on. When the family had it appraised, it turned out to be a rare, exquisitely decorated seventeenth-century lacquered coffer, created by master craftsman Kaomi Nagashige. Experts had been looking for the work for decades. It was ultimately bought by Amsterdam's renowned Rijksmuseum for over £6 million – roughly 60,000 times what it cost in 1970.

No such luck for milkman Ben Timperly, who was often handed sketches by one of his customers in Cheshire in the 1950s. The drawings held no appeal for Ben – 'a child could have done better' – and he promptly threw each and every one into the dustbin. It was only when he was visiting a doctor's surgery years later, and saw a reproduction of a painting by the renowned British artist LS Lowry, that the penny dropped – not to mention the fortune he'd dropped into the dustbin all those years before. Nowadays, a Lowry can reach prices of half a million pounds or more. Luckily, Ben adopted a philosophical attitude to his loss. No use crying over spilt milk.

One major artwork was rediscovered as a result of destroying another. In 1955, a new building was being opened at the Buddhist temple of Wat Traimit in Bangkok, Thailand, to house some of the temple's treasures. The largest of these was a three-and-a-half-metre-high statue of the

Buddha. During the move, the ropes supporting the heavy statue snapped, and disaster – the sacred statue crashed to the floor.

Well, as it turned out, not so disastrous, as the impact broke away several lumps of what was merely stucco covering over a majestic golden statue. At the very least, it solved the mystery of why the statue was so damn heavy. It's weight turned out to be five-and-a-half tons, and a valuation based purely on its gold content puts it in the

The five-and-a-half-ton golden Buddha of Wat Traimit.

region of a quarter of a billion dollars. And that's not accounting for its artistic and religious value, which make it literally priceless. Now that has to be the find of the millennium.

A LAW UNTO THEMSELVES

Let's turn to crime. In 2006, Nick Flynn was sitting at home in Cambridge when he saw his face on the news, with the caption, 'Have you seen this man?' Shocked as he was then, imagine how he felt when twenty policemen turned up at his house at seven one morning, and carted him off in handcuffs for an overnight stay in a cell.

His crime? A few months previously, he'd been visiting the Fitzwilliam Museum in Cambridge. He had tripped on an open shoelace and fallen down a stairway, colliding with three vases that were on display on a windowsill. All of the vases where shattered. Poor Nick assumed the vases weren't that valuable, considering they were displayed in such a vulnerable place. He dusted himself off and left, unaware he'd been captured on CCTV.

The museum hadn't had the vases valued in decades, and it turned out that they were actually seventeenth-century Qing dynasty vases, worth roughly half a million pounds. Police suspected that Nick had smashed the vases for publicity, but it was just one of those things, and Nick himself was shattered when he realised what he'd done. Anyway, the vases were completely restored and are on display again, presumably in a safer location. And one of the most popular attractions in the museum ever since has been ... the stairway where Nick tripped.

A genuine crime of mammoth proportions occured in Paris in 1911, when the world's most famous painting, the 'Mona Lisa', was stolen from the Louvre. And at one point, the number one suspect was none other than Pablo Picasso, then twenty-nine. Initially, French poet and art critic Guillaume Apollinaire had been arrested, presumably on the basis that he'd once called for the Louvre to be burnt down. He then implicated his friend Pablo (some pal he turned out to be). Picasso was arrested and questioned for several days before being released and exonerated, although suspicion remained that he'd knowingly bought two small Egyptian statues that had previously been stolen from the Louvre.

Anyway, the 'Mona Lisa' vanished for two years. Until, that is, a former employee of the Louvre, one Vincenzo Peruggia, turned up in Florence and tried to sell the missing masterpiece to the Uffizi Gallery. They agreed, kept the painting for 'safe-keeping' and promptly called the police.

At his trial, Peruggia claimed he'd stolen the painting for patriotic reasons, which won him a lot of brownie points with the public and the jury. He was sentenced to just one year in jail, and served only seven months. The 'Mona Lisa' was then toured around Italy to huge audiences, before being returned to the Louvre in 1913.

However, there was another fascinating theory about Peruggia's motives. American journalist Karl Decker later claimed that Argentine Eduardo de Valfierno, a well-known conman, was the brains behind the theft. De Valfierno reputedly hired master forger Yves Chaudron to make six copies of the painting, which he

The wall in the Louvre where the 'Mona Lisa' didn't hang for two years.

then distributed to various locations in the USA. As the real 'Mona Lisa' hadn't yet been stolen, all of these made their way through customs safely. He then hired Peruggia to steal the original painting, and once it had disappeared, he represented the forged works to potential buyers in the US, and sold each for $300,000. He then vanished.

The fact that none of the fakes has yet turned up casts doubt on this story, but then, who's going to admit that their father or grandfather was willing to buy a stolen 'Mona Lisa'? We'll never know, unless one of them shows up.

Crime and art often have one thing in common – neither of them pay in the long run. And such was the case involving a work by the great surrealist artist Salvador Dali. In 1965, Dali was due to give an art lesson to inmates of Riker's Island prison in New York's East River. Not feeling well, he cancelled the visit, but, eager not to let the prisoners down, he took up his brushes and painted a surrealist depiction of the crucifixion, which was then despatched to the inmates.

The painting was hung in the inmates' canteen near the trash bins and, over the years, became stained with tomato ketchup, mayonnaise and grease, until a subsequent warden decided to give the work the respect it deserved. He mounted it in a locked Perspex case in the prison's main entrance.

It seems, however, that the criminal tendencies of the inmates had rubbed off on several of the guards, who decided to stage their own inside job. One of them produced a crude copy of the painting and, one night in March 2003, they borrowed the warden's key to the Perspex box, distracted the other guards with a fire alarm, and switched the original with the fake.

It seemed they'd pulled off the perfect crime. Except that the original had been in a frame, and they hadn't bothered with this detail. Another slight problem was that their fake more resembled a child's finger painting than the work of a surrealist master.

The switch was noticed in just days, and an investigation begun. By June, the four conspirators had been arrested, and three of them would eventually receive sentences ranging from three to five years in prison.

As for the Dali? Well, the man who'd been charged with keeping it safe claimed that he panicked when the police started to investigate, and burned it. One way or another, it hasn't been seen since. It was worth about three to four hundred thousand dollars, not counting the loss to art. Clearly, the Dali prison heist was anything but a masterpiece of criminal planning.

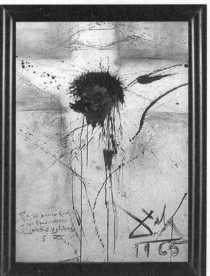

10

FORGOTTEN UNFORGETTABLE DISASTERS

....

We've all heard of the *Titanic*, Krakatoa, the Black Death, and so on. But for every disaster you're familiar with, there are ten more you probably haven't heard of, though they might well have been catastrophes of even greater magnitude. Certainly, some of these less famed disasters fall into the 'unusual', or more accurately, 'bizarre', category.

EIGHTEEN HUNDRED AND FROZE TO DEATH

....

In 1808, a volcano exploded somewhere. A big one. A super-volcano in fact. Nobody's sure exactly where it was. Either there weren't a lot of people around to witness it or, if there were, they didn't live to tell the tale. We know this because scientists have examined core samples from Greenland ice that reveal the markers for such an event. Two possible candidate locations are Greenland itself and a volcanic island in the vicinity of Tonga, which is about as remote as you can get on the planet.

The enormous amount of dust thrown skywards would cause global temperatures to drop for several years afterwards. That in itself wasn't so bad a disaster, but things were about to get much, much worse. Each of the successive years provided another major volcanic eruption, mostly in the Pacific ring, with major volcanic events in Indonesia, the United States, Japan and the Philippines. These further clouded the atmosphere with a sun-blocking layer of black dust, causing increased global cooling and massive failures of harvests.

But the biggest one was still to come. In 1815, the earth vented its greatest fury yet, with a colossal explosion on the island of Sumbawa in Indonesia. One hundred and sixty cubic kilometres of material was ejected into the sky. To put that in context, imagine a block that is roughly the size of Belgium on each side.

The actual eruption killed approximately 90,000 people. That was bad enough, but the cloud also caused worldwide temperatures to plummet. The following year, 1816, was called 'the year without a summer'. Europe, half a world away from the eruption, lost about a quarter of a million people.

The worst-affected country was Ireland. In a precursor to the famine four decades later, which would kill between one and one and a half million people, the main staple of the poor, the potato crop, was wiped out, leading to widespread starvation and a plague of typhus. One hundred thousand died.

The changing climate resulted in famines across Asia and the United States. Millions of acres of crops were lost, and whole herds of animals died due to lack of feed. In Connecticut, which often records temperatures in the high seventies in June, people were astonished when snow fell. A Reverend Thomas Robbins wrote in his diary:

On my way to work I was dressed throughout with thick wool-len clothes and an overcoat on, my hands got so cold that I was obliged to lay down my tools and put on a pair of mittens ... there

*was snow at the northward last Thursday ... my wife brought in
clothes left out to dry and they were frozen solid.*

The year became popularly known as 'eighteen hundred and froze to death.'

The world didn't return to normal for several more years, and the decade of 1810 to 1820 is the coldest on record. It is not known exactly how many people died as a result of the eruption, though one could comfortably speculate in the millions. But because the deaths didn't all occur in the same place on the same date, their cumulative, disparate nature relegated one of the biggest disasters in world history to the sidelines, behind the Battle of Waterloo, the births of Charles Dickens, Karl Marx, Queen Victoria and Otto von Bismarck, war between the US and Britain, and the financial panic of 1819 in the US.

But with today's incessant debate about climate change, this should unquestionably be a case of learning the lessons of history.

IN THE DRINK

At the other end of the scale in terms of fatalities, the London Beer Flood, which occurred during the same decade, sounds like the title of a slapstick comedy movie. But it was anything but funny for the people who perished, or were injured and traumatised.

In 1814, the neighbourhood of St Giles was like something from a Dickens novel. Slums holding up slums, impoverished families, barefoot children playing in the streets, dens of thieves, painted ladies of the night, dogs scampering after cats scampering after rats. A large proportion of the population of 'The Rookeries', as the area was known, were Irish immigrants.

On 17 October, in the cellar of one of those slums, an Irishwoman called Ann Saville, aged sixty, was weeping over the body of her two-year-old grandson John, who had recently died. Other mourners,

The rundown neighbourhood of St Giles in London.

mostly women and children, huddled around in the cramped basement, trying to console the Savilles. In the tenement above, a woman called Mary Banfield had just made a pot of tea and poured a cup for herself and her four-year-old daughter Hannah. In the street nearby, fourteen-year-old servant girl Eleanor Cooper was drawing water into a pot from the pump next to the towering wall of the Messrs. Henry Meux and Co. Brewery, locally known as the Horseshoe Brewery.

Within the factory walls, something terrible was brewing, and it wasn't beer. Late that afternoon, a brewery foreman, George Crick, saw that a metal hoop had fallen from one of the colossal porter vats. His supervisor told him to have it repaired whenever possible, but not to trouble himself about it otherwise. Crick was concerned, however. The rivets holding the hoop appeared to have popped free, which would require a great deal of pressure.

About an hour after his observation, there was a tremendous noise. Crick watched from a platform above the vat house as the giant container exploded into splinters, spilling one-and-a-half million litres of beer into the building. The huge wave crashed into several other vats, smashing their valves and releasing their contents in a disastrous chain reaction.

The explosion caused bricks and timbers to rain down on the homes and streets beyond, and demolished the wall below which Eleanor Cooper was filling her bucket. She was the first to perish.

A mini-tsunami of beer was unleashed into the narrow streets, sweeping away street stalls and carts, people, dogs and cats, flooding into homes and grocers and taverns, sending people scurrying up onto anything that would float.

A visiting American man provided a first-hand account:

> All at once, I found myself borne onward with great velocity by a torrent which burst upon me so suddenly as almost to deprive me of breath. A roar as of falling buildings at a distance, and suffocating fumes, were in my ears and nostrils. I was rescued with great difficulty by the people who immediately collected around me, and from whom I learned the nature of the disaster that had befallen me ... and from among the crowds which filled the narrow passages in every direction came the groans of sufferers.

London's *Morning Chronicle* reported that 'the cries and groans which issued from the wreckage were dreadful'.

The house where Mary and Hannah Banfield were sipping their tea was the first struck by the wave of beer, as the wall of liquid crashed through the wall of stone. Hannah was swept against an inner wall and killed, her mother washed out through the window, subsequently drowning. Another small child of hers, then in another room, was also carried away and almost drowned, but neighbours rescued the badly bruised child.

The basement hosting the wake of John Saville was the worst hit. The badly constructed slum building crumpled under the pressure of the huge wave, and five of the mourners below were either crushed or drowned. Those who perished were the grieving Ann Saville; Catherine Butler, a widow aged sixty-five; Elizabeth Smith, aged twenty-seven, a bricklayer's wife; Mary Mulvey, aged thirty; and her son, Thomas, aged three.

In the aftermath, beer-soaked Londoners scrambled desperately across the ruins of collapsed slum buildings, in search of neighbours and loved ones. Later reports of mobs imbibing vast amounts of the spilled beer were almost entirely invented. In fact, as the *Times* and *Morning Post* reported, the crowds fell silent when commanded, so that rescuers could hear the cries of those trapped in the rubble. Many were rescued by their efforts, and local hospitals were crowded with the injured for several days.

An inquest later found that the brewery held no responsibility for the tragedy – it was deemed an 'act of God'. And while the company lost a great deal of money, it was allowed to reclaim the excise duties it had already paid the Government for the production of the beer. The company soon recovered, and continued in business until 1921, when the factory was demolished. It was replaced by the Dominion Theatre, which ever since, thankfully, has been hosting much more enjoyable dramas than the tragic one played out in this corner of London two centuries ago.

The rebuilt Meux brewery in 1830.

BLACK DEATH

Another city, another bizarre wave, this time not of beer but of molasses, or black treacle. The Purity Distilling Company in Boston had just taken shipment of a cargo of Cuban molasses in January 1919, which it stored in an enormous circular metal tank, the height of a five-storey building and twice as wide. Molasses was an in-demand product at the time, for fermentation to produce beer (ironically, demand for it would increase in the Prohibition years to follow), and to make industrial alcohol for use in munitions and high explosives such as TNT – this was the intended use for the Boston molasses.

The supertank that held the viscous liquid had been made just three years earlier, but it was widely known by locals that sufficient care hadn't been taken with the joints. Children used to snap off hardened molasses fingers where the contents had seeped out, and some women used to fill pots from oozing leaks for use in home baking.

On 15 January 1919, there were nine million litres of molasses in the tank. All around the dockyard, men were going about their day's work. They were almost all Italian or Irish immigrants, and invariably poor. Labourers, drivers, blacksmiths, carpenters and stevedores were looking forward to their brief lunchtime break, relieved that the bitter sub-zero cold of the past days had finally abated. In the streets nearby, women went about their daily chores, and children ran home for lunch from school.

Suddenly, everyone looked up at the rat-tat-tat sound of rivets popping. Some survivors said it sounded like a machine gun. This was followed by the ground trembling, and a rumble like a train passing, and then came the mighty groan of thick

Boston's Purity Distilling Company's giant molasses vat.

metal sheets warping. They were bent and distorted like sheets of cardboard under the tremendous pressure. Finally came a deafening explosion, like a thunderclap, and hundreds of people watched in horror as the mountainous tank crumpled before their eyes.

Molasses is famously slow-moving, but because of the sheer volume involved and the pressures being exerted by the enormous mass, a huge wave gushed from the collapsed tank at a speed of almost sixty kilometres per hour. It was eight metres high, and because of its density, it easily picked up entire trucks, cars, barrels, carts, horses and, of course, people, and swept them away in a hideous, viscous black wave. Some men caught in the wave desperately tried to swim to keep their heads free, but it was impossible, because of the liquid's thickness. They were quickly dragged under and suffocated.

The wave picked up a railroad car, and smashed it into a fleeing ten-year-old boy called Pasquale Iantosca. Truck driver Cesare Nicolo wasn't found for ten days – he had been engulfed and swept into the water under a nearby wharf. Sixty-five-year-old Bridget Clougherty was hanging laundry from her porch in a nearby street when she was swallowed up and crushed against the building. A Stephen Clougherty, likely her son, also died that day.

Dockside buildings were reduced to splinters, brick buildings were crushed to rubble, work horses were seen thrashing about helplessly, and here and there, survivors reported seeing the black-coated shapes of men and women heaving and struggling beneath the uncaring mire, unable to free themselves.

When the wave finally settled, twenty-one people were dead and over 150 were injured, some horrifically. The area was virtually flattened, looking for all the world like some vile new explosive weapon had gone off, coating everything in black sludge.

The subsequent inquiry and court case dragged on for years, with the company claiming that Italian anarchists had bombed the tank. But ultimately this was dismissed as an attempt to wriggle out of their responsibility. In the end, a settlement of $300,000 was awarded, with each of the bereaved families receiving $6,000 – a large sum in those days.

The case marked a turning point in US legal history, as it was the first time a court had found against a large corporation, and it ultimately led to much stricter safety procedures and worker protection laws.

The tank was never rebuilt, and the area today has a pretty little park with a Little League baseball field. The only indication of what happened there is a small plaque recording the tragedy. Local lore holds that even now, on hot days, the sickly sweet scent of molasses still lingers in the warm summer air.

The horrific, treacly aftermath of the disaster.

THE EARTH'S VENOM

On the evening of 7 May 1902, twenty-seven-year-old Louis-Auguste Cyparis went for a few drinks in his local bar in St Pierre, on the Caribbean island of Martinique. Louis was a labourer and of Afro-Caribbean origin, and had had a few run-ins with the law before, a fact that probably saved his life. That night he had a few too many, and got into a bar fight. He was arrested and thrown in jail, which happened to be in the basement of an old fort with very thick stone walls.

The police were stretched at the time, and probably left him to sleep it off. They had been busy, dealing with the catastrophe that had befallen the town since Mount Pelée had started rumbling about a month beforehand. First came an invasion of yellow ants and giant centipedes, up to thirty centimetres in length, sweeping down from the hillsides into farms and homesteads. The centipedes had bitten countless people, especially farm workers, and although their venom was not fatal, it usually left its human victims in agonising pain for several days, requiring medical treatment.

After the creepy-crawlies had come a much more deadly menace – thousands of fer-de-lance snakes. These deadly pit vipers are up to two metres long, and unless human bite victims receive immediate attention, death is almost inevitable. The shifting earth higher on the mountain had driven them from their habitat to seek safety in the lower slopes.

By that hot May evening, more than fifty people had already been killed, along with 200 farm animals. Hundreds of others who had been bitten were suffering from horrible rashes, internal bleeding, fever, nosebleeds, impaired consciousness nausea and vomiting. Local medical staff were working flat out to treat the sick and dying.

They weren't aware that all their efforts would be in vain, as a much greater catastrophe was about to strike the island.

Louis-Auguste Cyparis possibly imagined that the deafening explosion ringing in his ears just before eight the next morning was a symptom of his hangover. He couldn't see the horizontal jet of flame and black smoke shooting from the side of Mount Pelée. A second plume then shot up vertically, darkening a 20,000-square-kilometre area of sky. Within minutes, a massive pyroclastic flow had surged down the mountain slopes and swallowed the town of St Pierre whole. The para-

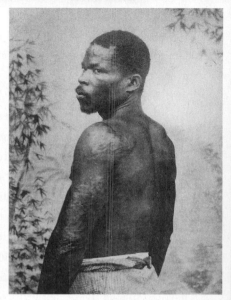

Louis-Auguste Cyparis, destined to become one of very few residents of St Pierre.

dise island was transformed into hell, as a deadly cloud of sulphurous gas enveloped the land and ash showered relentlessly from the skies. Léon Compère-Léandre, a shoemaker whose home was just beyond the edge of the deadly flow, described his experience:

> I felt a terrible wind blowing, the earth began to tremble, and the sky suddenly became dark. I turned to go into the house and felt my arms and legs burning, also my body. I dropped upon a table. At this moment four others sought refuge in my room, crying and writhing with pain, although their garments showed no sign of having been touched by flame. At the end of ten minutes, one of these, the young Delavaud girl, fell dead; the others left. I got up and went to another room, where I found her father dead. He was purple and inflated, but the clothing was intact. Crazed and almost overcome, I threw myself on a bed, inert and awaiting death. My senses returned to me in perhaps an hour, when I beheld the roof burning. With sufficient strength left, my legs bleeding and covered with burns, I ran to Fonds-Saint-Denis, six kilometres from St Pierre.

On another part of the island, little Havivra Da Ifrile, aged ten, was going on an errand for her mother when she witnessed three people perish in a minor vent on Mount Pelée's side. She ran towards the town and when she saw the main explosion and the glowing pyroclastic flow, she rushed to her brother's small boat and rowed along the shore to a cave she played in with her friends. There she hid until she passed out, probably from the effects of the gas. Her boat drifted out to sea, and she was later found alive by a French cruiser.

Back in what was left of the town, beneath tons of volcanic ash, Louis-Auguste Cyparis felt a jet of burning wind shoot through the small grate in his prison cell. He couldn't breathe and felt his skin burning, but then the heat abated and he collapsed into a corner, gasping for air. The thick walls of the old prison cell had protected him from the worst of the heat, and there was sufficient air for him to survive for several days, until rescuers arrived and dug him out.

Incredibly, he, the shoemaker and the little girl were the only three survivors from a population of 30,000 people. He was subsequently pardoned by the colonial governor and became a minor celebrity, eventually beginning a new career, touring America with Barnum's Circus and recounting his incredible tale of survival.

St Pierre, once known as 'the Paris of the West Indies', had been obliterated, all of its fine buildings demolished or buried. It never recovered its former glory, although it is now a pretty town, nestling in the corner of this island paradise. But looming over it always is the menacing bulk of the volcanic Mount Pelée.

The once-beautiful downtown St Pierre.

DEAD IN THE WATER

....

When it comes to maritime disasters, the first word that usually pops into people's heads is 'Titanic'. But if you're American, the first word that should enter your head is 'Sultana'. Okay, it doesn't sound as dramatic as the famed transatlantic liner, named after a race of powerful Greek gods, but it was the single greatest maritime tragedy in the US – and that includes wartime losses. The sinking of the *Sultana* is the naval disaster that history forgot.

Strictly speaking, the loss of the *Sultana* could be deemed a wartime event, as it took place in the closing days of the American Civil War, and there were a lot of soldiers involved. On the other hand, the war had nothing to do with the actual tragedy. But why was the disaster so poorly reported at the time? Well, it just happens that a few other news stories pushed it into the fringes of history.

On 9 April 1865, the Battle of Appomattox Court House took place in Virginia. General Lee's Confederate army suffered relatively minor losses of 500 dead. More importantly, his forces were completely surrounded and outnumbered, and he surrendered.

Less than a week later, on Friday, 14 April, President Abraham Lincoln arrived at Ford's Theatre in Washington DC, to watch a performance of the comedy *Our American Cousin*, by English dramatist Tom Taylor. His favoured bodyguard, William H Crook, was off duty that night, but later told reporters that the President had confided in him that he'd dreamt he was going to be assassinated for three nights running. He declined Crook's advice not to go, and a policeman called John Parker stood in for Crook. During the interval, Parker slipped away to a nearby tavern and didn't return, allowing stage actor John Wilkes Booth to walk into the President's private box and shoot him at point-blank range in the back of the head. Booth then escaped on horseback.

Twelve days later, on 26 April, General Joseph E Johnson surrendered the final remaining Confederate Army in North Carolina, effectively bringing the Civil War to an end. It was an eventful day, as the men of the Union Army's 16th New York Cavalry assigned to tracking down John Wilkes Booth learned that he was hiding on a farm with accomplice David Herold, near the town of Bowling Green, Virginia. They trapped the two men in the barn, and Herold surrendered. But Booth refused, so they set the barn alight, hoping to drive him out. Their orders were to take him alive. But one of the soldiers, Boston Corbett, went to a gap in the timbers and shot Booth in the back of the head. He was arrested and court-martialled but cleared, and he became a national hero.

Just over a week after Booth's death, Union forces captured Jefferson Davis, President of the Confederate States of America, as they were known, bringing the war to a final, bitter conclusion. Almost one million people lay dead across the battlefields of America.

Had the steamboat *Sultana* sunk a couple of months earlier or later, it would have been headline news around the United States. But for all the above reasons, the event, on 27 April 1865, was completely relegated to the back pages.

The large boat was of a familiar design for vessels trading on the Mississippi river: dual-funnelled, with three decks above the waterline, ornate wooden rails encircling its upper deck, its name *Sultana* emblazoned in two-metre high, wild-west-style lettering on the side. It was virtually a new boat, constructed only two years previously, and was intended for use as a cotton-trading vessel operating between New Orleans and St Louis.

On 21 April, the steamboat left New Orleans under the command of Captain J Cass Mason, with 100 passengers and a similar number of crewmen. Several days later, one of the *Sultana*'s four giant boilers sprang a leak, and the boat docked at Vicksburg in Mississippi.

While awaiting repairs, Mason was approached by Lieutenant Colonel Reuben Hatch of the Union Army, who had been assigned the task of getting 2,300 paroled Union soldiers back home to the

The *Sultana*, loaded with way too many soldiers.

north. He told Mason that the US Government would pay him five dollars a head to transport the soldiers. This would have normally entailed dividing the men between several boats on different days, but Hatch wanted rid of the problem, and also saw a way of making a lot of money. He suggested to Mason that he could arrange to have all 2,300 men at the dock the following day, if, firstly, Mason agreed to take the lot in one go, and secondly, if Mason agreed to give Hatch a one-dollar kickback for each man.

Mason readily agreed, despite the fact that the boiler hadn't been repaired, and that his boat's capacity was less than 400 passengers and crew, and already had over 100 civilians on board. If he delayed, the remaining soldiers would be picked up by other vessels. He told the mechanic to quickly patch up the damaged boiler, rather than fix it properly.

The following day, 24 April, soldiers began to board the *Sultana*. There was so little space on the three decks that the men were crammed together like sardines, but having endured the horrors of war and anxious to get home to loved ones, they endured their discomfort with little complaint. On 26 April, the boat stopped at Helena, and a photographer took a shot of the vessel. The crammed decks are clearly evident, and one has to assume the soldiers either slept in a standing position, or not at all.

The normally slow-moving Mississippi was in flood at the time, with reports that in places, trees on the riverbank were submerged. The waters beneath the boat were rushing by with tremendous force, requiring the engines to work harder and harder as they battled the current. The boat's boilers were also working at capacity, struggling to cope with hauling a mass far greater than was ever intended.

Finally the pressure told. At 2am on 27 April, the hastily repaired boiler exploded, in turn causing two of the other three boilers to explode. The initial blast wrecked a substantial part of the ship, and was responsible for hundreds of deaths. Many more were blasted into the dark river by the force of the explosion. The twin funnels collapsed, crushing hundreds more, and the wooden ship was soon ablaze forward, aft and mid-ships.

More than 1,000 people leaped overboard. Hundreds of these drowned almost immediately in the churning water. Most of the soldiers were malnourished, and had been standing in cramped conditions for two days. They were too weak to keep themselves afloat. Of those who made it to the submerged treetops, hundreds more died of hypothermia while waiting for help to arrive.

A minister, Barry Chester, later tracked down many of the survivors and recorded their memories of that terrible night. One soldier who gave an account was WP Madden:

On the morning of the 27th of April, 1865, at about two o'clock, I was asleep dreaming of home and loved ones, when I was awakened by an upheaval and crashing of timbers. I attempted to arise from my recumbent position and as I threw up my hands

to explore my surroundings I got them severely burned, and
was horrified to find that my efforts to extricate myself were
fruitless and the heat was stifling. I could not tell where I was,
but could hear the groans of the wounded and the shrieks of the
women mingling with the crackling noise of the flames and the
hissing of the white steam that enveloped the boat for a time.
No tongue can tell and pen is powerless to portray the agony of
those moments ...

Other boats came to the rescue, but at least 200 of the survivors were horribly burnt and later died in hospital. Captain Mason was among those who perished, and, as subsequent investigations revealed his part in the disaster, the feeling was that justice was in some small way served by his death. Hundreds of other bodies were washed downriver, and many were never recovered. The final death toll was 1,800, almost 300 more than died when the *Titanic* sank.

Parts of the blackened wreck of the *Sultana* were found in the 1980s under an Arkansas field, the Mississippi having shifted course since that fateful day. There is a memorial to those who died in the Mount Olive Baptist Church Cemetery in Knoxville, Tennessee. The tragedy remains the worst ever maritime disaster in United States history, in peace or wartime.

DANCING WITH DEATH

In 303 AD, St Vitus was martyred during the rule of Roman Emperor, Maximian. In the middle ages, it became popular in Germany, Poland and France to dance in front of his statue on his feast day, resulting in him eventually being named as the patron saint of dancers. The downside of this was that if anyone invoked his wrath, he would send down a plague of compulsive dancing from heaven.

So what's all this got to do with disasters, you may rightly ask. Well, the above may have had something to do with a mass psychosis that apparently gripped the town of Strasbourg in France in July 1518, when the population were possessed by a fevered dancing craze.

Yes, a *dancing craze*. This event is well attested to in council and church records, local historical accounts and the records of local physicians. That fine summer's day, a woman called Frau Troffea emerged from her cottage and began to dance fervently about the streets, and she continued dancing for about four days and nights. People who saw her were at first bemused, but one by one, others began to join her. Within a few days, almost forty of the town's residents were dancing in the street.

A few weeks later, there were 400 people boogying around Strasbourg's streets, the majority of them women, and the council met in

St Vitus's dance, as pictured in 1642.

emergency session to debate the matter. They decided that the best thing they could do was contain the problem and control it, so they opened the guildhalls, and hired musicians to play pipes and drums for the people to dance to. Having directed the dancers into the halls, they hoped that they would simply wear themselves out and everything would eventually return to normal.

What actually happened is that the older and weaker dancers began to collapse and die, mostly from heart attacks or dehydration. And yet this didn't deter the others and the dancing continued, right through August. The authorities then decided to load the dancers on to wagons and take them in batches to a nearby shrine (possibly to St Vitus), where they could plead for mercy.

This seems to have done the trick, and the dancing craze ended almost as quickly as it had started. It is not known how many people died as a result of the strange phenomenon, but given that the people were malnourished after a recent famine, the numbers are likely to have been high.

Two possible explanations have been offered. The first is the mass ingestion of ergot, a fungus that grows on rye, which could have tainted the town's bread supply. Ergot is known to trigger delirious behaviour, and can result in spasmodic limb movements. The second is related to superstition and religion, particularly St Vitus's curse, the belief in which may have induced mass hysteria among the town's population.

Stranger still, this was not a unique phenomenon, just the best documented. In 1237, a large group of children was similarly afflicted in the German town of Erfurt. They danced their way out of town, and didn't stop until they reached Arnstadt, about twenty kilometres away. In 1278, a couple of hundred German people began dancing frenetically on a bridge over the River Meuse, putting it under such strain that it collapsed. The survivors were nursed back to health in a nearby chapel of St Vitus, which fact might have contributed to the saint's legend and inspired future bouts of hysteria.

The biggest ever outbreak of dancing mania happened in Aachen in Germany in 1374. But it didn't stop there – the hysteria quickly spread to Cologne, before crossing borders into Flanders, Holland, France, Italy and Luxembourg.

One of the last major occurrences of the phenomenon was in Basel in Switzerland in 1536, involving another large group of children. Smaller outbreaks occurred throughout the seventeenth century, and then dancing hysteria disappeared completely.

A seventeenth-century professor of medicine, Gregor Horst, wrote an account of one outbreak:

> *Several women who annually visit the chapel of St Vitus in Drefelhausen, dance madly all day and all night until they collapse in ecstasy. In this way they come to themselves again and feel little or nothing until the next May, when they are again forced around St Vitus' Day to betake themselves to that place.*

Even allowing for the fact that we are dealing with uneducated, superstitious, religious people of the middle ages, you just have to marvel at the power of the human mind to make us behave in such a bizarre fashion.

11

HEAVEN, OR HELL, CAN WAIT

....

Perhaps because of death's inevitability, we all simply love a good old tale of the Grim Reaper being denied his prize, at least for a time. It's like we can briefly stick two fingers up to his dark, hooded visage and shout 'Na-na-nana-na!' Perhaps these tales give us all that little bit of hope – if we ever find ourselves in some grim scenario where death is hurtling towards us with near complete inevitability, at the back of our minds there's still just a teensy-weensy, one-in-a-billion chance that, somehow, we'll survive. Here are a few folk who stared the Pale Rider in the face – and lived to tell the tale.

HANGING IN THE BALANCE
....

Nowadays, Philip Street in Sydney is a chasm between skyscrapers, near the north end of which may be glimpsed the arching beauty of the Sydney Harbour Bridge. As you stroll along, it is hard to imagine just how different this place was two centuries ago. Back then, it was known as Back Row, and consisted of a few timber homes on a dusty street, with urchins scampering between the legs of horses as men and women plied their trades. But it was in this place, just after nightfall on 26 August 1803, that an event occurred that would be remembered in the footnotes of Australian history for two very different reasons.

Two years earlier, a man called Joseph Samuel was convicted of robbery in his native England and sentenced to transportation to Australia. Samuel escaped his captors sometime in 1803 and, along with several other men, burgled the home of a Mrs Mary Breeze, making off with £24 in cash, a sizeable amount back then. Burglary was a very serious offence at the time – it could merit a death sentence, depending on the circumstances.

A neighbour of Mrs Breeze was constable Joseph Luker, who himself had once been a criminal transported to Australia, and who subsequently reformed. He informed her of his suspicions that the culprit was a local ruffian called Isaac Simmonds. Luker set off into the night to investigate, and didn't return. The next day, he was found brutally beaten and dead, with his own cutlass piercing his skull. This is the first event of note here, as Joseph Luker officially became the first police officer to be killed on duty in Australia. A brief aside: After two centuries, Luker's final resting place was rediscovered beneath the town hall, making the place something of a memorial site for the city's police force.

Four men – Isaac Simmonds, William Bladders, Joseph Samuel and Richard Jackson – were arrested. Samuel and Jackson were charged with robbery, while the other two were accused of murder. Despite a lot of evidence being presented at their trial indicating Simmonds's guilt, including his blood-stained clothing, he was acquitted, as was Bladders. Jackson turned state's evidence against Samuel on the robbery charge, and he was acquitted. Samuel was sentenced to death by hanging, the sentence presumably so severe because of the policeman's murder, although Samuel insisted he had absolutely no knowledge of the crime.

At 9.30am on 26 September 1803, Samuel and another convicted thief, James Hardwicke, were brought in a cart from Sydney Gaol to the gallows at Brickfield Hill (now the Surry Hills suburb). A minister, having prayed for his eternal soul, then asked Samuel for information about the murder of Constable Luker. With the noose dangling beside him, Samuel denied any involvement and loudly accused Simmonds, who was present, of the killing. Many of the large crowd agreed with Samuel's assertion that a miscarriage of justice was about to occur, and Simmonds had to be protected by a number of constables.

Just then, a messenger arrived and handed the magistrate a paper. This turned out to be a last-minute reprieve for Hardwicke, who was taken down for return to the prison. Finally, proceedings were to get underway, and the noose was placed around Samuel's neck. The rope was made of strong hemp, and had previously been tested under weight, but when the order was given and the cart moved away, Samuel was left hanging for a few moments before the rope snapped and he crashed to the ground.

The crowd cried that Providence had intervened, and called for mercy. Samuel lay there, half-asphyxiated, while officials hurriedly returned the cart beneath the gallows, and two men dragged the condemned man to his feet.

Barely able to stand, he was placed on the cart again, and the noose put around his neck. Again the cart was pulled away, but this time the noose began to unravel. Samuel was left half-suspended, the tips of his toes touching the ground, before the noose slipped completely free of his neck and he again fell to the dusty earth.

The crowd were incensed and cried out for a reprieve, and the officials feared that they might be lynched themselves if they didn't get this over with quickly. Samuel was again readied for execution, but this time it required two men to hold him upright on the cart, as he was virtually unconscious. The cart pulled away and, incredibly, the rope snapped again.

With the threat of a near riot, the magistrate suspended proceedings and sent word to the governor about what had occurred. Sure enough, it was decided that divine intervention had been responsible for Samuel's survival, and his sentence was commuted to life imprisonment.

Later that day, the rope that had been used in the failed execution was again tested with a total weight of 400lb – about three times a man's weight. Much to the astonishment of officials, it failed to snap until two of its three strands had been severed.

Samuel was nursed back to health, only to be despatched to prison in Newcastle, where it was intended he remain for the rest of his days. A local newspaper, the *Gazette*, reported in 1806 that eight convicts had escaped from Newcastle, stealing a boat and rowing out beyond Port Stephens. Despite extensive searches, they were never heard of again. One of the men that escaped that night was called Joseph Samuel.

The three-strike rule seems also to have applied to John 'Babbacombe' Lee, a manservant in the home of Miss Emma Keyes, in the pretty seaside area of Babbacombe on the south coast of England. Lee was no angelic choirboy. He had previously served time for burglary, before securing work as a footman for the elderly Miss Keyes.

When his employer was brutally murdered on 15 November 1884, suspicion immediately fell on the nineteen-year-old Lee, if only because he was the only male in the household.

The victim, and the nature of the murder, made this a feast day for the press. They enthusiastically reported how Miss Keyes had been bludgeoned with an axe, had had her throat slashed, and that an attempt had even

John 'Babbacombe' Lee.

been made to burn down her house. The fact that she had once been a maid of honour for Queen Victoria, and that the Queen had once actually stayed in the house, gave the story some murky celebrity credentials.

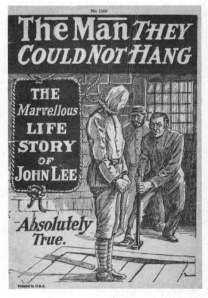

Despite the evidence being entirely circumstantial, and despite there being other strong suspects, Lee was convicted and sentenced to death, protesting his innocence all the way to the gallows. On 23 February 1885, Lee was led on to the scaffold at Exeter Prison.

Executioner John Berry pulled the bolt, but the trapdoor failed to open. Flustered officials removed Lee and tested the door again. It worked perfectly. The hooded prisoner was returned to the trapdoor, and the order was again given for the bolt to be drawn. Once again, the door failed to open. In one account, the officials stamped on the trapdoor to make it fall, but it simply wouldn't budge. The no-doubt highly distraught Lee was removed, and it was retested. The trapdoor worked perfectly again. A third attempt was made. No luck. The trapdoor simply wouldn't fall when Lee was standing on it.

The hanging was suspended and Lee was returned to his cell. Within a few days, the Home Secretary had commuted Lee's sentence to life imprisonment. He would serve a total of twenty-two years before being freed, aged forty-two.

Subsequent examination and testing of the trapdoor mechanism showed that the act of putting weight on the door caused it to shift slightly, so that it still rested on one eighth of an inch of the bolt. This narrow sliver of metal had separated Lee from death.

People who get shot in the head usually don't survive, especially if the bullet penetrates the brain and exits the other side. If the bullet is a large-calibre one, such as from a rifle, your chances of survival become seriously slim. Now imagine being hit in the brain by a bullet from, say, a Russian Gryazev-Shipunov GSh-23 anti-aircraft cannon, which is 23mm (almost an inch) in diameter and over 100mm long. Your chances of survival? Minimal would be an overstatement. Yet given his experience, Phineas P Gage might have remarked that such projectiles were for wimps.

On 13 September 1848, Gage, an intelligent, twenty-five-year-old with movie star looks, was working as a foreman on a crew laying a railroad in Vermont. The men were blasting a path through a large outcrop of rock, which involved repeatedly boring a deep hole, half filling it with gunpowder, topping this off with sand, and then compacting this down with a tool called a tamping iron. This instrument is pointed at one end, over three centimetres in diameter and one metre long, and weighs six kilograms.

As he was tamping down the material, the powder exploded prematurely and sent the iron hurtling upwards, penetrating the left side of his face, passing through his cheekbone and behind his left eye, entering the left frontal lobe of his brain and exiting though the top of his skull. The iron streaked through the air, landing some twenty metres away.

Not surprisingly, Gage collapsed and had a convulsion, but it soon passed. Amazingly, after a few minutes, he could speak to his fellow workers and walk with little assistance to a nearby wagon. Back in town, a Dr Edward H Williams was summoned, and Gage greeted him with the words, 'Doctor, here is business enough for you.' The doctor thought Gage's account of what had happened an exaggeration or a result of the trauma, as surely such an accident would be fatal, but he eventually realised that Gage was telling the truth. At one point, Gage felt very ill and had to vomit, the act of which, according to Williams, 'pressed out about half a teacupful of the brain, which fell upon the floor'.

Williams and another local doctor, John Harlow, treated Gage extensively for several hours. One of Harlow's notes from that evening reads: 'Mind clear. Constant agitation of his legs, being alternately retracted and extended like the shafts of a fulling mill. Says he does not care to see his friends, as he shall be at work in a few days.'

Within a month, Gage had apparently made a near-complete recovery, at least physically, although he was blinded in his left eye and bore a couple of impressive scars. Within two months, he was home on his parents' farm, doing manual work in the barn and even some ploughing.

According to friends and family, however, the injury had badly affected his character, and he was 'no longer Gage'. Dr Harlow noted that he 'uttered the grossest profanities' and 'showed little deference for his fellows'. He also took to alcohol.

He became an object of fascination for the medical community, and was even presented to the Harvard Medical School. He made some money by exhibiting himself and relating his amazing tale. He was refused his old job when he approached the railroad company, despite having been 'a model foreman'. Eventually Gage found regular employment in a stable in New Hampshire, and then emigrated to Chile, where he secured a job driving stagecoaches.

Much of his former social and personal skills seemed to return as the years passed. Sadly, while on a visit home to his mother in May 1860, he had a series of epileptic convulsions and died, aged just thirty-six. Even so, he'd survived a full twelve years beyond what would have been considered an almost certain fatal accident.

Gage has entered the folklore of neuroscience, and many modern textbooks still reference his incredible tale of brain injury survival. He

was among the first recorded cases to directly link specific personality changes to damage to specific areas of the brain.

Six years after Phineas Gage's early death, Dr Harlow got permission to exhume his body and remove his skull. He also had the original tamping iron in his possession, which caused the injury. Having written an extensive paper on the case, he donated both of these to Harvard's Warren Anatomical Museum, where they remain on display to this day.

Phineas Gage displays the tamping iron that, amazingly, didn't kill him.

FALLING ON ONE'S FEET

Tales of infant survival against incredible odds are as old as the hills – certainly as old as the hills of Rome, where Romulus and Remus were said to have been abandoned, only to be raised by a nice she-wolf and go on to found the Eternal City.

And at least once a year a story emerges, often nowadays captured on shaky phone or digital camera footage, of a baby being pulled alive from the rubble of a collapsed building, after an earthquake or a bomb. One diversion you can indulge yourself in, if you're so inclined, is watching startling YouTube videos of people catching babies falling from buildings, of which there are many. But here are a couple of brief baby survival tales to outdo even those, a couple of them tragic despite the happy outcome for the babies.

At the end of the Second World War, an American Baptist minister from Connecticut called Bob Vick, his wife Dorothy and their two small children, Teddy and Paul, travelled to China to work as missionaries. On 28 January 1947, the family boarded a China National Aviation Corporation plane in Shanghai, bound for Hubei Province, roughly 1,000 kilometres to the west. There were twenty-two other passengers on the plane. As it approached the Peng Bey area, towards the end of the flight, there was an explosion. The plane burst into flames and began to plummet to the ground.

The passengers had time to realise that they had little chance of surviving the impact, and they began to leap from the burning plane, one after the other. Likewise, Bob and Dorothy realised that they and their children had only one slim chance. Bob grabbed Paul and Dorothy grabbed Teddy, and they waited by the open door until the very last moment before leaping from the plane. Dorothy and Teddy died instantly, but Bob managed to shield sixteen-month-old

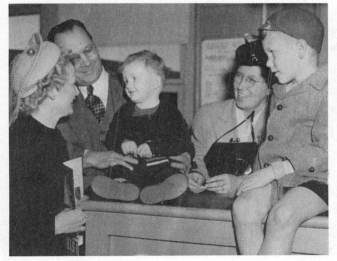

Paul Vick.

Paul with his body. Both survived the initial impact, and were taken to their mission's clinic in Tien Men (which means 'Gate of Heaven').

None of the other passengers survived and, sadly, Bob succumbed to his injuries after forty hours, refusing pain-killing medication to leave instructions that his son was to be raised by his grandparents in the US.

Thanks to his father's actions, Paul's only injuries were fractures to his legs and a concussion. He holds the record as the world's youngest sole survivor of a plane crash. Today Paul Vick is the treasurer of International Ministries for the Baptist Church. He recently returned to the spot where his parents and baby brother tragically died.

One more falling baby tale: In 1938, a street sweeper in Detroit called Joseph Figlock was working in an alley, bent over his sweeping. A baby climbed onto a fourth-floor window ledge above, fell and landed on the head and shoulders of Figlock. Both suffered minor injuries, but fully recovered.

Lucky baby, you may say, but compared to some of the falling babies on YouTube, the story is merely so-so. Ah, but you've only heard half the tale. Some time later, in a different part of town, two-year-old David Thomas managed to scamper over a window ledge and plummet towards almost certain death. But guess what broke his fall? Yes, there was Joseph Figlock again, sweeping away below, and David landed on his head and shoulders. Once again, both were injured, but not seriously. Oh baby.

DON'T LOSE YOUR HEAD

You're probably heard at least one joke about guillotines failing to drop and the executioner declaring it an act of God. The reality is that during the so-called 'Terror' of the French Revolution, many of the mob had simply abandoned their Christian faith (much of

Notre Dame was destroyed, for example, and turned into a temple to the Cult of Reason), so any appeals that Providence had intervened would have fallen on deaf ears. If the guillotine failed to work properly, the authorities simply summoned someone to fix it, while the terrified victims waited and watched.

This worked to the benefit of one very fortunate individual. Henri Chateaubrun lived in Paris with his beloved wife Marie, and although a Conservative, he was a strong believer in reform of the systems that had led the people into such abject poverty. His closest friend, Antoine Boyer, supported the Revolutionary cause enthusiastically.

As time passed, Boyer slowly began to fall for the beautiful Madame Chateaubrun. Boyer also began to argue politically with his friend about the course the Revolution was taking. Boyer later became very influential in the Revolutionary movement, and although Chateaubrun would never prove it, he would come to believe that when the soldiers knocked on his door to arrest him, Boyer was behind it.

Monsieur Chateaubrun was sentenced to death by the Revolutionary Court, and delivered along with twenty others to Revolution Square (Place de la Concorde), the site of the guillotine. Fifteen or so of the condemned were executed. When Monsieur Chateaubrun's turn came, the guillotine abruptly jammed. The crowd booed and wailed. They wanted to see more Royalist heads rolling.

A carpenter was summoned, and in the interim the prisoners, their hands bound behind them, were taken down from the scaffold. Minutes turned into hours, as the carpenter and his comrades worked to repair the guillotine. As evening drew in, the crowd grew restless. With their attention diverted from the guillotine, Monsieur Chateaubrun began to gently nudge his way backwards into the mob. In the fading light and with his fine clothing soiled from his time in prison, nobody noticed him as he slowly manoeuvred his way further and further from the instrument of death.

Then the executioner announced success in repairing the guillotine, and a huge cheer went up. With their eyes now firmly focussed on the execution of the remaining victims, the crowd failed to notice Chateaubrun vanishing into the shadows. If anyone realised the count of prisoners was short, they didn't make any fuss about it. No cry arose about a missing man – either someone didn't want to get into trouble, or there was simply no record of the number of executions due.

Willing himself to walk slowly, Henri made his way to the nearby Champs Elysées, where he approached a gentleman. Forcing himself to laugh, he told the man his friends had played a prank on him, tying his hands and stealing his hat (it was unusual for anyone to go about bare-headed at the time). The man laughed and severed Chateaubrun's bonds with a pocketknife, and the escapee vanished into the alleyways of Paris.

Assuming her husband was dead, Marie was naturally heartbroken. Antoine Boyer visited her with his condolences, and eventually professed his love, much to her shock. At this point, it dawned on her that he might have been behind her husband's arrest.

Some days later, a woman arrived at her door, claiming to be a friend of her husband and bearing the startling news that he was alive and living in the Netherlands. He had been too fearful to write a letter,

The crowd watches as Maximilien Robespierre, one of the architects of the French Revolution, awaits his turn at the Guillotine in Place de la Concorde.

in case the authorities intercepted it. Overjoyed, Marie immediately packed her bags and fled Paris without informing Boyer of her intentions. Two days later, she was joyfully reunited with her husband. Neither ever saw Boyer again.

The man who most likely betrayed Chateaubrun soon found his Revolutionary faction in conflict with others. He was eventually arrested and sent to the death he had intended for his closest friend.

SKIRTING DEATH

....

Sarah and her fiancé had a stormy relationship. They were constantly arguing, although it seems that Sarah, a barmaid at the Rising Sun pub in Bristol, was deeply in love. Her fiancé worked for the Great Western Railway. Sarah had apparently stormed into the rail yard sometime in early May 1885, and had a blazing row with him, telling him in her rage that she had lots of other potential suitors, all of a much higher standing than a mere porter. He was outraged, and that night he wrote Sarah a letter saying that he was finished with her. The engagement was off. He no longer loved her or wanted to be with her.

Each word stabbed Sarah Ann Henley like a knife in the heart. When her father found out, he sought out the porter and punched him on the nose. But it was no good – it was too late, no wedding bells, no happy ending.

Distraught, Sarah rushed out of her home in the Easton area of Bristol and made her way to the Clifton Suspension Bridge, two miles away. The bridge is an impressive piece of Victorian engineering, towering more than 100 metres above the River Avon. For Sarah, it was to be her bridge into the next life. Heartbroken, she made her way to its centre and peered down at the water far below.

Clifton Bridge was tolled, and its inspector, Thomas Stevens, was passing an otherwise uneventful day when to his horror he saw the

Clifton suspension bridge.

young woman clamber over the railings. He leaped to his feet, but it was too late. Sarah didn't ponder her decision for very long, and threw herself head-first to her presumed death.

Except it didn't quite work out like that.

There was a slight breeze blowing and, as she fell, she turned through 180 degrees. Local newspapers reported that witnesses described her crinoline skirt (the dreaded, deadly crinoline I lambasted elsewhere) filling with air and slowing her descent. She was blown off course, and instead of striking the water, Sarah came down in the soft mud just below the river's banks. Several men, including a constable, immediately rushed to her aid and hauled her from the riverbed. She was taken to the local infirmary and discovered to have several injuries, but nothing critical.

As she made her recovery in the following weeks, her story was recounted in the national media and her fame spread far and wide. Complete strangers made numerous proposals of marriage. Various showmen tried to tempt her to go on tour and recount her tale. They were all rebuffed.

Her ex-fiancé quietly slipped from the picture, and Sarah never returned to her job in the Rising Sun. Fifteen years later, she married a Mr Edward Lane, who worked at a Bristol wagon works. She lived a full sixty-two years beyond the day of her attempted suicide, and died aged eighty-five in 1948.

NOT QUITE DEAD, AND BURIED

We've had people surviving the gallows, the guillotine, 100-metre drops, metal bars through the brain, falling from balconies and bridges, so what's left? Oh yes, this ...

Essie Dunbar, a twenty-three-year-old South Carolinian woman, was prone to epileptic seizures. In the summer of 1915, she had a major attack, and a Doctor K Briggs was summoned, but arrived too late. He examined Essie, found no traces of life, and pronounced her dead.

The undertaker came, and Essie's body was placed in a coffin, her funeral scheduled for eleven the next day so that her sister, who lived out of town, would be able to attend. But Essie's sister arrived only in time to see the last shovels of dirt thrown on to the grave.

It was this chance event that saved the life of the 'dead' Essie. The woman was distraught at not saying her farewells to her beloved sister, and begged the ministers present to unearth the coffin again. They reluctantly agreed, and when the screws were unwound and the lid removed, to everyone's horror, Essie sat up, confused as to her whereabouts, and greeted her sister.

Frequent retelling of the tale locally has no doubt coloured what happened next, but it makes for a good story nonetheless. Apparently, all three ministers present were so shocked that they fell into the open hole, the one on the bottom suffering broken ribs as the other two trampled on him in their attempts to escape. The rest of the mourners, Essie's sister included, fled in terror at the sight of the 'ghost'. Their hysteria was compounded when they looked back and saw that Essie was running after them, pleading for an explanation.

Essie Dunbar.

Essie Dunbar returned home to live a long and fruitful life, although the more superstitious members of her community viewed her with uncertainty, always suspecting that she was a zombie of some kind. Anyway, she lived for a further forty-seven years and her death notice read 'Second funeral is held for South Carolina woman'.

No less remarkable is the tale of nineteen-year-old Frenchman Angelo Hays, who, in 1937, crashed his motorcycle and was hurled at a brick wall in the village of St Quentin de Chalais, near Bordeaux. The local doctor examined him, could find no pulse and declared him dead. Because he hadn't been wearing a helmet, his face was a virtual pulp, so much so that his distraught parents weren't allowed to view the body. He was buried in the local graveyard, and everyone thought that was the end of that.

For reasons that are unclear, the insurance company got an order to exhume his body two days later. When the coffin was opened, he was found to be still warm. At least there was no repeat of the dramatic scenes that accompanied Essie Dunbar's resurrection.

Angelo was rushed to the nearest hospital, where doctors declared that he was in a deep coma. This had apparently saved his life, as his body's diminished need for oxygen had allowed him to survive in the cramped confines of the coffin. Months of surgery followed and, incredibly, Angelo Hays made a near-complete recovery, although he was undoubtedly scarred.

He gained some celebrity in later life, having invented the 'security coffin', complete with food supply, small library, chemical toilet and radio transmitter. He didn't sell too many, as the coffin cost as much as a car. However, he did make a handsome profit from live displays and media appearances, and even demonstrated his invention from six feet under, live on TV in the 1970s. And who could blame him? It's not everyone who gets to profit from his or her own death.

12

PLAYING AT RANTUM-SCANTUM

According to Francis Grose's 1811 *Dictionary of Buckish Slang, University Wit and Pickpocket Eloquence*, the above title is a slang term for having sex from the mid-seventeenth century. From roughly the same period, we also get 'shot twixt wind and water', which sort of makes unpleasant sense when you think about it. As does 'play nug-a-nug' from 1501, and 'fadoodling' from 1611. 'Play the pyrdewy' (1512), 'play at rumpscuttle and clapperdepouch' (1684) and 'lerricompoop' (1694) are a lot less obvious. But the cutest slang expression for having sex has to be this from 1785: 'making feet for children's stockings'.

Yes, shocking it may be to young people, but their parents, grandparents and great, great, great grandparents, and indeed all their ancestors throughout the aeons, have all had sex at some point in their lives. They all had their own subtle language for describing the experience, just as 'Netflix and chill' will probably appear in some list of archaic slang in a century, leaving our great, great grandchildren scratching their heads.

History is laden with sex: ancient Greek homosexuality; Roman orgies; the *Kama Sutra*; kings and politicians brought down by sex scandals; and so on. From the most ancient times to the present day, sex has been one of the forces that make the world go round.

Of course, references to sex in history books are usually fleeting and superficial – we never really learn the meaty, sordid detail and many of the participants, certainly the scandalous ones, had a cloak drawn over their identities and their naughty bits. So let's see what we can uncover.

BUSINESSWOMEN

Charles II's sexual appetite was legendary, but besides his regular mistresses, of which there were many, where did the monarch go to satisfy his lusts? In fact, if you can believe the history books, where did much of his royal court, along with leading government officials and businessmen, go to play at rantum-scantum? Well, top of the list were the brothels run by perhaps England's most famous madam, Elizabeth Cresswell.

Born around 1625, by the age of thirty-three Cresswell was recorded

Madam Cresswell
Une Maquerelle
Vecelio refece

The very enterprising Elizabeth Cresswell, 'without rival in her wickedness'.

as a City of London brothel-keeper 'without rival in her wickedness'. At that point, she was arrested and tried. Among the evidence presented was the following: 'Witnesses told of seeing men and women going into rooms, the Woman having stript to her Bodice and Petticoat going into a room where they have shut the Casement and locked the Door,' and, 'whores in the habit of a Gentlewoman began to propose a Health to the Privy Member of a Gentleman ... and afterwards drank a Toast to her own Private Parts.' One can't but titter.

Cresswell got a stint in prison for that offence, but that by no means stopped her. A decade later, she had an entire network of brothels across London, her girls servicing many of the royal court and the noblemen of the capital. Her connections to Britain's elite royals, politicians, lawyers and businessmen acted as a shield against most of the religious, moral crusaders who wished the world rid of her and her kind.

She boasted 'Beauties of all Complexions', 'from the cole-black clyng-fast to the golden lock'd insatiate, from the sleepy ey'd Slug to the lewd Fricatrix', and that she sold 'strong waters and fresh-faced wenches to all who had guineas to buy them with'. Cresswell employed a network of 'talent scouts' across England to find suitable girls, who usually came from impoverished backgrounds, but were sometimes formerly well-off ladies who had fallen on hard times.

There was an attempt to put her out of business in 1668, when young apprentices rampaged through her brothels, assaulting prostitutes and smashing furniture. The event, known as the 'Bawdy House Riot' was supposedly a moral crusade against prostitution, but might also have been driven by the fact that apprentices, who at the time couldn't marry, could not afford the fees Cresswell charged for her girls.

Despite all such attempts to close her down, she continued to successfully operate her brothels until she was again arrested, later in life. She died in the Bridewell Prison in 1698, aged seventy-four.

The Prós Triumph, or Bawdy-House Battery

Among France's most famous madams was a woman called Marguerite Gourdan, a country girl who fell for an army officer and married him. They came to Paris in the mid-eighteenth century, and she prostituted herself with a nobleman with her husband's consent, presumably because they needed the cash. The affair produced a child and an allowance from the rich nobleman.

Having been introduced to the oldest profession, Gourdan now decided to make a career out of it. With the money from her allowance, she opened her first brothel in 1759. Probably uniquely, she hired different classes of girl to service different classes of client – from uneducated working-class girls to the wives of the gentry who wished for an income of their own. She also catered for homosexual and lesbian clients.

Having divorced her husband, she went into business with another madam – Justine Paris, who would be immortalised by the famous author and adventurer Casanova. Together they opened a string of brothels across Paris, which also offered couples in illicit affairs private rooms in which to have sex, and which were equipped with sex toys.

Gourdan is credited with having designed a wooden penis, nicknamed the 'Nun heirloom', presumably because people imagined that celibate nuns would be keen purchasers.

In 1774, Gourdan and Paris opened what became the most famous, luxurious and exclusive brothel in Paris – Chateau de Madame Gourdan.

A satirical depiction of a prostitute from 1796.

Situated in the Rue des Deux Portes, it was just a ten-minute walk from the Palais Royale, convenient for the many members of the royal court who frequented the place. The brothel encompassed several houses, and even extended into neighbouring streets. It featured several speciality rooms, such as the notorious 'Salon de Vulcan', where guests could indulge their tastes for BDSM.

In 1774, Justine Paris, then aged sixty-nine, contacted syphilis and died. Marguerite Gourdan continued to ply her trade to rich and poor, heterosexual and gay, royal and commoner, until 1783, when she also died. Her age at the time of her death is unknown.

Another madam duo was responsible for probably the most famous brothel in the United States at the beginning of the twentieth century. Sisters Ada and Minna Everleigh were born in the 1860s in either Virginia or Kentucky (depending on your source). Originally called either Simms or Lester, they changed their name to Everleigh because of their grandmother's habit of signing her letters 'Everly yours'. They were both well-educated, refined and attractive girls who had attended finishing school, married young into abusive marriages and divorced their husbands before they were thirty.

They initially turned to acting to survive, but having come from a well-to-do background, a yearning for a more luxurious lifestyle may have prompted them to open their first brothel in Omaha, Nebraska in 1895 – they simply saw it as good business, and clearly had no moral qualms.

That proved a successful venture, and when the five-month-long Trans-Mississippi and International Exposition (a type of world fair) was held in Omaha in 1898, they opened a second bordello. With two-and-a-half million visitors to the city, delegates also flocked to the exhibits on display in the brothel adjacent to the exposition. The sisters made a small fortune, and decided to move up in the world – the glamour of Chicago was beckoning.

In 1899, they located a suitable premises in South Dearborn Street in Chicago's Levee District, then a hub of seedy bars, brothels and dance clubs. But the sisters were determined that theirs would be different. They fired all the prostitutes working there at the time, and ploughed a fortune into renovating the large building in a highly luxurious manner:

> ... silk curtains, damask easy chairs, oriental rugs, mahogany tables, gold rimmed china and silver dinner ware, perfumed fountains in every room, a $15,000 gold-leafed piano for the Music Room, mirrored ceilings, a library filled with finely bound volumes, an art gallery featuring nudes in gold frames – no expense was spared.

Ada took care of business matters, including hiring of the girls who would work the place, and who they would call 'butterflies'. Minna was more outgoing, greeting and entertaining customers and training the girls in how to behave. This included advice along the following lines:

> ... forget why you are here, be charming and have a good time. Men are wired differently to women. They have physical needs as well as a longing for female companionship. Here at the Everleigh House we have a service to fulfil, both with grace and elegance. This is how we will compete with brothels in Chicago. If a man just wants sex, he can go down the street and pay less for it. Here we give them much more.

'Butterflies' were instructed to spend at least an hour talking with a client before taking him to a room upstairs, ostensibly to create the feeling for the man that he was talking to a 'real girl' as opposed to a prostitute, but also presumably to encourage him to spend money on food and alcohol. The girls were treated well by the sisters – they had regular health checks, and earned over $100 a week – a vast salary at the time.

A room in the Everleigh Club and, inset, sisters Ada and Minna Everleigh.

Patrons had to be very wealthy to use the Everleigh Club's services. Just getting in the front door cost ten dollars, at a time when the average weekly wage was eight dollars. Having spent your ten dollars, you would be required to spend at least forty more, or you would not be permitted to return. The club offered guests a high-class dinner for fifty dollars, wine for twelve a bottle and, most importantly, the 'company' of a 'butterfly' for fifty dollars. The Everleigh Club's luxuriousness and exclusivity allowed patrons to tell themselves that they were visiting a 'gentleman's club' rather than a seedy brothel.

The sisters' investment paid off handsomely, as the rich, powerful and famous flocked to sample its pleasures. Business tycoons, politicians, sports stars, writers and socialites all flocked to the club – Prince Henry of Prussia specifically requested to make a visit while on a trip to the US. A year after opening the Everleigh sisters were taking home an astonishing $15,000 a week – almost 2,000 times the average American wage.

The sisters forked out fortunes in bribes to keep moral crusaders at bay. Politicians, lawyers and judges were among the clients who enjoyed the services of the club gratis – and left the club with their pockets lined rather than empty. It worked perfectly for more than a decade, until growing pressure from the public and the media began to demand closure of the city's countless brothels and drinking dens.

The Chicago Vice Commission was established, and one of its first acts was to turn its gaze on the city's most famous bordello. The Everleigh Club's opulence and its wealthy and political patrons were an open secret in the city, and it was chosen as among the first of Chicago's brothels to close.

In 1911, the club shut its doors for the last time, and the Everleigh sisters walked off into the sunset with one million dollars in their pockets, possibly making them the most successful brothel entrepreneurs in history.

WORKING GIRLS

Of course, prostitutes don't only ply their wares within the walls of brothels. During the American Civil War, army-sized groups of girls would follow regiments as they moved about the country, preparing themselves for engagement. The soldiers, that is.

Many of these women were said to be wives of soldiers, who had to turn to prostitution to survive because their men were away for extended periods of time. Increasing numbers of brothels were opening up in cities since the war started, but by far the largest increase was in the neighbourhoods of rural towns where the army had set up camp.

Nashville, for example, then a relatively small Tennessee town, had a population of 200 prostitutes in 1860, and 1,500 a couple of years later. The Army of the Potomac, which had in excess of 100,000 troops, is said to have had a camp following of prostitutes numbering in their thousands, who trudged from place to place behind the marching boots of the men.

One of the army's commanders was Major General 'Fighting Joe' Hooker, and there were said to be so many prostitutes plying their trade around his army that they became known as 'Hooker's Division'. A common myth is that he also gave his name to the slang term for prostitutes, but actually, 'hooker' as a term had been around for a long time, and may have originated simply because girls were said to 'hook' men like fish.

One downside of all this paid-for sex is that, of the two million men who served in the Union Army, 200,000 had a venereal disease, usually either gonorrhoea or syphilis. A similar proportion of Confederate soldiers suffered the same fate.

While the identities of many madams are well documented, the working girls themselves have tended to be blotted out, remaining sadly anonymous, used and then discarded by history. But there are exceptions.

Perhaps the oldest known prostitute in written history is Phryne, who lived in ancient Greece around the middle of the fourth century BC. Her name and some biographical information survive, principally because her clientele included famed Greek writers and sculptors, who captured her beauty in sculpture or words, but also because she was the defendant in a well-known trial from the ancient world.

Among those clients was Praxiteles, who reputedly used the stunningly beautiful Phryne as the model for his famous sculpture Aphrodite of Knidos, said to have been the first life-sized statue of the nude female form. The later Roman scholar Pliny the Elder recorded that the statue's nudity so shocked the residents of Kos that they rejected it outright and instead it was taken by the far less prudish people of Knidos, where it became a must-see attraction for visitors. Another ancient literary source, the Erotes, relates a tale, probably apocryphal, that one young man was so taken with the sculpture's beauty and realism that he broke into the temple where it stood one night and tried to make love to it. One perhaps shouldn't try to imagine the outcome of that one.

The rhetorician Athenaeus (who lived five hundred years later, it must be said) related the tale of how, on the occasion of the festival of the sea god Poseidon, Phryne stripped naked before the crowds and walked into the sea as an offering to the god. This inspired the renowned painter Apelles to paint Venus Anadyomene, showing Venus rising from the sea – a creation that has inspired many other works, most notably 'The Birth of Venus' by Sandro Botticelli.

Phryne became exceptionally wealthy through prostituting herself to famous and wealthy men, and is said to have charged the men according to how much she liked or disliked them, or how wealthy they were. A rich but tyrannical ruler would be charged a fortune, but the great philosopher Diogenes went free because she so admired his mind.

Phryne's most famous moment was her trial. She had been accused of impiety, perhaps for her nude skinny dip in honour of Poseidon, and insulting the gods was an offence that carried the death penalty. The great orator Hypereides, who was also one of her clients, defended her. The effectiveness of his oration is unknown, but in what is perhaps another apocryphal tale, what swung the jury in her favour was the moment when she stood up and bared her breasts, asking the jury how a god could be offended by anything so beautiful, especially as it was the gods who had created her beauty in the first place.

This scene gave a few Victorian artists the excuse to paint a woman disrobing herself before an astonished male audience, or in the case of Frenchman Jean-Léon Gérôme, to portray Phryne baring all. Anyway, to finish the tale, the jury became fearful that the gods

Phryne, an excuse for painting a nude lady.

would be angry with them for killing such a wondrous creation, so they acquitted her. So it was smiles all round, especially for her many clients.

Next we move forwards a few hundred years, to one of the most famous events in history – the destruction of Pompeii by the eruption of Vesuvius in 79 AD. Not well publicised, particularly when they were first discovered, are some of the ruder graffiti left behind on brothel walls. Most of this was by customers,

A fresco from the wall of a Pompeii brothel.

and it was mostly extremely crude, but occasionally one of the girls recorded her name for posterity, or one of her clients paid her a compliment. Below are some of the messages found in the brothels and bars of Pompeii (some of what follows is not for prudish eyes):

Arphocras his cum Dracua bene futuit denario.
Harpocras has a good fuck here with Dracua, for a denarius.

Romula cum suo bic fellat et ubique
Romula sucks here and everywhere

Si quis hic sederit, legat hoc ante omnia.
Si qui futuere voluit Atticen, quaerat assibus IV.
If anyone sits here, let him read this first of all: if anyone wants a screw, he should look for Attice; she costs 4 sestertii.

Restituta bellis horibus
Restituta with the pretty face

Mula fututrix.
Mula, the fucktress.

Lucilla ex corpore lucrum faciebat.
Lucilla made money from her body.

Fortunata fillat
Fortunata sucks

Felicia ego hic futui
I fucked Felicia here

Restutus dicit: Pone tunica; rogo, redes pilosa cunnum
Restitutus says: Restituta, take off your tunic, please, and show us your hairy cunt.

Okay, it's not the greatest way for posterity to recall your name, but better than nothing. Most of these unfortunate girls were likely not prostitutes by choice, but either slaves or forced into it through poverty, and at least we know their names, and that they existed. There are hundreds more such graffiti, some much ruder, to be found around the streets and bars of the town.

Four hundred years after Pompeii, the Roman Empire would be no more. It was replaced largely by the Byzantine Empire, certainly in the east of Europe, and it is to here that we turn to find our next prostitute who left us a legacy of sorts.

Theodora was probably the most successful prostitute of all time, certainly in terms of where her initial profession eventually led her. Born around 500 AD, possibly in Syria or Cyprus, her father was a bear trainer and her mother an actress and dancer. When her father died, her mother sent her and her sister to Constantinople to enter the theatre.

While Theodora certainly worked as an actress, she also worked as a prostitute in a brothel from an early age, and her work as an 'actress' most likely involved sexually indecent stage performances. A contemporary of hers, the historian Procopius, wrote that one of her stage acts earned her widespread fame – a lewd portrayal of Leda and the Swan, the tale from Greek mythology in which Leda is raped by Zeus who has taken the form of a swan.

It must be said that Procopius wrote numerous accounts of Theodora, some in praise, some castigating her, and it is uncertain what can be

Theodora – empress, saint, working girl.

taken as a true portrayal. He described her as a prostitute who 'gave her youth to anyone she met, in utter abandonment'. Here is one description of her performing on stage that he has left us:

> Often, even in the theatre, in the sight of all the people, she removed her costume and stood nude in their midst, except for a girdle about the groin: not that she was abashed at revealing that, too, to the audience, but because there was a law against appearing altogether naked on the stage, without at least this much of a fig-leaf. Covered thus with a ribbon, she would sink down to the stage floor and recline on her back. Slaves to whom the duty was entrusted would then scatter grains of barley from above into the calyx of this passion flower, whence geese, trained for the purpose, would next pick the grains one by one with their bills and eat.

When she was sixteen, a Syrian official named Hecebolus took her as his courtesan while serving in Libya. There she remained for four years, during which time she was badly mistreated. She returned to her former profession in the next few years, as she worked her way back to Constantinople. A further excerpt from Procopius gives a flavour of her skills as she climbed the social ladder by climbing into the beds of increasingly wealthy and influential men:

Once, visiting the house of an illustrious gentleman, they say she mounted the projecting corner of her dining couch, pulled up the front of her dress, without a blush, and thus carelessly showed her wantonness ... And though she flung wide the gates to the ambassadors of Cupid, she lamented that nature had not similarly unlocked the straits of her bosom, that she might there have contrived a further welcome to his emissaries.

Around 520 AD, still only twenty or so, she found religion while travelling through Egypt, and converted to a type of Christianity, vowing to abandon her former lifestyle.

Two years later, she was back in Constantinople. Through her former high-ranking contacts, she was introduced to no less than Justinian, heir to the throne of the Byzantine Empire. He took her as his lover, but marriage was forbidden, because she was an 'actress'. When his uncle died in 527, he immediately repealed the law and married Theodora, making her Empress of the most powerful empire on the planet.

And she slotted well into the role, reputedly acting with the dignity, intelligence and grace expected of one in her position, all trace of her former behaviour abandoned. She eventually became one of the most influential women in the thousand-year history of the Byzantine Empire. She acted as advisor to Justinian at key moments of crisis, for which historians have generally remembered her kindly.

Theodora also left a reputation for the advancement of women's rights in some small way. She championed the cause of legislation prohibiting forced prostitution, as well as alterations to the divorce laws, making them more favourable to women. She served as Empress for over twenty years, until cancer, possibly breast cancer, claimed her life in 548, at the age of forty-eight, leaving the Emperor heartbroken.

Theodora was later elevated to sainthood in the Eastern Orthodox Church. The girl did well.

Another prostitute who expanded her horizons beyond satisfying men was the Renaissance era's Veronica Franco, who plied her trade with increasingly powerful men in late-sixteenth-century Venice. Well educated and refined, Franco's mother moulded her into a younger version of herself, a so-called *cortigiana onesta*, or 'honest courtesan', a kind of upper-class hooker, as opposed to the street walker-type prostitute. She mixed with Venice's finer society, and slept with a great number of them. Among those she seduced was Domenico Venier, a poet from a wealthy and influential Venetian family.

This affair ushered Franco into the world of the Venetian literati, allowing her to develop another talent, that of writing poetry. She published a book of poetry called *Terze Rime*, or 'verse letters', many of which had, for their day, what would have been regarded as erotic content.

> *So sweet and delicious do I become,*
> *when I am in bed with he who,*
> *I sense, loves and enjoys me,*
> *that the pleasure I bring excels all delight,*
> *so the knot of love, however tight*
> *it seemed before, is tied tighter still.*

Veronica Franco also bedded King Henry III of France, which was quite a feat, as there exists substantial evidence that Henry was homosexual. In 1565, a book detailing all of Venice's well-known prostitutes was published, which seems to suggest that prostitution was an accepted part of Venetian society. *Catalogo de Tutte le Principal et Più Honorate Cortigiane di Venetia*, or the 'Catalogue of All the Principal and More Honorable Courtesans of Venetia', lists Franco as one of the foremost in the city.

Franco was a firm believer in equality of the sexes, and often referred to such in her writings:

> When we too are armed and trained, we can convince men that we have hands, feet, and a heart like yours; and although we may be delicate and soft, some men who are delicate are also strong; and others, coarse and harsh, are cowards. Women have not yet realised this, for if they should decide to do so, they would be able to fight you until death; and to prove that I speak the truth, amongst so many women, I will be the first to act, setting an example for them to follow.

Not forgetting her own roots, she tried to have the city council open a home for poor women, but without success. The Inquisition put her on trial for witchcraft at one point, a common excuse used to put prostitutes to death, but she successfully defended herself, her connections in high places probably helping, and she was acquitted.

Veronica Franco died around 1591, when in her forties, most likely in poverty, and most likely abandoned by her former benefactors as her age advanced and her beauty declined, as is so often the case with women in the sex business.

One prostitute who bucked that trend was Liverpudlian Catherine 'Skittles' Walters. Born in 1839, when she was four her mother died in childbirth and her alcoholic father sent her to a convent. At some point, presumably when she was considerably older, she ran away and got a job in a bowling alley of sorts. The skittles, as the pins were called, earned her her nickname, which she would keep for the remainder of her days. She also worked in a stable, and acquired a high degree of equestrian skill.

She was petite but very beautiful, and had long, chestnut-coloured hair. Her horsemanship may well have first brought her to the attentions of the upper echelons of English Victorian society, and her sexual favours earned her a position as the mistress of Lord Fitzwilliam, who set her up in London. He eventually tired of her, but left her with an annual income of £300, a very considerable sum in those days. She wasn't one to squander her money, and never indulged in flashy displays of jewellery or gaudy clothing. She knew she was on to a good thing, and continued to behave as an educated and refined society lady.

She took as lovers Spencer Cavendish, the Duke of Devonshire; leading MP Aubrey de Vere Beauclerk; French finance minister Achille Fould; popular poet of the day Wilfrid Scawen Blunt; French Emperor Napoleon III; and Edward, Prince of Wales, who would later be crowned King Edward VII. And those are just the clients that we know about – many more politicians, businessmen and nobles were rumoured to be among her favoured lovers. The pattern she had established with her first lover continued, as her lovers bought her discretion with generous annual payments and luxury accommodation.

There was one area of fashion she did spend some cash on – clothing designed for riding that was skin tight, a fashion that still exists today, but that startled Victorian London. Her frequent gallops along Hyde Park's Rotten Row attracted crowds of onlookers, mostly male, who were enthralled by the sight of Walters's shapely, tightly clad thighs bouncing along on her mount, a thing unheard of at the time. The rumour was that so clinging were her riding tights that she surely wore no underwear. Some men were even moved to record the sight in letters to *The Times*:

The scandalous 'Skitties' Walters.

... Anonyma [Walters] and her ponies appear, and the crowd are satisfied. She threads her way dexterously, with an unconscious air, through the throng, commented upon by the hundreds who admire and the hundreds who envy her. She pulls up her ponies to speak to an acquaintance, and she is instantly surrounded by a multitude ...

Because she didn't squander her money, Walters managed to live in considerable luxury for her entire life, even when her beauty was a long distant memory. She continued to live among London's elite in the fashionable Mayfair area, until she died at the grand old age of eighty in 1820.

PARTY ANIMALS

You can't beat a good old-fashioned orgy. Just ask Roman emperors Tiberius, Caligula or Nero, to mention but a few. Their group horizontal tangos are well documented, so we won't dwell on the sordid details of those infamous nights in the Eternal City. But don't worry, we will explore plenty of the sordid details of other orgies, revels that probably didn't make it into your history books.

Let's continue where we began, in Rome, albeit a millennium after the fall of the great Empire, with an orgy that occurred in probably the last place you'd expect it. On 30 October 1501, Cesare Borgia, son of Pope Alexander VI (born Rodrigo Borgia), decided to throw a big party for his father in the Palazzo Apostolico in the Vatican. This is the building from which present-day popes often deliver prayers or make appearances after they've been elected. Cesare Borgia didn't have anything so sacred in mind. He ordered a lavish banquet and invited all the senior Vatican hierarchy, including cardinals, bishops, priests and influential lay people. He then hired fifty prostitutes to entertain the guests.

A so-called Protonotary Apostolic (an honorary title conferred by the Pope) called Johann Burchard had the task at the time of recording all events in the Vatican, which normally involved recounting diplomatic visits or annual ceremonies. Thankfully for posterity, Johann dutifully recorded the details of what was to become known as 'The Ballet of Chestnuts':

On the evening of the last day of October, 1501, Cesare Borgia arranged a banquet in his chambers in the Vatican with 'fifty honest prostitutes', called courtesans, who danced after dinner with the attendants and others who were present, at first in their garments, then naked. After dinner the candelabra with the burning candles were taken from the tables and placed on the floor, and chestnuts were strewn around, which the naked courtesans picked up, creeping on hands and knees between the chandeliers, while the Pope, Cesare, and his sister Lucretia looked on. Finally, prizes were announced for those who could perform the act most often with the courtesans, such as tunics of silk, shoes, barrets, and other things.

It's a bit of a shame that events such as the above tainted an otherwise successful papacy, in which Alexander VI reformed the Curia, the body responsible for the running of the church, and brought a degree of political stability. He also initiated a new era of artistic and architectural endeavour, employing the likes of Michelangelo and Raphael. He encouraged educational development that resulted in the establishment of several universities. He was ahead of his time in his liberal attitude to Jews, welcoming thousands of that faith into Rome after they'd been exiled from Spain and Portugal.

Some later historians, particular of the Victorian era, believed that the wilder aspects of 'The Ballet of Chestnuts' were exaggerated by the Pope's enemies to show how immoral he'd become. Then again, Victorians were often publicly squeamish when it came to matters of sex, so they probably would say that, wouldn't they?

'The Sin', Heinrich Lossow's imaginative 1880 depiction of 'The Ballet of Chestnuts'.

Predating the orgies of the Borgias by at least a couple of hundred years are Europe's Maypole celebrations. The Maypole usually conjures up images of brightly dressed country folk, hopping and skipping merrily around a towering, colourful pole. Yes, they certainly have toned it down a bit since the late middle ages. You see, the Maypole is actually representative of a giant phallus protruding from the Earth, and the annual festival is an appeal to the gods of fertility, in the hope that the recently planted seeds will produce a bountiful harvest.

So all across Europe as May began, peasants would unite in gay abandon, indulging in drinking, singing, dancing and much copulating. The idea was that you danced around the Maypole, indulged in a few drinks and songs, and then spread out into the surrounding furrows to have sex with whoever was willing, which by all accounts, was pretty much the entire peasantry. In short, everyone really let their lice-ridden hair down.

An English, sixteenth-century Puritan spoilsport, one Phillip Stubbes, had something of a rant about the vile, pagan practices in his book *Anatomy of Abuses in England*, published in 1583. His outrage is evident:

> ... but wherescre shuld the whole towne, parish, village, and cuntrey ... make such gluttonous feasts as they doo? And therefore, they are to no end, except it be to draw a great frequencie of whores, drabbes, thieves, and varlets together, to maintaine whoredome, bawdrie, gluttony, drunkermesse, theft, murther, swearing, and all kind of mischief and abomination! ... to adventure the whole week, spending it in drunkennesse, whoredome, gluttony and other filthie Sodomiticall exercises ... For what clipping, what culling, what kissing and bussing, what smouching and slabbering one of another, what filthie groping and uncleane handling is not practifed every where in these dauncings ... fornication and adulterie in all sortes shamefully practized ...

What Stubbes believed to be a fairly recent phenomenon had been going on thousands of years. The ancient Mesopotamians, Romans and Greeks all had similar fertility festivals, and the ancient Celts celebrated the festival of Beltane. The Irish Gaelic word for May is actually Bealtine, which derives directly from this festival, celebrating the start of spring. On the appointed day, young maidens would roll naked in the grass to gain the benefit of the early morning dew, which they believed would prolong their beauty and sexual attractiveness.

Beltane heralded the approach of summer, and the Celts believed that the world was alive with energy and passion. To prove it, adults took to the fields and made love among the newly planted seeds, planting a few million seeds of their own. Any child that resulted from such a coupling was thought to be blessed by the gods, a gift rather than an unwanted consequence.

Fifteen hundred years before the Celts, we come to the recently identified Hatshepsut Festival of Drunkenness in Egypt. Hatshepsut has been described as one of the first great women of history, and one of only a handful of female pharaohs who ruled alone. Among her accomplishments was the opening up of previously closed trade routes – to Sinai to the east, to Somalia, Eritrea and Sudan to the south and to Lebanon to the north. She also commissioned hundreds of building projects throughout Egypt, many of which tourists still snap with their cameras today, such as her stunning mortuary temple at Deir el-Bahari.

But we're here to talk about drinking and sex, not architecture. In the last decade or so, archaeologists have uncovered strong evidence that during Hatshepsut's reign, the people held a festival to celebrate their salvation from the goddess Sekhmet. The myth goes like this: the bloodthirsty Sekhmet almost destroyed all humans, but the sun god Re tricked her into drinking ochre-coloured beer, thinking it was blood. Sekhmet became so inebriated, she passed out and was transformed into the goddess Hathor, who personified the principles of feminine love, pleasure and motherhood – and humanity was saved.

The festival of drunkenness therefore involved a lot of beer drinking and sex. In fact, the whole idea was to abandon oneself totally to gluttony and lust. Archaeologists are unsure whether sex was actually part of the festival, or just a result of alcoholic abandonment, but they know a great deal of it took place, thanks to inscriptions left behind, which include many references to 'travelling through the marshes', a cute ancient euphemism for sex. There is also graffiti depicting various sexual positions.

This indulgence actually served a purpose, which was to get so drunk you could see and experience the deities. The morning after you'd eventually collapsed unconscious, a drummer would walk around, pounding out a deafening beat and waking the revellers to the joy of the world, just as Hathor had in the myth. You can just imagine the horrible moans and groans, as the masses awoke with pounding heads under a beating sun.

While that festival was an annual event, the Etruscans, who predated the Romans by a few hundred years, liked to party all year round. Greek historian Theopompus was shocked by some of their practices, which seemed to be fairly universal in the Etruscan world:

> Among the Etruscans, who were extraordinarily pleasure-loving, the slave-girls wait on the men naked ... and it is normal for the Etruscans to share their women in common. The women take great care of their bodies and exercise bare, exposing their bodies even before men ... for it is not shameful for them to appear almost naked. The women dine [meaning 'frolic' or 'fornicate' in this context] not only with their husbands but with any man who happens to be present, and they toast any one they want to. The Etruscans raise all the children who are born not knowing who is the father of each one. It is no shame for them to be seen having sexual experiences, for this too is normal – it is the local custom. When they come together in parties with their relations and when they stop drinking and are ready to go to bed, the slaves bring in to them – with the lights left on! – either prostitutes or very beautiful boys or even their wives.

Clearly from this account, homosexuality was flaunted in Etruscan society. The Tomb of the Bighe in Tarquinia originally depicted several scenes of a chariot race, one featuring two men openly having sex. Another tomb in Tarquinia shows a pair of threesomes, which also depict whipping as a sexual practice. One image shows a woman embracing a man while a second man penetrates her from behind. The other shows a woman bent over, fellating one man while being penetrated from behind by another, who is also hitting her on the backside with a whip.

A scene depicted in a tomb in Tarquinia.

From the outrageous, orgiastic carry-on of those savage Etruscans, let us leap forward and explore the outrageous, orgiastic carry-on of some civilised eighteenth-century Englishmen.

Sir Francis Dashwood was Chancellor of the Exchequer in 1762–63, and a sexual libertine. His wealthy background allowed him to indulge his passion for worshipping ancient Roman and Greek deities, along with some of their wilder rituals, albeit secretly. Around 1740, Dashwood visited the excavations at Herculaneum in Rome, an experience that may have fuelled his fascination with ancient gods. The garden of his home at West Wycombe contained many statues and shrines to different deities, including Priapus, the Greek fertility god, depicted with an enormous phallus; Dionysus, Greco-Roman god of wine and ritual abandonment; and Venus, the Roman goddess who encompassed beauty, love and sex. Actually the Temple of Venus in Dashwood's estate was on a hill representative of the mons veneris (pubic mound), and the grotto below it – called Venus's Parlour – was accessed through a distinctly suggestive entrance.

In the 1740s, Dashwood founded what would later become widely known as the Hellfire Club, whose motto was 'Fais ce que voudras', meaning 'do what thou wilt'. It originally had just twelve members, all prominent nobles and politicians like himself. In 1751, he leased Medmenham Abbey in Buckinghamshire, north of London, and his club took up residence there, becoming known afterwards as the 'Monks of Medmenham'. There were some small caves beneath the abbey, and Dashwood had these expanded significantly into a series of 'rooms', including one called the River Styx – the mythological boundary between the earth and the underworld – and beyond it an inner chamber. Club members addressed each other as 'brother', and the leader as 'abbot'.

Unfortunately, little is officially recorded of what went on in the caves. Stories abounded of bacchanalian orgies, pagan sacrifices and demon worship, but if these happened, they were probably in a mocking manner – a bit like sexual role-playing. A lot of drinking and whoring almost certainly did take place, and prostitutes, who were known to members as 'nuns', regularly entertained the members. Respected contemporary historian Robert Walpole wrote:

> ... practice was rigorously pagan: Bacchus and Venus were the deities to whom they almost publicly sacrificed; and the nymphs and the hogsheads [large casks of ale] that were laid in against the festivals of this new church, sufficiently informed the neighborhood of the complexion of those hermits.

The 'Temple of Venus' in Sir Francis Dashwood's estate.

SCARLET WOMEN

....

It is okay for powerful men to lust after women – in fact, it is almost expected, if you are to believe the antics of political leaders and monarchs down the centuries. But as soon as a woman does it – scandal! Women just don't do that sort of thing. But, of course, there are exceptions, women who have breached the taboo and exhibited a lust for sex and power to rival any man. While male Lotharios are often regarded with admiration, or at worst cause tittering, history has branded their female equivalents as harlots, Jezebels and scarlet women. So let's remember a few of these fine, scandalous ladies.

Catherine the Great was undoubtedly one of Russia's finest leaders, her thirty-four-year reign responsible for the modernisation of the country, the expansion of its territories, advances in education, the arts and literature, and the building of much of the country's finest classical architecture. Yet many people hear her name and immediately think 'sex nymph'.

Catherine was a real go-getter. German by birth, her family were relatively minor nobles, yet her mother used her connections to wangle an introduction to the Russian Grand Duke Peter, heir to the emperor's throne. At the age of sixteen, she was happy to marry Peter to escape her mother, who reputedly was a cold, manipulative woman, happy to use her daughter merely as a means to advance her social status.

Catherine soon found that she couldn't stand her husband, and they lived in separate parts of the castle. She also despised her husband's politics. As soon as he was crowned Emperor, she was plotting his downfall. Just six months into his reign, she engineered a coup d'etat, in which he was killed, although not on her orders.

That was 1762, when Catherine was in her thirties. But her affairs had started long before that. The first nine years of the marriage had failed to produce any heirs. In 1754, when she announced her pregnancy, the child was widely believed to belong to Sergei Saltykov, a

Russian officer and noble. He would be the first in a long line of lovers for the voracious Catherine that also included her coup d'etat co-conspirator Grigory Orlov, a multitude of other Russian aristocrats, a Polish king, a sixteen-year-old boy and the famous General Grigory Potemkin. Her final lover, when she was sixty, was the twenty-two-year-old Prince Platon Zubov. Catherine reputedly had twenty-two lovers – at least, they're the ones we know about.

What makes her dalliances even more intriguing is the involvement of two of her leading ladies, Countess Praskovya Bruce and Countess Anna Protasova. Countess Bruce had been friends with Catherine from an early age, and became her closest confidante when she was Czarina. Catherine shared all her secrets with Bruce, including her bedroom antics. The Czarina wrote that she was 'the person to whom I can say everything, without fear of the consequences.'

Eventually, Bruce was given the (unofficial) position of 'l'éprouveuse' or tester – incredibly, she would physically vet all of Catherine's lovers in advance, firstly having them checked by a doctor for venereal disease, then having sex with them to ensure that they were sufficiently skilled in bed to satisfy Catherine.

It is unknown how many of Catherine's lovers were 'vetted' by Bruce. There was an unwritten rule that once Catherine had taken a man to her bed, Bruce was to take a back seat and have no more involvement with the man. Ultimately this proved her undoing, as Bruce, at the age of fifty, continued to have a sexual relationship with Ivan Rimsky-Korsakov (ancestor of the famous composer), who was twenty-four at the time. Catherine, also fifty, reputedly caught the pair naked and in the act, and immediately banished her long-time friend to Moscow.

She filled the vacant spot in her staff with a new maid of honour – Anna Protasova, a woman of thirty-four. She and Catherine formed a close bond, almost as strong as that with Bruce, and Protasova was eventually given the job of 'l'éprouveuse', a role she fulfilled until

Catherine finally quit taking lovers in her sixties. But she remained close to the Czarina until her death in 1796, at the age of sixty-seven.

The tale is told of a secret 'erotic cabinet' of Catherine's, a room filled with all manner of indecently designed furniture – chairs and tables with penis legs, snuff boxes with pornographic images on the inner panels, chairs whose arms were formed by spread-eagled naked women, and all manner of other items decorated with pornographic imagery. Pre-Second World War Russian witnesses confirmed the room's existence, and two Wehrmacht officers also reputedly saw the room in 1941, but the furniture has long since vanished. Maybe it will turn up yet and give us all a titter.

French biographer Charles Masson, a first-hand witness to goings-on in St Petersburg, wrote of Catherine that 'she had two passions, which never left her but with her last breath: the love of man, which degenerated into licentiousness, and the love of glory, which sunk into vanity'.

Russia never featured in the travels of English aristocrat Jane Digby, but pretty much every other country in Europe did, and even Syria was on the itinerary of her love quest. Born into a wealthy family of nobles in 1807 in Dorset, Jane was determined to rail against the attitudes of the age, which denied women many rights. Her father was a captain in the British Navy, and had actually commanded a vessel under Nelson at the Battle of Trafalgar. Thanks to various postings around Europe, the teenage Jane got her first experiences of international travel.

The beautiful young woman was presented to society when she was sixteen, and it didn't take long before she was being courted by Edward Law, 2nd Baron Ellenborough, a man seventeen years her senior. They were married the following year, in haste it must be assumed, as almost immediately the immature Jane realised what a mistake she'd made.

Not long into the marriage, Law began to neglect her badly, and Digby responded by amusing herself, attending balls and parties alone, and attracting the attention of many male admirers. The first lover she took was Colonel George Anson, her first cousin and something of a Don Juan character. Before long she found herself pregnant, and the paternity of the child, Arthur, is unknown, as she and her husband were still sleeping together at the time. The child would not survive infancy.

The beautiful Jane Digby.

Anson soon grew tired of her and dumped her, leaving her distraught – but not for long. Within months, she was having another fling, with an Austrian diplomat called Prince Felix Schwarzenberg. They managed to keep their affair quiet initially, but soon their indiscretions became just that, indiscreet, and eventually her husband got wind of it all. When he learned that she was again pregnant, he immediately began divorce proceedings, and the juicy details were enthusiastically recorded on the front page of *The Times*:

> Q. (To husband) What did you hear then?
> A. I could hear them kissing, and a noise that convinced me that the act of cohabitation was taking place.

Digby fled to Switzerland. The child, Mathilde, was born in Basel, and would ultimately be raised by Schwarzenberg's sister. The couple had a second child, Felix, who died soon after birth. At this point, Schwarzenberg deserted her. By now divorced and alienated from family and society, the twenty-three-year-old Digby travelled to Munich, where her aristocratic connections brought her to the attention of King Ludwig I of Bavaria. and another affair was set in motion.

While at court, a German Baron called Carl Venningen began to pursue her. He was next on her list of conquests after the King, and once again she ended up pregnant. She reluctantly agreed to marry Venningen to give herself and her child respectability, although apparently he'd been no more than a fling for her.

Venningen moved in Munich's elite circles, and there she met the famed French novelist Honore de Balzac, who would base an erotic character called Lady Arabella Dudley on Digby. The pair may also have indulged in a brief affair.

Next up was a fling with a Greek count named Spiridon Theotoky, who she met at a masked Oktoberfest ball. Her husband found out about the affair and challenged Theotoky to a duel, in which the Greek was wounded. Venningen then divorced Digby, and took responsibility for the two children she'd borne him.

Jane married Theotoky and moved to Athens, where they had a son, Leonidas. Not long into their marriage, Theotky began to neglect her, spending his evenings dining and drinking to excess with friends. When she discovered that he also had other lovers, she managed to become the mistress of her second King – Otto of Greece. Leonidas was tragically killed at the age of six when he fell from a balcony, and between the trauma of this and her husband's affairs, the relationship broke down.

Digby began an affair with a Thessalian general called Christodoulos Hatzipetros, which led briefly to a life of adventure, Digby experiencing the outdoor life, living in tents, riding horses and hunting. But the discovery of his unfaithfulness with his maid brought that episode to an end.

She was now forty-six, but her wanderings and love quest were not over yet. She travelled to Syria, where she met and began an affair with Sheik Abdul Medjuel el Mezrab, who was only twenty-six, but who was besotted by the still attractive and exciting Englishwoman. Although she never converted to Islam, they were married in a Muslim ceremony and she became Jane Elizabeth Digby el Mezrab. She adopted Arab dress and learned Arabic, and spent six months of each year living the life of a nomad, the other six in the sheik's Damascus villa. Finally her sexual wanderings were at an end, and she and the sheik remained happily married for twenty-eight years. After four marriages and innumerable affairs, the outrageous Jane Digby died in August 1881, aged seventy-four.

Jane Digby in the middle east.

Depending on which historian you choose to believe, Faustina the Younger was either a model of all that was finest in ancient Roman womanhood, or a shameless, sex-crazed, murderous hussy. If you haven't heard of Faustina, you've more than likely heard of her husband, Marcus Aurelius, the philosopher emperor, or the guy played by Richard Harris in 'Gladiator'. Marcus was reputedly devoted to his wife, despite being aware of her numerous sexual dalliances, though according to some historians, these were somewhat exaggerated, or entirely fictitious.

Those who claim Faustina was a virtuous woman and mother point to the fact that she had thirteen children (and, given infant mortality rates at the time, probably multiple other unsuccessful pregnancies), whose rearing wouldn't have left much time for fooling around. But that doesn't really hold any water, as wealthy Roman matrons left the care of their kids to wet nurses and slave nannies. Rumours persisted that at least some of the children weren't fathered by the Emperor, including the future Emperor Commodus, who may have been the offspring of a gladiator, but we'll get to that.

Marcus Aurelius's devotion to her goes against the notion of her as a sex-mad seductress – when she died he had a statue of her

The Romans sure knew how to party – 'Bacchanalia' by Auguste Levêque (c.1890).

sculpted and placed in the hallowed Temple of Venus in Rome. A separate temple was also built in her honour, and he even opened special schools to cater for orphaned girls, called Puellae Faustinianae. Hardly the reward a frequently cheating wife might expect.

But the ancient Roman historians largely vilified the Empress. According to the *Historia Augusta*, written in the fourth century, Faustina was a wicked poisoner, plotter and sex-mad playgirl. According to that and other historical records, when visiting the seaside town of Caieta to the south of Rome, Faustina liked to wander among the sailors and gladiators around town, choose one she fancied and take him home to her bed. She was accused of having affairs with mime actors and senators, which might explain how she was so frequently pregnant.

She reputedly got rid of enemies by means of poison and execution, and was supposedly the instigator of a revolt in the east (modern-day Turkey) against her husband by one of the Emperor's top generals, Avidius Cassius. Believing her husband to be near death, she apparently urged Cassius to seize the empire and proclaim himself Emperor so that she could be sure of her young son Commodus's future succession.

The revolt failed, Cassius was murdered and she was forgiven. She died that same year (175 AD) of natural causes at the age of about forty-five, in the ancient town of Halala. Marcus Aurelius had the place renamed Faustinopolis – more evidence that at least some of her bad girl reputation was scurrilous fabrication.

On the subject of scurrilous historical gossip, let's have the juiciest, goriest tale concerning Faustina. According to ancient historical records, at one point the Empress believed that Marcus Aurelius was on the point of death. Torn by guilt, she confessed to him that she had recently seen a bunch of gladiators pass by in the street, and 'was inflamed for love of one of them', who she immediately commanded to her chamber. Undoubtedly the gladiator was only too happy to comply, although he would pay dearly for his pleasure.

Marcus Aurelius didn't die, and in fact recovered completely. He immediately went to the Chaldeans, or soothsayers, who advised that the only way to purify his wife of her transgression was to have the gladiator executed and then have Faustina bathe in his blood, after which they should copulate. He duly followed their advice, and the unfortunate gladiator ended up hanging over Faustina's bath, being bled dry. After her 'bath', she went immediately to her husband's bed. It seemed the treatment worked miracles, as a few weeks later, she discovered she was pregnant. The fact that the child would turn out to be the cruel and unstable Commodus, the looper who liked to fight gladiatorial battles, led ancient gossips to speculate that he could not be the son of the great Marcus Aurelius, but surely must be the offspring of the lowly, executed gladiator. But we'll simply never know.

A couple of centuries before Faustina, the daughter of the first emperor Augustus, Julia the Elder, enjoyed an equally scandalous reputation, and we can say with somewhat more certainty that hers was no mere product of gossip and exaggeration.

A scandalous Roman matriarch, Julia the Elder.

Julia had been married off a few times to suitors who served her father's political purposes. Her first two husbands died of natural causes, and her third, the future Emperor Tiberius, turned out to be very unsatisfactory – they both quickly found that they hated each other.

But Julia was a woman who liked her sex, and with her husband seemingly proving so disappointing in that regard, she went and found it elsewhere. According to the dramatist and philosopher Seneca, a contemporary of hers, she had 'adulterers by the herd', and she:

... covered the imperial home with scandal: lovers admitted in droves, nightly orgies throughout the city, daily meetings beside the statue of Marsyas, where, worse than an adulteress, a mere prostitute, she claimed her right to every shamelessness in the arms of the first passer-by.

Ironically, Julia's father, Augustus, had around this time provided the Roman people with a treatise on morality and family values, encouraging marital fidelity and outlawing adultery. He had actually made his original delivery from the Rostra, the common speaking platform in the Forum, the very platform on which Julia publicly and frequently prostituted herself, indulging in 'night time orgies and drinking parties', according to historian Dio Cassius.

When Tiberius took himself off to Rhodes to indulge in his own hedonistic pursuits, Julia essentially had the run of the place, and is said to have taken lovers by the dozen. She wore skimpy, body-hugging silk dresses in public and wandered around accompanied by a retinue of men, much to the shock of Rome's conservative upper-class ladies.

Julia was also recorded by Pliny the Elder as having sex 'on the statue of Marsyas', a Greek mythological satyr in the form of a muscular, nude male. Pliny says the statue 'groaned under the weight of her lewdness'.

Eventually, his daughter's excesses became too great an embarrassment for Augustus, especially as among her lovers were such prominent citizens as nobleman Sempronius Gracchus and the son of Mark Anthony, Iullus Antonius. Although he loved his daughter, he had her exiled to a tiny island with no men, where she remained for five years. He also had many of her lovers either exiled or forced to commit suicide.

She was eventually allowed to return to the mainland, but never reconciled with her father. When her now ex-husband, Tiberius, came to power, she died of malnutrition, possibly having been starved to death by his order.

Although Marie of Romania may not have been able to match Julia of Rome in terms of numbers of lovers, it wasn't for the want of trying. Despite her title, she was actually born in 1875 of a union between the British and Russian royal families, and was officially known as Princess Marie of Edinburgh. She would become one of Romania's most beloved women, and well able to match male royals in the illicit-affair stakes.

Her parents initially tried to marry her off as a teenager to Prince George of Wales, later to become King George V. When that didn't work out, a very different match was found for her in Crown Prince Ferdinand of Romania. Ten years her senior, he was something of a softie and a limp fish if accounts are to be believed. It took roughly a week for the newly married couple to realise that they were totally unsuited.

Although just seventeen when she wed, Marie would mature into a tough, assertive beauty. She was unkindly nicknamed the 'man-queen', because of her strength of character and her frequent insistence on taking leading roles in affairs of state, normally a preserve of men.

Ferdinand, on the other hand, was shy and weak-willed, and it wasn't long before Marie was ruling the roost.

During the First World War, Marie truly won the adoration of the people. First, she persuaded her husband, now King Ferdinand, to enter the war in opposition to Germany. Then she worked as a Red Cross nurse, wearing the uniform and personally helping to transport wounded soldiers to hospital. She also devised a plan for her country's defence, and after the war was largely responsible for negotiating a treaty that expanded Romania's territories considerably.

But Marie is remembered as much for her racy personal life as her political and humanitarian achievements. Her marriage to Ferdinand being such a damp squib, the young princess soon began to find diversion elsewhere. By the time she was nineteen, she'd already given birth to two children by her husband, although historians would later question the lineage of many of her offspring.

A couple of years after the birth of her second child, she met Lieutenant Zizi Cantacuzene, probably through their shared passion for horse-riding. They were soon sharing another passion as before long

Marie was pregnant, and it was common knowledge that Ferdinand hadn't been around to do the deed. She left court to have the child, which was either stillborn or sent off to an orphanage upon birth. That episode didn't temper her behaviour. Her affair continued, and her second daughter, born when she was twenty-four, was widely believed to be her paramour's.

After that fling ended, Marie is said to have taken a string of lovers to the royal bed, including millionaire businessman William Waldorf Astor;

The hugely impressive Marie of Romania.

Grand Duke Boris Vladimirovich of Russia, grandson of the Tsar; Italian architect Fabrice; and Canadian adventurer and businessman 'Klondike' Joe Boyle. Gossip at the time had her sleeping with visiting Russian dukes, German envoys, Polish counts and even common hussars. Her husband, Ferdinand, is believed to have known about her many affairs, but wisely turned a blind eye – he needed her political nous and leadership skills.

Marie's best-known affair was with Romania's future Prime Minister, the handsome and dashing Barbu Stirbey, who would be her close confidant and political adviser in the war years. In fact, they were close in many respects – Marie's last two children bore a striking resemblance to him, a cause of much tittering among the masses.

Ferdinand died in 1927, and Marie lived for a further eleven years. She died of natural causes in 1938 at the age of sixty-two, with several of her children at her bedside. Her country would soon be thrown into the horror of another world war, after which the monarchy would be swept away by the Soviet-supported Communist Party of Romania. But those who lived during her reign and who witnessed how much she achieved for her country still fondly remembered her colourful time in the spotlight.

RANDOM SEX

Fitting in no particular category, there follows a collection of naughty bits and bobs from the fascinating history of all things sexual, from pubic wigs to 400-year-old sex manuals to prehistoric sex toys.

In the pre-Islamic Arabic world, a common practice to improve the bloodline of one's family was that of wife-lending. It worked like this: some ordinary, everyday guy, perhaps a carpenter or a camel-herder, would present his wife to someone considered 'a man of distinction' – perhaps a wealthy merchant or a local politician. Having inspected the woman, and determined that she was pretty enough to have sex with, this big shot would agree to take her into his home and do his best to get her pregnant. The trooper.

After a while the wife would be returned to her husband, and he had to agree to abstain from having sex with her for a time. If she was discovered subsequently to be pregnant, it could then be said with certainty that the 'man of distinction' had impregnated her. However, tradition recognised the offspring as the natural child of the husband and not the biological father.

The abstaining husband might not have been so sexually bored had he lived about 1,500 later, when he could have aroused himself by watching the world's first ever pornographic movie, the 1896 *Le Coucher de la Mariée*, or 'The Bride's Bedtime'. It starred, and I'm not making this up, Louise Willy.

It didn't take porn-makers long to capitalise on the wonders of moving pictures, as the film was released just months after the world's first public screening of a projected motion picture. This was probably the movie entitled *Workers Leaving the Lumière Factory in Lyon*, a title which sort of gives the plot away. Actually, it's a fascinating short documentary, showing hundreds of men and women pouring through factory gates after a hard day's work.

The plot of *Le Coucher de la Mariée* involves a man, presumably the groom, encouraging his shy new wife to undress before bedtime. This she does only when he agrees to go behind a screen, from where he takes naughty little peeks. The good news is that you can watch Louise shedding her kit on YouTube. The bad news is that the last five minutes of the seven-minute movie had been left to degrade in the French Film Archives, so we only get to see Louise strip down to one of her innumerable undergarments.

A steamy moment from *Le Coucher de la Mariée*.

If pornography wouldn't satiate your appetite and you required the real thing (this assumes you were male), and if you happened to live in eighteenth-century London, you'd most likely turn to *Harris's List of Covent Garden Ladies*. This was a hefty enough annual publication, more than 150 pages, detailing the services of almost 200 prostitutes in and around central London, from 1757 to almost the end of the century. It contained vital gems of information such as this description of the charms of Miss Dowd of No. 6, Hind-court, Fleet Street:

> ... she is, indeed, turned of forty, rather fat and short, yet she looks well, dresses neat ... and if you are not soon disposed for the attack, she will shew you such a set of pictures, that very seldom fails to alarm the sleeping member. Then may you behold the lovely fount of delight, reared on two pillars of monumental alabaster; the symmetry of its parts, its borders, enriched with wavering tendrils, its ruby portals, and the tufted grove, that crowns the summit of the mount, all join to invite the guest to enter ... That experience this lady has and is perfectly skilled in every delightful manoeuvre, knowing how to keep time, when to advance and retreat, to face to the right or left, and when to shower down a whole volley of love.

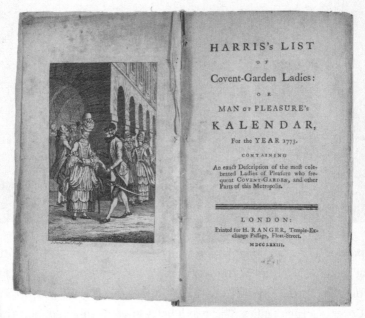

HARRIS's LIST
OF
Covent-Garden Ladies:
OR
MAN OF PLEASURE's
KALENDAR,
For the YEAR 1773.

CONTAINING

An exact Description of the most celebrated Ladies of Pleasure who frequent COVENT-GARDEN, and other
Parts of this Metropolis.

LONDON:
Printed for H. RANGER, Temple-Ex-
change Passage, Fleet-Street.
MDCCLXXIII.

The credited author, Covent Garden pimp Jack Harris, didn't actually do any of the writing, but probably contributed to the copious amounts of detail contained within. The true author was probably an Irishman called Samuel Derrick, a hack writer and failed actor who enjoyed a few literary connections in Samuel Johnson and James Boswell. Derrick found some financial success through *Harris's List*, as estimates of the book's sales have been put at a quarter of a million across its lifetime.

Now, I said that you'd turn to this book if you wanted the real thing, but in reality many of the sales were surely to enjoy the book's descriptions as pure pornography. As he sat alone by his fireplace, what red-blooded eighteenth-century gentleman wouldn't be stirred by the depiction of Miss Rufus, of No 1, Poland Street:

> *Here youth and beauty are combined, and unadorned by education or art; what she feels in the amorous encounter cannot be feigned. Her natural simplicity is yet so unstained, and her*

knowledge of the world so very little, that it is almost impossible
for her to dissemble; her hair, eye-brows and eyes, are of the
deepest black; her complexion of the roses red, and her neck and
breasts of the purest white; her limbs are nobly formed, every
joint possessing the most enchanting flexibility, which she man-
ages with uncommon dexterity, and her Venus Mount is so nobly
fortified, that she has no occasion to dread the fiercest attack,
nor does she.

What is perhaps surprising is the inclusion in some editions of information pertaining to lesbian services on offer for London ladies. While
male homosexuality was illegal at the time, and punishable by severe
penalties, lesbianism was not on the statute books. Two sisters, Anne
and Elanor Redshawe of Tavistock Street, ran what they described as
an 'extremely secretive discreet House of Intrigue', catering for 'Ladies
in the Highest Keeping', which was frequented by well-off women in
disguise. Another girl, Miss Wilson of Cavendish Square, is also evidently a ladies' lady, her description running as follows:

Her hands and arms, her limbs indeed, in general are more
calculated for the milk-carrier than the soft delights of love;
however, if she finds herself but in small estimation with our sex,
she repays them the compliment, and frequently declares that 'a
female bed-fellow can give more real joys than ever she experi-
enced with the male part of the sex.' Many of the pranks she has
played with her own sex in bed, where she is as lascivious as a
goat, have come to our knowledge.

Let's finish with one more of the hundreds of wicked descriptions of
the delights on offer to eighteenth-century gentlemen:

Miss Betsy Rawlins, No. 12, Little Tichfield Street ... she can com-
mand a Paradise of bliss; a fair eye, and beautiful complexion,
together with firm panting breasts, busy hand, which loves to be

busily employed in inviting the tumid guest to her dear land of delight; the two grand supporters of which always unfold at the approach of this never unwelcome visitor, whose knocking and entrance is generally performed at the same time.

One of the items working girls like Betsy probably employed while entertaining their gentlemen was a merkin, or pubic wig. These have been around since at least the fifteenth century, according to the *Oxford Companion to the Body*, but have probably existed much longer. Their principal use was for reasons of hygiene, pubic lice being quite a problem for prostitutes in olden times. The idea was to keep the pubic area shaved and thus lice-free, and replace the hair with a little wig, as girls were expected to be hairy in that anatomical locality back then.

Another more repugnant reason to wear a merkin was to conceal sores that were the symptoms of venereal diseases such as syphilis and gonorrhea, the two most common sexually transmitted diseases of the time.

There is no real reference surviving as to how the merkin was attached, but it's likely some form of animal glue was used, made by boiling animal connective tissue. Ugh.

On a more cheerful note, there is a comical reference to a merkin in Alexander Smith's 1714 *A Complete History of the Lives and Robberies of the Most Notorious Highwaymen*':

> ... this put a strange Whim in his Head; which was to get the hairy circle of a prostitute's Merkin ... this he dry'd well, and comb'd out, and then return'd to the Cardinal, telling him he had brought St. Peter's Beard.

Whether the Cardinal fell for the ruse or not is unknown.

A working girl earning her crust.

Around the same time as the aforementioned Betsy Rawlins was doing her thing with London's gentlemen, a chap in Geneva was making a name for himself as a writer, composer and philosopher. He was Jean-Jacques Rousseau, regarded as one of the greatest philosophers of the eighteenth century. His work influenced the Enlightenment, the French Revolution, the US Constitution and the development of modern political thinking. Not a bad CV, you'd have to admit.

What a shame that Jean-Jacques's copybook was blotted by his rather odd sexual behaviour, which involved exposing his bare backside to groups of ladies passing in the street. He provided an explanation of sorts in his autobiography, confessing that as an eight-year-old, his adoptive mother, a Mademoiselle Lambercier, had put him over her knee and spanked him, causing him to become aroused:

She had often threatened it [a spanking], and this threat appeared to me extremely dreadful; but I found the reality much less terrible than the idea, and what is still more unaccountable, this punishment increased my affection for the person who had inflicted it ... and [I sought] by fresh offences, a return of the same chastisement, for a degree of sensuality had mingled with the smart and shame, which left more desire than fear of a repetition ... Who would believe this childish discipline, received at eight years old, from the hands of a woman of thirty, should influence my propensities, my desires, my passions, for the rest of my life, and that in quite a contrary sense from what might naturally have been expected?

The experience never left Rousseau, and as an adult he discovered that he required his bottom to be spanked before he could become aroused. Thus the mooning at genteel, shocked ladies. 'What they saw was not the obscene thing, I never even thought of that, it was the ridiculous thing,' he wrote, meaning that he never flashed his genitals at them, just his backside.

What he craved was for one of the ladies to smack him on the bottom, he explained, just as Mademoiselle Lambercier had done. His adult relationships involved mother-like figures, who would dominate and spank him. The first of these, Francoise de Warens, was a decade older than he. He called her 'Mamam', and to her he was 'mon petit' or 'my little one'. He wasn't shy about telling the world about his fetish:

To fall at the feet of an imperious mistress, obey her mandates, or implore pardon, were for me the most exquisite enjoyments, and the more my blood was inflamed by the efforts of a lively imagination the more I acquired the appearance of a whining lover.

While Rousseau's obscene public expression of his sexual desire was a bit much, many will regard his spanking fetish as pretty mild stuff. At the other end of the fetish spectrum is the case of Thomas Granger, who holds the distinction of being the first known juvenile to be executed in the United States. His crime was bestiality, or having sex with animals. And it was very much in the plural, and also across a whole range of species, if you are to believe the only written record of the episode.

In 1642, Granger was about sixteen or seventeen, a servant to a wealthy butler called Elder Love Brewster in the recently formed Plymouth Colony in Massachusetts. Apparently, one of the colonists chanced upon Granger having sex with a mare. Given the puritanical colonists' views on simple extra-marital sex, bestiality must have caused the poor chap or maiden pass out. Granger was quickly arrested, and charged with an offence against God and nature.

According to the Bible, to which the colonists adhered rigidly: 'If a man shall lie with a beast, he shall surely be put to death: and ye shall slay the beast.' Granger was interrogated 'in private' by magistrates, so who knows how they wrung the disturbed young man's further confessions from him. After initial denial of the offence, it seems he broke down and confessed his crimes in full. As the written record tells it:

> He was this year detected of buggery, and indicted for the same, with a mare, a cowe, two goats, five sheep, two calves, and a turkey.

Yes, you read that correctly. A *turkey*. He furthermore confessed, both in private and then in open court, that his indiscretions with said animals had been on multiple occasions. He was sentenced to 'death by hanging until dead.'

According to biblical law, the defiled animals had to be put to death along with the defiler. So a large pit was dug near the place of execution. The entire flock of Brewster's sheep was paraded before the condemned man, and he was required to differentiate the guilty sheep from the innocent ones:

...he ancient Madhya Pradeshis.

...he sculptures on the temples' walls ...ously proportioned male and female ...o numerous that you could spend days ...ty ones, and many people do. Although ...idered fairly conservative in matters of se... ...ly weren't shy about such things.

...ent Hindus, the French have long had quit... ...beral ...ers sexual, certainly when compared to ... ...of their ...neighbours, who traditionally believed in ... Calvinist/ ...n-style restraint or Catholic-style dread ... ...ternal hellfire ...ns of the flesh.

That's not to say that the French weren't m... Catholic, just that ...ays seemed to have a dispensation ... ...n it came to matters ...inly they acted like they di... Nowhere was this more ...ase of royal mistres...

And whereas some of the sheep could not so well be knowne by
his description of them, others with them were brought b
him, and he declared which were they, and which were
A very sade spectakle it was; for first the man and th
cowe, and the rest of the lesser catle, were kild before h
according to the law, and then he him selfe was execu
catle were all cast into a great and large pitte that wa
purposs for them, and no use made of any part of th

Much happier, certainly for one guy, is the tale of
saint, Drukpa Kunley (1455–1529), who is the patro
country would love to have, or certainly the one eve
his country to have. Let me explain. He was know
Divine Madman', 'The Saint of 5,000 Women' and
Dragon Lineage', all of which begin to make ser
about the man.

Drukpa Kunley was a Buddhist monk. As
religion seeks the attainment of the sublime
quenching of the three fires of passion, av
this particular Buddhist monk was fairly u
anti-institutional attitudes, and his ques
Buddhism and the path to Enlightenme
'avadhūta' – a yogi known for using u
who often acts contrary to standard s

Kunley was a mendicant, wandering fro
ing that spiritual happiness is only achieved by letting g
conventions, particularly when it comes to women and alcohol.
simple terms, drink as much as you like and indulge in lots of sex.

To this end, he convinced thousands of women that the path to
enlightenment ran straight through whatever bed he happened to be
sleeping in, and to help them on the way he used the 'Thunderbolt of
Flaming Wisdom', aka his erect penis. Really, that's what it's known as.

A demonstration of the athleticism of

Although only ten percent of
involve sex, nudity and gener
figures, the sculptures are s
just examining the naug
India is nowadays con
their ancestors clea

Like those an
view of mat
European
Luther
for

musical instr
in the 'sixty-nine' pos   n, having
orgies, more oral sex, s   with animals, and g
every conceivable positio

The kind of thing you're likely to see in Bhutan – giant phalluses adorning the walls.

This also earned Drukpa Kunley the reputation of 'fertility saint', as countless women travelled from near and far to seek his blessing in the form of sex.

His practices led directly to the tradition of phallus paintings in Bhutan – you'll find phalluses everywhere in the country – on restaurant walls, on people's homes, on store signs – and in souvenir shops you can buy yourself a large wooden phallus the way you might buy a model of the Eiffel Tower in Paris. Drukpa Kunley died an enlightened and no doubt very happy man at the grand old age for the time of seventy-four.

Staying in the same neck of the woods, at least in global terms, the Khajuraho Hindu Temples of Madhya Pradesh in India give us many insights into the everyday lives of ordinary people of that region around the end of the first millennium. The exteriors of many of the temples are covered in hundreds of sculptures, mostly of people going about their daily lives – farming, getting married, playing musical instruments, dancing, washing their hair, having oral sex in the 'sixty-nine' position, having threesomes, foursomes, outright orgies, more oral sex, sex with animals, and generally having sex in every conceivable position.

A demonstration of the athleticism of the ancient Madhya Pradeshis.

Although only ten percent of the sculptures on the temples' walls involve sex, nudity and generously proportioned male and female figures, the sculptures are so numerous that you could spend days just examining the naughty ones, and many people do. Although India is nowadays considered fairly conservative in matters of sex, their ancestors clearly weren't shy about such things.

Like those ancient Hindus, the French have long had quite a liberal view of matters sexual, certainly when compared to most of their European neighbours, who traditionally believed in grim Calvinist/Lutheran-style restraint or Catholic-style dread of eternal hellfire for sins of the flesh.

That's not to say that the French weren't mostly Catholic, just that they always seemed to have a dispensation when it came to matters of sex, or certainly they acted like they did. Nowhere was this more evident than in the case of royal mistresses.

While Rousseau's obscene public expression of his sexual desire was a bit much, many will regard his spanking fetish as pretty mild stuff. At the other end of the fetish spectrum is the case of Thomas Granger, who holds the distinction of being the first known juvenile to be executed in the United States. His crime was bestiality, or having sex with animals. And it was very much in the plural, and also across a whole range of species, if you are to believe the only written record of the episode.

In 1642, Granger was about sixteen or seventeen, a servant to a wealthy settler called Elder Love Brewster in the recently formed Plymouth Colony in Massachusetts. Apparently, one of the colonists chanced upon Granger having sex with a mare. Given the puritanical colonists' views on simple extra-marital sex, bestiality must have made the poor chap or maiden pass out. Granger was quickly arrested, and charged with an offence against God and nature.

According to the Bible, to which the colonists adhered rigidly: 'If a man shall lie with a beast, he shall surely be put to death: and ye shall slay the beast.' Granger was interrogated 'in private' by magistrates, so who knows how they wrung the disturbed young man's further confessions from him. After initial denial of the offence, it seems he broke down and confessed his crimes in full. As the written record tells it:

He was this year detected of buggery, and indicted for the same, with a mare, a cowe, two goats, five sheep, two calves, and a turkey.

Yes, you read that correctly. A *turkey*. He furthermore confessed, both in private and then in open court, that his indiscretions with said animals had been on multiple occasions. He was sentenced to 'death by hanging until dead.'

According to biblical law, the defiled animals had to be put to death along with the defiler. So a large pit was dug near the place of execution. The entire flock of Brewster's sheep was paraded before the condemned man, and he was required to differentiate the guilty sheep from the innocent ones:

And whereas some of the sheep could not so well be knowne by his description of them, others with them were brought before him, and he declared which were they, and which were not ... A very sade spectakle it was; for first the mare, and then the cowe, and the rest of the lesser catle, were kild before his face, according to the law, and then he him selfe was executed. The catle were all cast into a great and large pitte that was digged of purposs for them, and no use made of any part of them.

Much happier, certainly for one guy, is the tale of Bhutan's patron saint, Drukpa Kunley (1455–1529), who is the patron saint that every country would love to have, or certainly the one every man would love his country to have. Let me explain. He was known variously as 'The Divine Madman', 'The Saint of 5,000 Women' and 'The Madman of the Dragon Lineage', all of which begin to make sense as you learn more about the man.

Drukpa Kunley was a Buddhist monk. As you probably know, the religion seeks the attainment of the sublime state of nirvana, or the quenching of the three fires of passion, aversion and ignorance. But this particular Buddhist monk was fairly unique in his scepticism and anti-institutional attitudes, and his questioning of many aspects of Buddhism and the path to Enlightenment. He was a 'nyönpa' or an 'avadhūta' – a yogi known for using unusual teaching methods, one who often acts contrary to standard social etiquette.

Kunley was a mendicant, wandering from village to village preaching that spiritual happiness is only achieved by letting go of earthly conventions, particularly when it comes to women and alcohol. In simple terms, drink as much as you like and indulge in lots of sex.

To this end, he convinced thousands of women that the path to enlightenment ran straight through whatever bed he happened to be sleeping in, and to help them on the way he used the 'Thunderbolt of Flaming Wisdom', aka his erect penis. Really, that's what it's known as.

Now, it's common knowledge that many kings (and a few queens) had a bit on the side, or several bits. As previously mentioned, England's randy old Charles II had at least nine mistresses, and his successor James II carried on that fine tradition, having at least five. Poland's Augustus II the Strong (1670–1733) had at least eleven ladies at his beck and call, and was rumoured to have fathered hundreds of children. Egypt's Ramses II supposedly had 200 mistresses, producing 150 children. His rampant sexual appetite also resulted in his name adorning the Ramses brand of condom.

But while most kings and princes sought to keep their marital infidelities out of the limelight, no such fears of scandal afflicted the French. Around 1600, or during the reign of Henry IV, it was decided to make the position of royal mistress official, i.e. adulterous sex was openly condoned by the French monarchy. And this was done in full view of the Catholic Church.

The official title was 'Maîtresse-en-titre', and it entitled the lady to her own royal apartments, plenty of money, expensive clothes and a generally luxurious lifestyle – all she had to do was satisfy the King's lusts every once in a while. Oh, and probably bear a few of his bastard children.

There were lots of takers for the post. During Henry's reign, nine willing ladies filled the position, and his successors Louis XIV and Louis XV each had no less than fifteen 'Maîtresses-en-titre'. Louis XIV's girls included three of the five celebrated and beautiful Mancini sisters – Olympe, Marie and Hortense, who he took as mistresses almost in succession. Hortense incidentally was also a mistress of Charles II of England – the girl liked to mix it up a bit. He also took as mistresses Henrietta of England, who happened to be his sister-in-law, and Isabelle de Ludres, who incongruously posed semi-nude for a portrayal of Saint Mary Magdalene, presumably depicting the biblical character in her original profession of prostitute.

Three of the five de Mailly sisters, depicted as mythological nude ladies.

Louis XV also liked to take sisters as mistresses, outdoing his predecessor by taking four of the five de Mailly sisters in succession – Louise Julie, Pauline, Diane and Marie Anne. Each was a year or two older than the next, suggesting that Louis simply took another, fresher, younger model when he grew tired of the older one.

Louis also had a lot of his mistresses painted by the same artist, Jean Marc Nattier, who liked to depict them in mythological attire, i.e. very little or very skimpy clothing, presumably so that Louis could nostalgically gaze upon their bare breasts long after they'd left his court.

The post of 'Maîtresse-en-titre' sort of drifted out of fashion around the time of the French Revolution, as not too many girls wished to have their heads removed by the guillotine. But the term is still often jokingly used by the French press when referring to mistresses of French Presidents and other politicians.

Another brief royal over-indulgence concerns King Fatafehi Paulah of Tonga, who died in his eighties in the late eighteenth century. Captain Cook paid a visit to the King while travelling among the myriad of islands in 1777, and among the things he brought back was the word 'taboo', whose origin lies in some of the cultural practices of the Tongans:

> Not one of them would sit down, or eat a bit of any thing ... On expressing my surprise at this, they were all taboo ('tapu', in Tongan), as they said; which word has a very comprehensive meaning; but, in general, signifies that a thing is forbidden.

But one thing that wasn't taboo, particularly for the King himself, was sex. Quite the opposite in fact. The octogenarian King Paulah told Captain Cook that the King had not only the right but also the royal duty to deflower all the girls in his kingdom, and in his efforts to do his duty, he had sex with eight or ten virgins every day.

Now, this is all very well, but it does seem to suggest that incest wasn't taboo either – you can only imagine, as the generations passed and the King's offspring grew up, that he might have had trouble finding a mate who wasn't his half-sister. That aside, on a conservative estimate, King Fatafehi Paulah had sex with 37,000 virgins in his lifetime, if we're to believe the old guy's claims.

Tonga's King Fatafehi Paulah, on the left, and one of his grateful subjects, on the right.

Another of history's bizarre sexual practices, at least to western, twenty-first-century eyes, was the voluntary sacred prostitution practised in the ancient near eastern cultures of Mesopotamia. Now, this wasn't prostitution as we know it, but it was required that every female in the land of reproductive age would be paid for sex by a stranger in the temple of Mylitta (another version of the Greek Aphrodite, goddess of love and beauty), as a sacrifice to honour the goddess. Numerous ancient historians recorded the cult, including the Greek Herodotus, who was horrified by the practice:

> The foulest Babylonian custom is that which compels every woman of the land to sit in the temple of Mylitta and have intercourse with some stranger at least once in her life ... there is a great multitude of women coming and going; passages marked by line run every way through the crowd, by which the men pass and make their choice. Once a woman has taken her place there, she does not go away to her home before some stranger has cast money into her lap, and had intercourse with her outside the temple. So she follows the first man who casts it and rejects no one. After their intercourse, having discharged her sacred duty to the goddess she goes away to her home; and thereafter there is no bribe however great that will get her ... the women that are fair and tall are soon free to depart, but the uncomely have long to wait because they cannot fulfil the law; for some of them remain for three years, or four.

It's evident that sexual satisfaction for males has historically been pretty easy to come by. However, very few such releases existed for females with strong libidos, mostly because of the consequences of pregnancy or the stigma of being a so-called loose woman. Women have therefore had to seek satisfaction by other means, such as the sex toy.

Now, you might imagine that dildos and the like are a relatively recent phenomenon, but in fact, they've been around pretty much as long as humanity has existed. Yes, Stone Age man, or should I say woman, if you are to believe archaeological experts, may have been using stone dildos as long as 28,000 years ago.

At least that's one of the possibilities suggested by the recent find of a twenty-centimetre-long, three-centimetre-diameter siltstone

You see all kinds of behaviour on Greek vases.

phallic object in a cave in Germany, which may be the earliest known sex toy. Alternatively, it might just have been a tool of a different sort, used for knapping flints, but that's a really boring explanation.

It is undisputed, however, that dildos as sex aids have existed since ancient times. There are depictions on objects such as Greek vases of women carrying gigantic phalluses, or preparing to use them on themselves.

The origin of the word 'dildo' is uncertain. It could be derived from the Latin *dilatare*, meaning to dilate or open wide, or the Italian word *diletto*, meaning delight, but the most amusing etymology is that it comes directly from the word 'dill', which is a pickled cucumber and obviously phallic in shape. Whatever its origin, the word has been around for a long time. It is used by Shakespeare in *A Winter's Tale*, and by Ben Jonson in *The Alchemist*, both of which were written in the early seventeenth century.

Swedish archaeologists recently uncovered a phallus carved from an antler, estimated to be about 6,000 years old. It is speculated that this may indeed have been a sex toy, as Stone Age male fertility symbols are very rare.

A more recent addition to the world's historic dildo depository is the well-preserved leather and wood dildo uncovered near Gdansk in Poland in 2015. This one is estimated to be about 250 years old, and that society definitely did not produce phalluses as fertility symbols, suggesting it can have had only one purpose. Records exist of dildos as sex aids made from wood, leather, bone and even, in Greco-Roman times, from bread – they were called *olisbokollikes*, presumably not too freshly baked however.

Ah, ancient Greece, which gave the world so much in terms of architecture, culture, democracy and kinky sexual practices. Aristophanes's most renowned play, *Lysistrata*, features the titular woman formulating a plan to get all the other women in the land to deny their husbands sex until they make a peace treaty and end the war that has been raging. In the course of her meeting with the other women, she says the following (by the way, this is a tame translation – other versions are much more graphic; 'olisbos' means 'leather penis'):

> Since the day we were betrayed by the Milesians, I have not once seen even an eight-inch olisbos as a leathern consolation for us poor widows.

In case you haven't had enough of dildos, there exists a representation of a group of seventeenth-century women standing in front of what looks like a market stall, examining a display of large dildos that are either spread on the counter or hanging at eye level. This can be found in an extraordinary sex manual written in 1680, which seems to have been designed for the enlightenment of women in all things sexual, and is not at all shy about telling it as it is.

It is called *The School of Venus or the Ladies' Delight Reduced into Rules of Practice*. The title page says it is a translation of a French book entitled *L'École des Filles*, or 'The Girls' School'. The book takes the form of a dialogue between two young women, Frances and Katherine, with the experienced Frances (Frank) educating the innocent virgin Katherine (Katy) on matters of sex, in advance of her marriage. Early on, Katy is given a quick anatomy lesson:

Frank: *You must therefore know that the thing with which a man pisses is sometimes called a prick ...*

Katy: *Oh Lord Coz [cousin]! You swear?*

Frank: *Tut, you are very nice, if you are minded to hear such discourse you must not be so scrupulous.*

Katy: *I am contented. Speak what you will.*

Frank: *I must use the very words cunt, arse, prick, bollocks etc.*

Katy: *I am contented.*

Frank: *Then let me tell you, the thing with which a man pisses is sometimes called a prick, sometimes a tarse, sometimes a man's yard, and other innumerable names. It hangs down from the bottom of their bellys like a cow's teat, but much longer, and is about the place where the slit of our cunt is.*

Katy: *Oh strange!*

That's one of the milder passages in the 160- page manual, which the famous diarist Samuel Pepys found so shocking that he immediately burned his copy. Or at least that's what he claimed. Interestingly, Pepys had found his copy in an ordinary bookshop, suggesting that it was sold, at least initially, not as a seedy piece of back-street pornography, but as an ordinary, mainstream book, available to all and sundry. The book was eventually banned by the powers that be, but not before a great many innocent ladies were educated by passages such as this:

The School of Venus

Frank: In short, 'tis thus it often happens a couple of young lovers meet in some place, where they have not the convenience to fuck, they therefore only kiss and roul their tounges in one anothers mouths, this tickleth their lips and proves the youth so, that it makes his Prick stand, they still continuing kissing, and it not being a convenient place to fuck in, he steals his Prick into her hand, which she by rubbing gently (which is called figging) makes the man spend in her hand.

Katy: Hey day! Must a woman of necessity know of all these things?

Frank: Yes, and a great deal more for, After a little repose they try another conclusion to please another.

Katy: You tell me of a variety of pleasures, how shall I do to remember them, how it say you doth the women fuck the man?

Frank:	*That is when he lyes down backward, and the women gets astride upon him and riggles her arse upon his prick.*
Katy:	*That's a new way. It seems this pleasure has many postures.*
Frank:	*Yes, above a hundred, have you but a little patience and I will tell you them all.*

And indeed she does, and in ways that are surprisingly biased towards the woman's satisfaction, given the attitudes of the day.

Although no author is credited, many of the sexual tips and the tone of voice suggest it possibly had a female author, or at least a female advisor. Oh, and in case seventeenth-century ladies needed still further advice, the book also features graphic depictions of various sexual positions.

In case you want to study this remarkable publication, in the interests of furthering your historical knowledge, you'll be glad to hear that Google have kindly digitised the entire manual. It'll give you something new to read, now that you've reached the end of this book.

Off you go.

SOURCES

....

Chapter 1

Death by antiquity

Haaren, John. *Famous Men of Greece.* New York: The American Book Company, 1904.

J Figueira, Thomas. *The Strange Death of Draco on Aegina.* Michigan: University of Michigan Press, 1993.

"The Brutal Draconian Laws of Ancient Greece." Ancient Origins: Reconstructing the Story of Humanity's Past. 20 November 2014.

Laertius, Diogenes. Chapter 1, section IX, *Lives of the Eminent Philosophers.*

Fairweather, Janet. *The Death of Heraclitus* North Carolina: Duke University Press, 1973.

brainyquote.com/quotes/heraclitus_121940

McKeown, J.C. *A Cabinet of Greek Curiosities: Strange Tales and Surprising Facts from the Cradle of Western Civilization.* Oxford: Oxford University Press, 2013.

"List of Unusual Deaths." Wikipedia: The Free Encyclopedia. 13 June 2018.

"Ancient Greece – Aeschylus." Classical Literature: A Basic Level Guide to Some of the Best Known and Loved Works of Prose, Poetry and Drama and Classical Antiquity. 2009.

Bloody mess

wikipedia.org/wiki/Capital_punishment_in_Denmark, 10 November 2017.

"Denmark's Last Public Execution." 1001 Stories of Denmark: kulturarv. dk/1001fortaellinger/en_GB/soelvbjerghoej/stories/denmark-s-last-public-execution.

"1892: Jens Nielsen, the last in Denmark." 2018: executedtoday. com/2008/11/08/1892-jens-nielsen-the-last-in-denmark/.

Berry, James. *My Experiences as an Executioner.* Bradford and London: Percy Lund, Humphries & Co. 1892.

"Bradford's Victorian Executioner." *The Local Leader.* December 17 2013.

Engel, Howard. *Lord High Executioner: An Unashamed Look at Hangmen, Headsmen, and Their Kin.* Ontario: Firefly Books, 1996.

Uncredited. 'Head Severed By The Rope'. *San Francisco Chronicle.* April 27, 1900.

Thomas Ketchum

"1901: "Black Jack" Tom Ketchum, who was left in three pieces." executedtoday. com/2010/04/26/1901-black-jack-tom-ketchum-clayton-hanging/.

Stanley, Frances. *No Tears for Black Jack Ketchum.* Santa Fe: Sunstone Press, 2008.

Eva Dugan

"Cheerful Eva." *Time* magazine. 3 March 1930.

"1930: Eva Dugan, her head jerked clean off." February 21, 2011. executedtoday. com/?s=Eva+Dugan+.

Guillotine

"The Men Behind the Word." BBC Radio World Service. May 18 1992.

"Guillotine." 14 June 2018: wikipedia.org/wiki/Guillotine#Invention.

"Antoine Louis." 31 January 2018: wikipedia. org/wiki/Antoine_Louis.

H, Neil. "A man is beheaded cleanly by a guillotine. Is it possible that there follows a period of awareness, albeit of only a few nanoseconds?" *The Guardian,* 2011.

madameguillotine.org.uk/2011/07/17/charlotte-corday-17th-july-1793/.

guillotine.dk/Pages/30sek.html.

"1905: Henri Languille, a man of science." June 26, 2008: executedtoday. com/2008/06/28/1905-henri-languille-a-man-of-science/.

"Living Heads." June 18, 2017: newworldencyclopedia.org/entry/Guillotine#Living_heads.

"Blowing from a gun." 6 April, 2018: wikipedia.org/wiki/Blowing_from_a_gun#cite_ref-1.

"Execution by cannon in Iran" 1890s URL: http://world-inpics.blogspot. com/2017/02/execution-using-cannon-in-iran.html

Uncredited. "British Retaliation in India." Page 21 - 23. *The Advocate of Peace Journal,* January – February, 1858.

Dying for a laugh

Reynolds, Reginald. *Beards: Their Social Standing, Religious Involvements, Decorative Possibilities, and Value in Offence and Defence Through the Ages.* Doubleday, 1949.

"List of unusual deaths." Wikipedia: The Free Encyclopedia. 13 June 2018.

Uncredited. "King-sized meal: a cautionary tale." *Nordstjernan*, January 2005. Accessed 2018.

"Adolf Frederick: King of Sweden." Encyclopedia Britannica. May 2018.

Vallandigham, James L. *A Life of Clement L. Vallandigham*. Baltimore: Turnbull Brothers Publishers, 1872.

"Victorian Strangeness: The lawyer who shot himself proving his case." BBC News. 16 August 2014.

Andrew Marshall, 'The Queen and I', *Weekend Australian*, 12–13 March 2005.

Duthel, Heinz. *Duthel Thailand Guide IV: Chakri Dynasty*. Germany: Books on Demand, 2015. Accessed: 2018.

Socrates, Walford, Edward and de Valois, Henri. *The Ecclesiastical Histories of Socrates*, "Chapter XXXVIII: The Death of Arius." Bohn, 1853.

Muehlberger, Ellen. *The Legend of Arius' Death: Imagination, Space and Filth in Late Ancient Historiography*. Oxford: Oxford Journals, May 6, 2015.

"Who was Arius.". 2005. URL: http://arian-catholic.org/arian/arius.html

Sex and death

Penn, Imma. *Dogma Evolution & Papal Fallacies*. Indiana: Authorhouse, May 30, 2007.

"Pope Leo VII." New Advent Catholic Encyclopedia. 14 June 2018.

Logan, Donald F. *A History of the Church in the Middle Ages*. New York: Routledge, 2013.

"Pope John XII." New Advent Catholic Encyclopedia. 14 June 2018.

DeCormenin, Louis Marie; Gihon, James L. *A Complete History of the Popes of Rome, from Saint Peter, the First Bishop to Pius the Ninth*. Philadelphia: James L. Gihon, 1857.

"Pope Paolo ll." The Papal Encyclopedia. 2000.

Ceilán, Cynthia. *Thinning the Herd: Tales of the Weirdly Departed*. Surrey: Lyons Press, 1st November 2007.

"Pope Paul II." Wikipedia: The Free Encyclopedia. 16 March 2018.

"My Homosexual Brother." Chiesa Espressonline. 12 February 2015. URL: http://chiesa.espresso.repubblica.it/articolo/1350992bdc4.html?eng=y

Bogle, Joanna. "The cardinal who died in a prostitute's home." *The Catholic Herald*. 9th April, 2015. 2018.

President Félix François Faure

"Félix Faure." Wikipedia: The Free Encyclopedia. 21 March 2018.

"Marguerite Jeanne Steinheil." murderpedia.org, 4 March 2011.

Storey, Neil R. *The Little Book of Death*. Ireland: The History Press, 2013.

"16 Février 1899 : La Fellation Fatale Du Président Félix Faure." LCI. 16 February 2015.

Madame Marguerite Steinheil

'Fascinating Women: Marguerite Steinheil." Edwardian Promenade: La belle enoque in our modern world. 22 August 2010. URL: http://www.edwardian-promenade.com/sex/fascinating-women-marguerite-steinheil/

'Private lives in the public eye (Lord Palmerston),' by Norman Smith. BBC Radio 4, December 31, 2008

Chorley, Matt. "Cameron vows not to copy the last PM who increased his majority." *The Daily Mail*. 15th July 2015. Accessed: 2018.

Gibbon, Edward. *The History of the Decline and Fall of the Roman Empire*. CreateSpace Independent Publishing Platform, 25 September 2013.

Siegel, Lee. "Rocks Off!" *New Yorker Magazine*. 1 April 2012. Accessed: 2018.

D. McFadden, Robert. "New Details Are Reported on How Rockefeller Died." *New York Times*. 29 January 1979.

Frank, Jeffery. "Big Spender: Nelson Rockefeller's grand ambitions." *New Yorker Magazine*, 13 October 2014.

Chapter 2

Spin doctors

Gordon, Richard. *Great Medical Disasters*. London: Hutchinson and Co. 1983

Soniak, Matt. "'Time Me, Gentlemen': The Fastest Surgeon of the 19th Century." *The Atlantic*. 4 October 2012.

"Pioneers: Robert Liston 1794-1847." History of surgery and anesthesia: an ODP's perspective. 2001. URL: http://historyofsurgery.co.uk/Web%20Pages/0413.htm

Coppeman, W.S.C. "Andrew Ure M.D" *Proceedings of the Royal Society of Medicin.* August 1951. Pages 655–662.

"Andrew Ure galvanizing the body of the executed murderer." Getty Images.

Lewis, Roger. "Raising the Dead: the men who created Frankenstein." *The Daily Telegraph*, 19 July 2008.

Victoria, Moore, "Dr Barry's deathbed sex secret: The extraordinary truth about a great war hero and medical pioneer." *Daily Mail*, 10 March 2008.

Pain, Stephanie. "Histories: The 'male' military surgeon who wasn't." *New Scientist*, 5 March 2008.

Geoghegan, Tom. "Five British heroes overlooked by history." *BBC Magazine*, 17 November 2009.

Brandon, Sydney. "Barry, James (c.1799–1865)" Oxford Dictionary of Biography. 2018.

Hume, Robert. "The Anatomy of a Lie: The Irish woman who lived as a man to practice medicine" *Irish Examiner*, 1 August 2014.

"Pennsylvania Surgeon Operates on Himself, Successfully Removing his Appendix" *New York Times*, 16 February 1921.

"Dr. Kane Recovering." *New York Times*. 17 February 1921.

Thompson, Larry. "When The Surgeon Is His Own Patient." *The Washington Post*, 3 March 1987.

Ericson, John. "Incredible Self-Surgeries In History." *Medical Daily*. 27 Aug 2013.

"Medicine: Country Surgeon." *Time Magazine*. 18 January 1932.

K. Hutchens, John. "Notes on the Late Dr. John R. Brinkley, Whom Radio Raised to a Certain Fame." *New York Times*, 7 June 1942.

Lee, R. Alton. 'The Bizarre Careers of John R. Brinkley." Kentucky: The University Press of Kentucky, 2002.

"John R. Brinkley. "Goat gland doctor," radio pioneer. 1885-1942."

Kansas Historical Society. 2018. www.kshs.org/index.php?url=kansapedia/john-r-brinkley/11988

Boese, Alex. "Did they really do that?" *The Scientist Magazine*. 7 September 2007.

"Carlos Finlay and Yellow Fever: Triumph over Adversity." *The Society of Federal Health Professionals Magazine*. 1 September 2004.

Rhatigan, Joe. "Book of Science Stuff: Wacky Experiments, Shocking Discoveries, Odd Facts and Other Outrageous Curiosities (Book of Stuff)." Bournemouth: Imagine Publishing, 1 October 2010.

'Kiss' held an intoxicant', *Chicago Tribune*, December 27 1900

"Crusade against kissing: New York Lady Doctor says it is Barbarous." *The Northants Evening Telegraph*, 29 December 1900.

Just what the doctor ordered

"Charles Romley Alder Wright – The Forefather of Heroin." DrugAbuse.com, 2018.

'The Pharmaceutical Company Bayer and the Invention of the "Non-Addictive" Drug Heroin'. healthimpactnews.com, 31 July, 2014.

Selby, Jenn. "Peaches Geldof, drug addiction, and a very brief history of heroin." *The Independent*, 23 July 2014.

"History of Heroin." The United Nations Office of Drugs and Crime. January 1 1953. unodc.org/unodc/en/data-and-analysis/bulletin/bulletin_1953-01-01_2_page004.html

"Mrs. Winslow's Soothing Syrup." *New York Times*, August 30, 1910, Page 6.

Chase AW, MD. *Dr. Chase's Recipes*. Michigan: Ann Arbor, 1870.

Beasely, H. *The Druggist General Recipe Book*. Philadelphia: Lindsey and Blackingston Press, 1878.

Higginbottom, John. Mothers, Doctors, and Nurses. Nottingham: T. Kirk, 1843.

"Mrs. Winslow's Soothing Syrup For Children Teething.; Letter From A Mother In Lowell, Mass. A Down-town Merchant." *New York Times*. December 1, 1860.

"Mrs. Winslow's Soothing Syrup." The Wood Library-Museum. 2018. woodlibrarymuseum.org/museum/item/529/mrs.-winslow's-soothing-syrup.

"Piles and Prolapsus Ani." *The Medical Times and Gazette*, Volume 2 (1863), p.381.

"Atkinson's Registered Rectum Supporter." The Quack Doctor: Stories from Medicine's Past. 9 July 2009. thequackdoctor.com/index.php/atkinsons-registered-rectum-supporter/

"Heidelberg Alternating Current Belt." Museum of Quackery.com. 13 April 2013. URL: http://museumofquackery.com/

ephemera/heidelberg.htm.

"Franz Mesmer." Wikipedia: The Free Encyclopedia. 5 June 2018.

Tartakovsky, Margarita. "Psychology's History of Being Mesmerized." Psych Central.com. 2004.

Lamb, Jonathan. *Preserving the Self in the South Seas, 1680–1840.* Chicago: University of Chicago Press, 2001.

"A Timeline of Scurvy" by Jason Allen Mayberry.

Food and Drug Law Class and 3L Paper, Harvard Law School, 27 April 2004.

"The Emergence of Scurvy." BBC History. 17 February 2011. bbc.co.uk/history/british/empire_seapower/captain-cook_scurvy_01.shtml

"Scurvy" Wikipedia: The Free Encyclopedia. 18 June 2018.

"Big Think Interview With Rachel Maines." Big Think. May 2017. www.bigthink.com/videos/big-think-interview-with-rachel-maines.

Maines, Rachel P. *The Technology of Orgasm: "Hysteria," the Vibrator, and Women's Sexual Satisfaction.* Baltimore: The Johns Hopkins University Press, 1999.

Pearson, Catherine. "Female Hysteria: 7 Crazy Things People Used To Believe About The Ladies' Disease" *The Huffington Post.* 21 November 2013.

"Hysteria and the Strange History of Vibrators". *Psychology Today.* 1 March 2013.

Epstein, Michael S, Danny G. Miles, Jr. and Lee L. Yu "What Were They Drinking? A Critical Study of the Radium Ore Revigator" *Journal of Applied Spectroscopy.* Vol. 6, Issue 12 (2009): pp. 1406–1409.

"Medicine: Radium Drinks." *Time Magazine.* 11 April 1932.

'Radioactive Drinking Water Cures Insanity' quackery.umwblogs.org/quackery-from-the-1800s-1960s/.

"Death Stirs Action On Radium 'cures'." *New York Times*, 2 April 1932.

Bitter pills to swallow

McKeown, J. C. *A Cabinet of Roman Curiosities.* Oxford: Oxford University Press, 2010.

Pliny the Elder. *Natural History.* Vol. 3, Books 28-32.

"An update on the management of acne vulgaris" NCBI. 17 June 2009.

URL: https://www.ncbi.nlm.nih.gov/pubmed/21436973.

"The Historic Panorama of Acne Vulgaris" U.S. National Library of Medicine, June 17 2009.

International Journal of Advanced Ayurveda, Yoga, Unani, Siddha and Homeopathy Volume 2, Issue 1 (2013): pp. 99-104, Article ID Med-92 ISSN: 2320-0251.

"Epilepsy: On the Sacred Disease." The Internet Classics Archive. 2009. URL: http://classics.mit.edu/Hippocrates/sacred.html.

"De-coding the Black Death" BBC News, October 3, 2001. Accessed: 2018

Medieval Plague Cures

"Black Plague Cures". gohistorygo.com/black-plague-cures.

"What were the cures for the black death" HubPages.com. 31 July 2012. libguides.ucd.ie/ld.php?content_id=31366730.

"Plague Doctor Costume." Wikipedia: The Free Encyclopedia. 15 June 2018.

Clendening, Logan. *Source Book of Medical History.* New York: Dover Publications Inc. 1942.

"John of Arderne: the Father of English Surgery" University of Glasgow Library. 25 September 2012. libguides.ucd.ie/ld.php?content_id=31366730.

"The Fifteenth Century Manuscript of John Aderne's Medical Treatises England" University of Glasgow, May 2006.

Wilde, Lady Francesca. *The Properties Of Herbs And Their Use In Medicine & Medical Superstitions And Ancient Charms.* Ticknor & Co. Publishers, 1888.

Left to their own devices …

Tiemann, George. American Armamentarium Chirurgicum & Co, James M. Edmonson George Tiemann & Co New York 1379.

Holt's Divisor:

"Ivory Holt's Divulsor by Maw." Phisick. 2018. phisick.com/item/ivory-holts-divulsor-by-maw/.

Haemorrhoid forceps:

Carol Parry. "Victorian Hemorrhoid Forceps. 'Glasgow Surgical Instrument Makers' Royal College of Physicians and Surgeons of Glasgow, 18 September 18 2015. heritageblog.rcpsg.

ac.uk/2015/09/18/glasgow-surgical-instrument-makers/surgicaltechnologists.net

Double lithotomy cache

Drake, Daniel. 'Double lithotomy cache: Operations for the Removal of Urinary Calculi Article 4' *The Western Journal of Medical and Physical Sciences* Volume 7 (1834).

Double Lithotome Cache by Tiemann. Phisick. 2018. phisick.com/item/double-lithotome-cache-by-tiemann/.

'The world of Shakespeare's humors' U.S. National Library of Medicine. 19 September 2013. nlm.nih.gov/exhibition/shakespeare/fourhumors.html.

Seigworth, Gilbert R. 'Bloodletting Over the Centuries' *New York State Journal of Medicine*, December (1980).

"Bloodletting" Science Museum. 1999. broughttolife.sciencemuseum.org.uk/broughttolife/techniques/bloodletting.

Boston Medical and Surgical Journal Volumes 8-9 Instruments (1833): Page 263.

Prioreschi, Plinio. "Primitive and Ancient Medicine Trepanning" *History of Medicine*, Volume 1, (1995).

"Trephine Drill with Ebony Handle 19th Century." Phisick. 2018. phisick.com/item/trephine-drill-with-ebony-handle-19th-c/.

'Trephination' Ancient History Encyclopedia. May 2013. ancient.eu/Trephination/.

Wergland, Glendyne R. *One Shaker Life: Isaac Newton Youngs, 1793-1865*. Massachusetts: University of Massachusetts Press, 2006.

"German Spermatorrhea Ring Screw Catch" Phisick. 2018. phisick.com/item/german-spermatorrhoea-ring-screw-catch/.

"Vaginal Speculum" Surgical Instruments from Ancient Rome, University of Virginia. 2007. exhibits.hsl.virginia.edu/romansurgical/.

Eveleth, Rose. 'Why No One Can Design a Better Speculum'. *The Atlantic Magazine* November 17, 2004. Accessed: 2018. theatlantic.com/health/archive/2014/11/why-no-one-can-design-a-better-speculum/382534/.

"From jewel-capped teeth to golden bridges – 9,000 years of dentistry". 8 March 2014. ancient-origins.net/human-origins-science/jewel-capped-teeth-golden-bridges-9000-years-dentistry-001427.

Morris, Thomas. 'The gruesome and mysterious case of exploding teeth" BBC *Future*. March 2, 2016. Accessed: 2018. bbc.com/future/story/20160301-the-gruesome-and-mysterious-case-of-exploding-teeth.

W. Ermatinger, James. *The World of Ancient Rome: A Daily Life Encyclopedia*. Vol. 2, Denver: Greenwood, 1959.

"Tooth Extraction Devices" Medical Discoveries. 2018. discoveriesinmedicine.com/To-Z/Tooth-Extraction-Devices.html.

Jarus, Owen. 'Blackbeard's Booty: Pirate Ship Yields Medical Supplies'. *Live Science Magazine*, 26 January 2015. Accessed: 2018.

"Treatment of Venereal Disease during the Civil War" Medical Antiques.com. 2015. medicalantiques.com/civilwar/Civil_War_Articles/Civil_War_Venereal_Disease_treatment.htm.

Medicine on the Mary Rose: maryrose.org/meet-the-crew/the-surgeon/medicine/

Chapter 3

Edwin Booth

S. Goff , John. *Robert Todd Lincoln: a man in his own right*. Oklahoma:

University of Oklahoma Press, 1968. Klein, Christopher. 'How Boston embraced the Booth brothers', *The Boston Globe*, 12 April 2015. Accessed 2018.

"Edwin Booth". 30 May 2014. biography.com/people/edwin-booth-39624#synopsis.

"Mary Devlin Booth" Live Journal. 21 February 2010. ebooth-myhamlet.livejournal.com/16789.html.

"Edwin Booth" 3 June 2018. britannica.com/biography/Edwin-Booth.

Albert Goering

Hastings Burke, William. 'Albert Göring, Hermann's anti-Nazi brother' *The Guardian*, Saturday, 20 February 2010. Accessed 2018. theguardian.com/lifeandstyle/2010/feb/20/albert-goering-hermann-goering-brothers.

Brennan, Zoe. 'The Goering who saved

Jews.' *Daily Mail*. April 9, 2010. Accessed, 2018. dailymail.co.uk/news/article-1264738/The-Goering-saved-Jews-A-new-book-reveals-Hermann-masterminded-Final-Solution-brother-Albert-rescued-Gestapo-victims.html.

Winer, Stuart and Sue Surkes 'Top Israeli honor eludes Goering's brother, who heroically saved Jews' *The Times of Israel*, 25 January 2016. Accessed 2018. timesofisrael.com/top-israeli-honor-eludes-goerings-brother-who-heroically-saved-jews/.

'The Good Brother – A true Story of Courage.' Albert Goering. March 2013. goering.dk/.

'The Good Brother.' Auschwitz.dk. 2013. auschwitz.dk/albert.htm.

Pauline Bonaparte

Knopf, Flora Fraser. *Pauline Bonaparte: Venus of Empire*. New York: Anchor Books, 24 February 2009.

Laurel Thatcher Ulrich. "The Notorious Pauline Bonaparte." Scandalous Women. 13th May 2008. scandalouswoman.blogspot.com/2008/05/notorious-pauline-bonaparte.html.

"Pauline Bonaparte." 5 June 2018. britannica.com/biography/Pauline-Bonaparte.

Bingham, D. 'A Selection from the Letters and Dispatches of Napoleon Bonaparte' London: Chapman & Hall, 1884.

Daylight robbery

Huntford, Roland. *Shackleton*. New York: Carroll & Graf, 1998.

'Shackleton Jr stole crown jewels" by Jerome Reilly.

Irish Independent, January 13, 2008.

O'Byrne, Robert "The mystery of the missing Crown Jewels".

The Irish Times, March 26, 2002. Accessed: 2018. irishtimes.com/culture/the-mystery-of-the-missing-crown-jewels-1.1055099.

sydenham.org.uk/frank_shackleton.html.

"Frank Shackleton." History Ireland. 2018. historyireland.com/20th-century-contemporary-history/frank-shackleton/.

A law onto themselves

McArthur, Jeff. *Two Gun Hart: Lawman, Cowboy, and Long-Lost Brother of Al Capone*. California: Bandwagon Books,
January 8 2015.

Bergreen, Laurence. *Capone: The Man and the Era*. New York: Simon & Schuster, August 1996.

"James Vincenzo Capone" Wikipedia: The Free Encyclopedia. 2 June 2018. en.wikipedia.org/wiki/James_Vincenzo_Capone.

Uncle Adolf

Gardner, David 'Found: The REAL Hitler diaries ...'

The Mail on Sunday, 20 September 2014. Accessed, 2018.

Gardner, David. 'Getting to know the Hitlers'.

The Telegraph, 20 January 2002. Accessed 2018. telegraph.co.uk/news/worldnews/northamerica/usa/1382115/Getting-to-know-the-Hitlers.html.

'Corpsman Hitler, US Navy?' AmericaInWWII.com. 2018. americainwwii.com/articles/corpsman-hitler-us-navy/.

'Patrick Stuart Houston.' Wikipedia: The Free Encyclopedia. 16 June 2018. en.wikipedia.org/wiki/William_Stuart-Houston.

"William Patrick "Willy" Stuart-Houston, born Hitler enlisted and fought in World War II with the USA forces." World War Two Graves. 7 April 2017. ww2gravestone.com/william-patrick-willy-stuart-houston-born-hitler-enlisted-and-fought-in-world-war-ii/.

Chapter 4

Letting the cat out of the bag

C. Madrigal, Alexis. "Operation Acoustic Kitty: The CIA's Would-Be Cat Spy' *The Atlantic Journal*, 8 May 2013. Accessed 2018.

Farberov, Snejana. 'Operation Acoustic Kitty: How the CIA's attempt to turn CATS into cyborg spies ended abruptly after the cat was run over by a cab' *The Daily Mail*, 9 May 2013. Accessed 2018. dailymail.co.uk/news/article-2321693/They-monstrosity-How-CIA-tried-failed-turn-CATS-cyborg-spies-Operation-Acoustic-Kitty-ended-disaster.html.

'Views on Trained Cats Use' Memorandum, U.S. Central Intelligence Agency, March 1967.

"Acoustic Kitty" Wikipedia: The Free Encyclopedia. 20 April 2018. en.wikipedia.org/

wiki/Acoustic_Kitty.

That sinking feeling

Marshal, Andrew. 'The strange sinking of the Nazi Titanic.' *The Telegraph* March 5 2010. Accessed, 2018. telegraph.co.uk/culture/tvandradio/9124111/The-strange-sinking-of-the-Nazi-Titanic.html.

Nazi Titanic. Directed by Oscar Chan. 2012. History Channel, 2012.

'The Titanic on Film.' A Life at the Movies. 19th April 2012. libguides.ucd.ie/ld.php?content_id=31366730.

Lebovic, Matt. 'Goebbels' 'Titanic' cinematic disaster turns 70' *The Times of Israel*. 1 October 2013. Accessed 2018. timesofisrael.com/goebbels-titanic-cinematic-disaster-turns-70/.

'SS Cap Arcona.' Wikipedia the Free Encyclopedia. 13 June 2018. libguides.ucd.ie/ld.php?content_id=31366730.

No kidding

Hebblethwaite, Margaret. *Paraguay*. Buckinghamshire: Bradt Travel Guides, 19 October 2010.

D.R., 'Paraguay's awful history - The never-ending war.' *The Economist*, 22 December 2012. Accessed 2018. economist.com/christmas-specials/2012/12/22/the-never-ending-war.

Appleby Matt. 'Paraguay: The Legacy of Francisco Solano López' *Pulsamerica* March 28, 2014. Accessed 2018. pulsamerica.co.uk/2014/03/paraguay-the-legacy-of-francisco-solano-lopez/.

'Battle of Acosta Nu.' Wikipedia the Free Encyclopedia. 12 June 2018. en.wikipedia.org/wiki/Battle_of_Acosta_Nu.

The mind boggles

Keller, Mitch. 'The Scandal at the Zoo' *New York Times* August 6, 2006. Accessed 2018. nytimes.com/2006/08/06/nyregion/thecity/06zoo.html.

Coard, Michael. 'Ota Benga, an African, caged in a U.S. zoo' *The Philadelphia Tribune*. 19 March 2016. Accessed 2018. phillytrib.com/commentary/ota-benga-an-african-caged-in-a-u-s-zoo/article_ad3fd3d9-e86b-5c36-b04e-fd451f179245.html.

Newkirk, Pamela. 'The man who was caged in a zoo' *The Guardian*, 3 June 2015. Acessed 2018. theguardian.com/world/2015/jun/03/the-man-who-was-caged-in-a-zoo.

Hornaday, Ann. 'A Critical Connection to the Curious Case of Ota Benga' *Washington Post*, 3 January 2009. Accessed 2018. washingtonpost.com/wp-dyn/content/article/2009/01/02/AR2009010202444.html.

Hale, Beth. 'Caged in the human zoo: The shocking story of the young pygmy warrior put on show in a monkey house - and how he fueled Hitler's twisted beliefs,' *Daily Mail*, 31 October 2009. Accessed 2018. dailymail.co.uk/news/article-1224189/Caged-human-zoo-The-shocking-story-young-pygmy-warrior-monkey-house--fuelled-Hitlers-twisted-beliefs.html.

'Mbuti People.' Wikipedia: the Free Encyclopedia. 8 June 2018. en.wikipedia.org/wiki/Mbuti_people.

Samuel Phillips Verner: geni.com.

No win situation

Schlosser Christoph, Friedrich and David Davison. *History of the eighteenth century and of the nineteenth till the overthrow of the French empire. With particular reference to mental cultivation and progress.* London: Chapman and Hall, 1843.

'Did You Know The Austrian Army Defeated Itself In The 1788 Battle Of Karansebes?' 25 April 2017. worldatlas.com/articles/did-you-know-the-austrian-army-defeated-itself-in-the-1788-battle-of-karansebes.html.

'Battle of Karansebes.' Wikipedia: the Free Encyclopedia. 31 May 2018. en.wikipedia.org/wiki/Battle_of_Kar%C3%A1nsebes#cite_note-1.

Dressed to kill

'Fashion victims: History's most dangerous trends,' BBC Culture. June 24 2015. www.bbc.com/culture/story/20150624-when-fashion-kills.

'Cage Crinoline' Glasgow Museums exhibit.

'Crinoline and whales' *The Dublin University Magazine: A Literary and Political Journal* Volume 52. Page 537.

'Burnt to death', *The Times*, November 14 1863.

'The tragedy of Oscar Wilde's half-sisters' Irish Identity. 2018. irishidentity.com/index.htm.

'Crinolines, Fashion History' Fashion Era. 2014. fashion-era.com/crinolines.htm.

'The Crinoline Period, 1850–1869' History of Fashion and Dress. January 2013. maggiemayfashions.com/belleepoque.html.

Chapter 5

Fire 'em up

Uncredited Article. '5 ways elephants changed history: A brief history of stomping victories and disastrous reversals' *The Independent*, 5 December 2013. Accessed 2018.

White, Matthew. *Atrocitology: Humanity's 100 Deadliest Achievements.* Edinburgh: Canongate Books, 2011.

Bauer, S. Wise. *The History of the Renaissance World.* New York: WW Norton & Co, 2013.

'Capture of Delhi (1398)' Timur: Wikipedia the Free Encyclopedia. 14 June. 2018. en.wikipedia.org/wiki/Timur.

On a wing and a prayer

Copping, Jasper. 'Honoured: the WW1 pigeons who earned their wings' *The Telegraph*, 12 January 2014. Accessed 2018. telegraph.co.uk/history/world-war-one/10566025/Honoured-the-WW1-pigeons-who-earned-their-wings.html.

'Animals during the war'. BBC Schools, WW1. 20 January 2014. bbc.co.uk/schools/0/ww1/25403861.

Dash, Mike. 'Closing the Pigeon Gap' Smithsonian. 17 April 2012. smithsonianmag.com/history/closing-the-pigeon-gap-68103438/.

'Famous Pigeons' The Pidgeon Insider. 2013. pigeonracingpigeon.com/uncategorized/famouspigeons/.

'The pigeon telegram' Letters of Note. 25 May 2010. lettersofnote.com/2010/05/for-heavens-sake-stop-it.html.

Wanderlust

Witz, Leslie. 'The making of an animal biography: Huberta's journey into South African natural history, 1928-1932' *Kronos Journal*, Page 138-166. Accessed 2018.

Dreyer, Nadine. *A Century of Sundays: 100 Years of Breaking News in the Sunday Times, 1906-2006.* South Africa: Zebra Press, 2006.

'Huberta.' Amathole Museum. 2018. museum.za.net/index.php/displays/huberta.

Snakes on a boat

'Battle of Ager Falernus/Carthaginian' Wikipedia: the Free Encyclopedia. 13 May 2018. en.wikipedia.org/wiki/Battle_of_Ager_Falernus.

Sabin, Philip. 'The Cambridge History of Greek and Roman Warfare' *Cambridge University Press*, Volume 1 (2007). Pages 441-442.

Campbell, Brian and Lawrence A. Tritle.'The Oxford Handbook of Warfare in the Classical World' *The Oxford University Press*, (2013). Page 194.

'Fightin' Fauna: 6 Animals of War' Britannica. 2018. URL: britannica.com/list/6-animals-of-war.

Ruffling the enemy's feathers

Beevor, Antony. *The Battle for Spain: The Spanish Civil War 1936-1939* Phoenix Books, 1 June 2006.

Thomas, Hugh. 'The Spanish Civil War'. Revised Edition. London: Penguin, 2001.

'Siege of Santuario de Nuestra Señora de la Cabeza.' Wikipedia: the Free Encyclopedia. 3 Feburary 2018. en.wikipedia.org/wiki/Siege_of_Santuario_de_Nuestra_Se%C3%B1ora_de_la_Cabeza.

On their high horse

K. Sagala, Sandra. 'Buffalo Bill v. Doc Carver: The Battle Over the Wild West.' *Nebraska State Historical Society* (2004).

'William Frank Carver.' Wikipedia: the Free Encyclopedia 13 December 2017. en.wikipedia.org/wiki/William_Frank_Carver#cite_note-Sagala1-3.

Trimble, Marshall. 'Who was Doc Carver?' *True West.* 9 December 2014. Accessed 2018. truewestmagazine.com/who-was-doc-carver/.

Drury, Flora. 'The mane attraction, 1920s-style' *Daily Mail*, 20 March 2015. Accessed 2018.

Kent, Bill. 'The Horse Was in Charge' *New York Times.* 4 May 1997. Accessed 2018.

nytimes.com/1997/05/04/nyregion/the-horse-was-in-charge.html.

Goldberg, Barbara. 'Atlantic City high-diving horses revival scrapped after protests' *Reuters*, 16 February 2012. Accessed 2018. reuters.com/article/uk-usa-horses-diving-idUSL-NE81F01020120216.

Footage: 'Diving Horse (from a 60ft platform)' British Pathé.

'Sonora Webster Carver.' Wikipedia: the Free Encyclopedia. 6 February 2018. en.wikipedia.org/wiki/Sonora_Webster_Carver.

A horse of a different colour

Bondeson, Jan. 'The Feejee Mermaid and Other Essays in Natural and Unnatural History.' *Cornessl University Press* (1999). Pages 2–20.

Howey, M. Oldfield. *The Horse in Magic and Myth*. London: William Rider & Sons, 1923.

Grace Elliot. 'Marocco - the Horse Accused of Witchcraft.' English Historical Fiction Authors. 6 February 2014. englishhistoryauthors.blogspot.ie/2014/02/marocco-horse-accused-of-witchcraft.html.

'Bankes's Horse.' Wikipedia: the Free Encyclopedia. 1 March 2018. wikipedia.org/wiki/Bankes's_Horse.

Shakespeare, William. *Love's Labour Lost*, Act 1, Scene 2: 'the dancing horse will tell you'.

Laughed out of court & Not giving a rat's arse

Evans, E.P. *The Criminal Prosecution and Execution of Animals* London: W. Heinemann, 1906.

Cohen, Esther. 'Law, Folklore and Animal Lore'. *Oxford Academic*. February 1, 1986.

Longley, Sean. 'The Hartlepool Monkey.' *The Independent*, 29 February 2008. Accessed 2018. independent.co.uk/arts-entertainment/books/reviews/the-hartlepool-monkey-by-sean-longley-789385.html.

Leafe, David. 'The town that hanged an elephant'. *Daily Mail*. 14 February 2014. Accessed 2018. dailymail.co.uk/news/article-2559840/The-town-hanged-elephant-A-chilling-photo-macabre-story-murder-revenge.html.

J. Krajicek, David. 'Fed up' circus elephant Big Mary lynched for 'murder' in 1916' *New York Daily News*. 14 March 2015. tronc.com/gdpr/nydailynews.com/.

Humphrey, Nicholas. 'Bugs and Beasts Before The Law'. *Oxford University Press* (2002). Chapter 18.

L. Carson, Hampton. 'The Trial of Animals and Insects. A Little Known Chapter of Mediæval Jurisprudence' *Proceedings of the American*. *Philosophical Society*. Vol. 56, No. 5 (1917). pp. 410-415.

Teubner, Gunther. 'The Rats of Autun' Lecture on January 17, 2007. *University of Frankfurt*.

'Autun.' Autun Office de Tourisme. 2018. autun-tourisme.com/en/discover/autun.

Chapter 6

Aimin' high

L.A. Times Staff Reporter. 'U.S. presidential assassinations and attempts.', *Los Angeles Times*. 22 January 2014. Accessed 2018. timelines.latimes.com/us-presidential-assassinations-and-attempts/.

"Presidential Assassinations and Assassination Attempts." Thought Co. 2018. thoughtco.com/presidential-assassinations-and-attempts-10543.

James, Marquis. *Andrew Jackson - Portrait Of A President*. New York: Grosset & Dunlap, 1937.

C. Rohrs, Richard. 'Partisan Politics and the Attempted Assassination of Andrew Jackson.' *Journal of the Early Republic*. Vol 1, No.2. (1981) pp. 149-163.

Latson, Jennifer. 'How Divine Providence—and a Heavy Stick—Saved a President's Life'. *Time Magazine*. 30 January 2015. Accessed 2018. time.com/3676512/andrew-jackson-assassination-attempt/.

'This day in history. 1835 - Andrew Jackson narrowly escapes assassination.' history.com/this-day-in-history/andrew-jackson-narrowly-escapes-assassination.

'Maniac in Milwaukee shoots Col. Roosevelt; He ignores wound, speaks for an hour, goes to hospital' *New York Times*.

13 October 1912.

'It Takes More Than That to Kill a Bull Moose: The Leader and The Cause' Theodore Roosevelt Association. 2018. theodoreroosevelt.org/site/c.elKSIdOWIiJ8H/b.8090799/k.C003/Home.htm.

Remey, Oliver. Henry Cochems and Wheeler Bloodgood. *The Attempted Assassination of ex-President Theodore Roosevelt.* Wisconsin: The Progressive Publishing Company of Milwaukee, 1912.

Royal screw-ups

Vickers, Miranda. *The Albanians: A Modern History.* London: Tauris & Co, 1995.

Binder, David. 'Albanian Premier Shot' *New York Times.* 24 February 1924. Accessed 2018. nytimes.com/1982/01/03/world/us-aides-suspect-albanian-premier-was-killed.html.

"King Zog Returns Home – Albanians congratulate ruler on escape from assassins in Vienna.' New York Times. 21 March 1931. Accessed 2018. nytimes.com/1931/03/21/archives/king-zog-returns-home-albanians-congratulate-ruler-on-escape-from.html.

Cavendish, Richard. 'The events leading up to King Zog I's coronation on September 1st, 1928'. *History Today Magazine.* Vol. 58, Issue 9. (2008).

'King Zog of Albania Holds to His Throne in a One-Man Country' by G. E. R. Gedye, *The New York Times Magazine,* 5 September 1937.

'Zog I of Albania.' Wikipedia the Free Encyclopedia. 21 June 2018. en.wikipedia.org/wiki/Zog_I_of_Albania#cite_note-Shaw-12.

Thomas Murphy, Paul. ',' *The Express.* 16 September 2012. Accessed 2018. express.co.uk/news/uk/365118/The-men-who-tried-to-kill-Queen-Victoria.

Doran, Sarah. 'Who tried to shoot Queen Victoria? The real story of the 1840 assassination attempt' *Radio Times.* 9 October 2016. radiotimes.com/news/2018-06-28/who-tried-to-shoot-queen-victoria-the-real-story-of-the-1840-assassination-attempt/.

'5 Things You May Not Know About Queen Victoria'. history.com. 28 June 2013. history.com/news/5-things-you-may-not-know-about-queen-victoria.

'Queen Victoria's Would-Be Assassins' The Victorian Web. 2012. victorianweb.org/history/victoria/murphy.html.

'Cane that wounded royalty. Pate's infamous attack on Queen Victoria recalled to mind' *New York Times.* 15 January 1899.

'The Trial of Arthur O'Connor.' New York Times, 12 April 1872.

Paul Thomas Murphy. 'Arthur O'Connor's illness' Shooting Victoria. 1 May 2012. shootingvictoria.com/post/22207171834/arthur-oconnors-illness.

Barbara J. Starmans. '7 Assassination Attempts On Queen Victoria'. The Social Historian. 2015. thesocialhistorian.com/7-assassination-attempts-queen-victoria/.

'Giuseppe Marco Fieschi' The Notable Names Database. 2014. nndb.com/people/344/000102038/.

Aanslag door Giuseppe Marco Fieschi en zijn helse machine op de Franse koning Lodewijk Filips, 1835, anonymous. 1835 Diagram of Infernal Machine. rijksmuseum.nl/en/collection/RP-F-OB-88.600.

Bouveiron, A. *An Historical and Biographical Sketch of Fieschi.* London: Fb&c Limited 2015.

Description of 'Infernal Machine'. 'Giuseppe Marco Fieschi, the attempted assassin of King Louis-Philipp' *The Landmark.* 23 September 1835

'Giuseppe Marco Fiesch' Wikipedia: the Free Encyclopedia. 21 May 2018. en.wikipedia.org/wiki/Giuseppe_Marco_Fieschi#cite_note-Bouveiron67-68-6.

In the wars

de Piero Pietro, Umanita Nova. 'Gino Lucetti and his attempt to assassinate Benito Mussolini (Il Duce) 11 September 1926' ChristieBooks. 1986.

'Gino Lucetti' Wikipedia: the Free Encyclopedia. 19 April 2018. en.wikipedia.org/wiki/Gino_Lucetti.

Uncredited. 'El joven anarquista' The young anarchist'. El Territorio, 10 April 2015.

'Anteo Zamboni'. World Heritage Encyclopedia. 2002. worldheritage.org/article/WHEBN0008037096/Anteo Zamboni.

'Michael Schirru and the attempted

assassination of Mussolini'. February 2016. libcom.org/history/articles/murder-michael-schirru.

'Michele Schirru' Wikipedia: the Free Encyclopedia. 2017. it.wikipedia.org/wiki/Michele_Schirru.

McManus, Darragh. 'The Irish woman who shot Mussolini'. *Irish Independent*, 3 April 2016. independent.ie/life/the-irish-woman-who-shot-mussolini-34588698.html.

'The Irishwoman Who Shot Mussolini'. RTE Radio (Irish National Radio) documentary. Aired 21 June 2014.

'Census 1901: 'Residents of a house 12 in Merrion Square North (Trinity, Dublin)' The National Archives of Ireland. Accessed 2018. census.nationalarchives.ie/.

Uncredited. 'Profile: Violet Gibson, the Irish woman who shot Mussolini.' *Belfast Telegraph*. 2 April 2016. Accessed 2018. belfasttelegraph.co.uk/life/features/profile-violet-gibson-the-irish-woman-who-shot-mussolini-34591366.html.

McNally, Frank. 'A shot to nothing – An Irishman's Diary on the Dublin woman who tried to assassinate Mussolini'. *The Irish Times*. 9 Apr 2016. Accessed 2018. irishtimes.com/opinion/a-shot-to-nothing-an-irishman-s-diary-on-the-dublin-woman-who-tried-to-assassinate-mussolini-1.2603844.

Last, Alex. 'The German officer who tried to kill Hitler' BBC *World Service*. 20 July 2014. Accessed 2018. bbc.com/news/magazine-28330605.

'6 Assassination Attempts on Adolf Hitler' Hisroy.com. 29 April 2015. history.com/news/6-assassination-attempts-on-adolf-hitler.

Mort, Terry. *Hitler pornography plot: Hemingway at War: Ernest Hemingway's Adventures as a World War II Correspondent*. New York: Pegasus Books, 2016.

'The Final Attempts On Hitler's Life, Before He Killed Himself' War History Online. 20 July 2016. warhistoryonline.com/war-articles/clothing-rationing-wwii.html.

wikipedia.org/wiki/Heinrich_Grunow.

'Otto Strasser and Heinrich Grunow' *New York Daily News Photo Archive*.

Callan, Paul. 'Plotting against the Führer:

Meet the men who tried to assassinate Adolf Hitler' *The Express*. 1 October 2014. Accessed 2018. express.co.uk/news/history/137228/The-men-who-tried-to-kill-Hitler.

Worthington, Daryl. 'Hitler Narrowly Escapes Suicide Bomber' *New Historian*. 20 March 2016. Accessed 2018. newhistorian.com/.

Robinson, Martin. 'Death by chocolate: Revealed, the fiendish German WWII booby-traps' *Daily Mail*. 30 September 2015. Accessed 2018. dailymail.co.uk/news/article-3254580.

Reynolds, Paul. 'Nazis' exploding chocolate plans' BBC *News*. 4 September 2005. Accessed 2018. news.bbc.co.uk/2/hi/uk_news/politics/4204980.stm.

Losing the plot

Tacitus. 'The death of Agrippina' Book 14, Chapters 1-12 & Suetonius, Chapter 34.

Buckley, Emma and Martin Dinter. A *Companion to the Neronian Age*. New Jersey: Wiley-Blackwell, 2013.

'Agrippina the Younger' Wikipedia the Free Encyclopedia. 16 June 2018. en.wikipedia.org/wiki/Agrippina_the_Younger.

'Julia Agrippina, Roman Patrician' Britannica. 3 April 2018. britannica.com/biography/Julia-Agrippina.

Rex Brown, Stephen. 'Fidel Castro survived over 600 assassination attempts, Cuban spy chief said'. *New York Daily News*. 26 November 2016. Accessed 2018. tronc.com/gdpr/nydailynews.com/.

'Fidel Castro: Dodging exploding seashells, poison pens and ex-lovers,' BBC *News*. 27 November 2016. Accessed 2018. bbc.com/news/world-latin-america-38121583.

Campbell, Duncan. 'Close but no cigar: how America failed to kill Fidel Castro' *The Guardian*. 26 November 2016. Accessed 2018. theguardian.com/world/2016/nov/26/fidel-castro-cia-cigar-assasination-attempts.

'Assassination Attempts on Fidel Castro' Wikipedia: the Free Encyclopedia. 21 June 2018. wikipedia.org/wiki/Assassination_attempts_on_Fidel_Castro.

Paton Walsh, Nick. 'Book tells how John Wayne survived Soviet assassination'. *The Guardian*. 1 August 2003. Accessed

2018. theguardian.com/world/2003/aug/01/film.russia.

'Stalin tried to kill John Wayne.' BBC News, July 2003.

'Sindercombe, Miles,' *Dictionary of National Biography*, 1885-1900, Vol. 52.

'Twenty-Two Turbulent Years 1639-1661' by David C. Wallace, Page 160-161 (Fastprint Publishing, 2013).

'Miles Sindercombe, d.1657': British Civil Wars, Commonwealth and Protectorate. bcw-project.org/biography/miles-sindercombe.

'The interregnum (AD 1648-1660) : studies of the commonwealth, legislative, social, and legal'. Frederick Inderwick, Pages 303-311 (Sampson Low, Marston, Searle & Rivington, London, 1891).

'Discipline and Punish' by Michel Foucault, Chapter 2, Page 54 (Vintage Books, a division of Random House, 1975).

'The Rise of the Dutch Republic - Complete (1555-84)' by John Lothrop Motley (Dent, 1909).

Balthasar Gérard: wikipedia.org/wiki/Balthasar_Gérard#cite_note-8.

Chapter 7
Never heard of her

constitutionfacts.com/us-declaration-of-independence/the-five-riders/.

biography.com/people/paul-revere-9456172.

paul-revere-heritage.com.

Paul Revere's deposition to the Massachusetts Provincial Congress, circa 1775.

www.findagrave.com.

Sybil Ludington, the Female Paul Revere: The Making of a Revolutionary War Heroine by Paula D. Hunt. Pages 187-222. *New England Quarterly Journal*, May 2015.

The Danbury Museum: The American Revolution and Sybil Ludington. danburymuseum.org/danburymuseum/Ludington.html.

Sybil Ludington, A Younger, Feminine Paul Revere. New England Historical Society. newenglandhistoricalsociety.com.

Getting the wrong angle

wikipedia.org/wiki/Pythagoras#cite_note-3.

Pythagoras: Dictionary of Greek and Roman Biography and Mythology, edited by William Smith (1849).

Pythagoras' theorem: BBC Bitesize KS3 Maths.

'"Sulba Sutra" of Vedic India and Pythagorean Principle of Mathematics' by Bipin R. Snah. academia.edu.

Astronomy and Mathematics in Ancient China: The 'Zhou Bi Suan Jing' by Christopher Cullen, Pages 74-80 (Cambridge University Press, 1996).

The earth moved

britannica.com/biography/Nicolaus-Copernicus.

'Aristarchus of Samos, the ancient Copernicus,' by Sir Thomas Heath (The Clarendon Press, 1913).

'The works of Archimedes,' by Sir Thomas Heath (Cambridge University Press, 1897).

'The Sand Reckoner'. Archimedes, Third century BC.

wikipedia.org/wiki/Aristarchus_of_Samos.

Ringing hollow

'Bell did not invent telephone, US rules,' by Rory Carroll. *The Guardian*, June 17, 2002.

'Ahead of Bell and Gray.' Uncredited. *New York Times*, January 22, 1887.

United States Congress H-Resolution. 269 on Antonio Meucci, 11 June 2002.

'A brief history of electroacoustics, pt. 1: The birth of electroacoustics and early telephones,' by Bjorn Kolbrek. Acoustics Research Centre Magazine, 22 June 2015. acousticsresearchcentre.no.

britannica.com/biography/Elisha-Gray.

wikipedia.org/wiki/Elisha_Gray.

Missing the fame gene

'Why does Charles Darwin eclipse Alfred Russel Wallace?' by Kevin Leonard. BBC News, February 26, 2013.

'The Alfred Russel Wallace revival club,' by Liz Leyden. *The Boston Globe*, 24 November 2013.

'Alfred Russel Wallace: A very rare specimen,' by Stephanie Pain. *New Scientist*, Issue 2942, November 2013.

Understanding Evolution, Berkeley University.

'Natural Selection: Charles Darwin & Al-

fred Russel Wallace.'
evolution.berkeley.edu/evolibrary/article/history_14.

Land ahoy
Captain James Cook (1728-1779): BBC History.
bbc.co.uk/history/historic_figures/cook_captain_james.shtml.
'The First Discovery of Australia With an account of the Voyage of the Duyfken,' by T.D. Mutch. Pages 31-34. Journal of the Royal Australian Historical Society, Vol. XXVIII., Part V. 1942.
Janszoon, Willem: Dictionary of Australian Biography.
gutenberg.net.au/ebooks15/1500721h/0-dict-biogI-K.html#jansz1
'Willem Jansz Lands on the Australian Mainland and Sets Off a Century of Dutch Exploration of the Region,' by Ellen Elghobashi.
wikipedia.org/wiki/Janszoon_voyage_of_1605–06.
Abel Tasman, biography: New Zealand History.
nzhistory.govt.nz/people/abel-tasman.
britannica.com/biography/William-Dampier.
wikipedia.org/wiki/Alexander_Selkirk.
'Alexander Selkirk - the Real Robinson Crusoe?' BBC History.
bbc.co.uk/history/scottishhistory/europe/oddities_europe.shtml.
'How Was Australia Named?': National Library of Australia: nla.gov.au/faq/how-was-australia-named.
'The Spanish quest for Terra Australis.': New South Wales State Library Archive.

Lost in space
'Girls Rebel!: Amazing Tales of Women Who Broke the Mold,' by Heather E. Schwartz. Pages 4-5 (Capstone Press, 2014).
'The first American woman in space said this was the dumbest question the media ever asked her,' by Julia Calderone. Business Insider Magazine, 2 February 2016.
'Russian female cosmonaut gets angry at 'hair' question in space press conference,' by Raziye Akkoc. NASA Video

of press conference, The Telegraph, 26 September 2014.
'Sally Ride and Valentina Tereshkova: Changing the Course of Human Space Exploration,' NASA, 14 June 2013.
nasa.gov/topics/history/features/ride_anniversary.html.
'Valentina Tereshkova, 76, first woman in space, seeks one-way ticket to Mars,' BY Robin McKie, The Guardian, 17 September 2013.
'Prominent Russians: Valentina Tereshkova.': Russiapedia.
russiapedia.rt.com/prominent-russians/space-and-aviation/valentina-tereshkova/.
Encyclopedia of World Biography.
notablebiographies.com/St-Tr/Tereshkova-Valentina.html.
'Russian astronaut becomes the first woman to walk in space,' by Seth Mydans. New York Times, 26 July 1984.

Glued to the seat
'Jackie's words echo thru years,' by Michael Daly. New York Daily News, 15 April 2007.
'Irene Morgan Kirkaldy, 90, Rights Pioneer, Dies,' by Richard Goldstein, New York Times, 13 August 2007.
'The Freedom Rider a Nation Nearly Forgot,' by Carlo Morello, The Washington Post, 30 July 2000.
'Before Rosa Parks there was Claudette Colvin, who deserves presidential recognition,' by Phillip Hoose. Portland Press Herald, 5 April 2016, via the Washington Post News Service and Bloomberg News.
'From Footnote to Fame in Civil Rights History,' by Brooks Barnes, New York Times, 25 November 2009.
'Negro Girl convicted: She Is Held Guilty of Refusing to Move to Back of Bus.' Uncredited. New York Times, 19 March 1955.
'She would not be moved,' by Gary Young. The Guardian, 16 December 2000.

Leading lights
'Thomas Edison and the Canadian connection of the Electric Incandescent Light Bulb.' Documentary, The History Channel.
'Lamp Inventors 1880-1940: Carbon Fila-

ment Incandescent.'
americanhistory.si.edu/lighting/bios/
swan.htm.
'Joseph Swan's lightbulb moment came
before Thomas Edison's,' by Dr. Ian West.
Letters, The Guardian, 19 January 2016.
'Descendants of North East inventor
Joseph Swan gather for centenary,' by
Tony Henderson. The Journal, 27 May
2014.
'James Bowman Lindsay'. Dundee City
Website.
dundee.com/dundee-ambassadors/inno-
vators/james-bowman-lindsay.html.
'A History of Wireless Telegraphy' by J.J.
Fahie. Page 13 – 25 (William Blackwood
& Sons, Edinburgh & London. 1901).
wikipedia.org/wiki/James_Bowman_
Lindsay.
'Obituary: Warren de la Rue,' by Huggins,
M.L. The Observatory, Vol. 12, Pages 245-
250 (1889).
wikipedia.org/wiki/Warren_De_la_Rue.
'Early Incandescent Lamps' by Edward J.
Covington. iar.unicamp.br/lab/luz/ld/
Lampadas/Early_Incandescent_Lamps.
pdf.
John Wellington Starr: 'History of Light
Bulbs - Development of Incandescent
Light Bulb.' historyoflighting.net.
'Robert-Houdin: the magic of the bulb':
interview of Sylvain Lefavrais with André
Keime Robert-Houdin.
mediologie.org/cahiers-de-mediolo-
gie/10_lux/houdin.pdf.
Woorward & Evans: 'Some bright ideas are
Canadian,' by Tom Villemaire.
historylab.ca/historylab_wp/some-
bright-ideas-are-canadian/.

Chapter 8

It all adds up

'The Irish man who discovered quaternion
algebra,' by Aoibhinn Ní Shúilleabháin.
The Irish Times, 26 October 2016.
britannica.com/biography/William-Row-
an-Hamilton.
'Sir William Rowan Hamilton.' Waterways,
(TV Series): The Royal Canal. RTE Television. October 2011.
'William Rowan Hamilton, a discourse,'
Iggy McGovern. Trinity College Dublin,
2005.
wikipedia.org/wiki/William_Rowan_
Hamilton.

The calculator kids

'Two Vermont Prodigies Astounded the
19th Century,' by Chris Costanzo. The
(Vermont) Herald, 22 December 2011.
'The Story of Zerah Colburn, Child Math
Wizard,' by Jane Brown.
The North Star Monthly (Vermont), March
2011.
'A memoir of Zerah Colburn; written by
himself.' (G&C Merriam, 1833).
'Truman Henry Safford,' by Arthur Sear-
le. Article in the Proceedings of the
American Academy of Arts & Sciences,
Volume 37.
'Obituary: Truman Henry Safford.' Un-
credited. The Observatory, Vol. 24, pages
307-309 (1901).
'Memorial Addresses: Truman Henry
Safford,' by Ernest B. Skinner. Pages
620–623. Transactions of the Wisconsin
Academy of Sciences, Arts and Letters ,
Volume 12, Part 2, University of Wiscon-
sin, 1901.

The Boy Fiend of Boston

'Singular Case in Boston A Mere Child
Pleads Guilty to Mutilating Other Chil-
dren.' Uncredited. Boston Journal, 21
September 1872.
murderpedia.org/male.P/p/pomeroy-jes-
se.htm.
'Jesse Pomeroy: The Boy Fiend of Boston.'
The Huffington Post, 12 February 2015.
'Shall Pomeroy Hang?' Uncredited. Boston
Daily Globe, 14 April 1875.
'Bay State Softens Pomeroy's Punishment.'
Uncredited. New York Times, 25 January
1917.
'The Wilderness of Ruin' by Roseanne
Montillo. Book Review by Kate Tuttle.
Boston Globe, 19 March 2015.
'Records show that Jesse Pomeroy did not
deserve sympathy,' by Louis Lyons. Daily
Boston Globe (1928-1960); 2 October 1932.
'The Autobiography of Jesse H. Pomeroy.'
Publisher unknown, 1920.

Bang, you're dead

'Kentucky 6-year-old tried for murder,' by
Andrea Tortora. The Cincinnati Enquir-
er, 5 March 2000.
'Mahan Case Finished in Kentucky, Is Be-

lief: Boy Apparently Free.' Uncredited. *The Cincinnati Enquirer*, 27 June 1929.
'Mahan Boy Called Before Court Again. 6-Year-Old Sentenced To Prison For Killing Playmate.' Uncredited. *New York Times*, 1 July 1929. murderpedia.org/male.M/m/mahan-carl-newton.htm.

Young blood
'The execution of Michael and Anne Hammond, ages seven and eleven.' *British Journal of Criminology*, 1965, volume 5, pages 198–207.
'The execution of children and juveniles,' with input by Michael Stern. capitalpunishmentuk.org/child.html.
Child Rights International Network: Minimal Ages of Criminal Responsibility Around The World. crin.org/en/home/ages.
Executed Today: 1629: John Dean, boy arsonist. 23 February. executedtoday. com/2011/02/23/1629-john-dean-boy-arsonist/.
'Top Five Notorious Hangings in the UK/John Dean,' by Lydia Smith. *International Business Times*, 13 August 2014.
'Sixty Spooky, Strange and Surprising Stories about Abingdon,' by Judy Stubley. Page 62 (Matador, 2013).
Tsarevich Ivan Dmitriyevich: Russian People Executed By Hanging. histropedia.com/timeline/jdqttpg9bg0t/Russian-people-executed-by-hanging. wikipedia.org/wiki/Tsarevich_Ivan_Dmitriyevich.
'Facing the Death Penalty: Essays on a Cruel and Unusual Punishment,' edited by Michael Radelet. Page 46-47, Hannah Ocuish (Temple University Press, Philadelphia, 1989).
Murderpedia: Hannah Ocuish. murderpedia.org/female.O/o/ocuish-hannah.htm.
'Death penalty for juveniles,' by Victor L. Streib. Pages 82–83. James Arcene (Indiana University Press, 1987). wikipedia.org/wiki/James_Arcene#cite_note-streib-1.
'Exonerated, 70 years too late,' by Ashley Collman, *Daily Mail*, 17 December 2014.

Toy soldier
'The Youngest Soldier In WWI Was A Serbian Boy, Aged 8,' by Nicola Budanovic. War History Online, 13 March 2016. warhistoryonline.com.
'Momcilo Gavric as an eight year old soldier in World War I. *The Telegraf* (Serbia), 4 October 2015.
'The forgotten youngest corporal,' by Саша Трифуновић, 21 September 2008. politika.rs/scc/clanak/56567/Zaboravljen-najmladi-kaplar-Momcilo-Gavric.
'Momčilo Gavrić - probably the youngest soldier in WW1.' Macedonia 1912-1918.

Puer ferus
'Elagabalus' Gibbon, Edward. Decline and Fall of the Roman Empire, Chapter VI (Strahan & Cadell, London, 1788-89).
'The Queerest Roman Of Them All - The Emperor Elagabalus,' by Harold Covington. (The Gay History Series, Lesson 10) (the Northwest Publishing Agency).
'Move over, Caligula! Book reveals the story of cross-dressing boy emperor Elagabalus,' by David Leafe. *Daily Mail*, 28 December 2011.
'Men Who Cultivated Their Eccentricity.' Uncredited. *New York Times*, 17 March 1929.
'Elagabalus Emperor of Rome,' by N.S. Gill. ancienthistory.about.com/cs/biocategory/a/elagabalus.htm. wikipedia.org/wiki/Elagabalus.

Chapter 9

Without a shadow of doubt
'Not pretty, but is it art?' Uncredited. *New York Times*, 22 August 1927.
'Pictures painted to 'show up' the critics bring fame to mythical modernistic artist.' Uncredited. *The Lawrence Daily Journal - World* (Kansas), 27 January 1931.
'International art hoax bared by Los Angeles author,' by Alma Whitaker, *Los Angeles Times*, 14 August 1927.
'Times Square and Other Stories,' by William Baer, p.37, 'Disumbrationism' (Abel Muse Press, 2015).

Aping the greats
'Art: Zoo story.' Uncredited. *Time* magazine, 21 February 1964.
'The Worlds Fastest Spookiest Smelliest Strongest Book,' by Jan Payne. 'The Most

Talented Chimp' (Buster Books, 2008).
'Pierre Brassau, Monkey Artist.' Uncredited. *The Gettysburg Times*, 13 March 1964.
thevintagenews.com/2016/11/06/pierre-brassau-the-chimpanzee-painter-who-fooled-the-avant-garde-world/.

Clever dicks

'Reconsidering the 'Obscene': The Massa Marittima Mural,' by Matthew Ryan Smith. *Queen's Journal of Visual & Material Culture*, Issue 2, 2009.
'Yes, this is a tree full of penises and, no, it's not a joke,' by Yvette Caster. *Metro 108 News*, 20 October 2014.
'Does this strange mural depict witches battling beneath a penis tree?' atlasobscura.com/places/massa-marittima-mural.
'Italian art experts accused of censoring phallic fresco,' by Nick Squires. *The Telegraph*, 21 August 2011.
'From Fertility Symbol to Political Propaganda - Decoding the Massa Marittima Mural,' by Andrew Lawless.
beyond-the-pale.org.uk/zxMassa.htm.
Greek Homosexuality, by Kenneth James Dover, pages 125–127 (Harvard University Press, 1978).
'Why the men in ancient statues all have small penises,' by Catriona Harvey Jenner. *Cosmopolitan*, 9 July 2016.
'This is why ancient statues always have small penises,' by Alison Lynch. *Metro 108 News*, 11 July 2016.
'The Clouds' by Aristophanes, written 419 BCE.

Big is beautiful

'Did Rubens make big beautiful?' by Dr Cordula van Whye, University of York.
bbc.co.uk/guides/zt6jq6f.
'What if the old masters' nudes were today's skinny models?' by Jonathan Jones. *The Guardian*, 11 March 2012.
Class in America: An Encyclopedia [3 volumes], edited by Robert E. Weir. Volume 1, Page 89-90, Body Image (Greenwood Press, 2007).

The naked truth

'Men with breasts,' by Jill Burke. 25 February 2011.
renresearch.com.
'Michelangelo: Naked Truths?' by Ann

Landi, Artnews, 1 February 2011.
'What the Good Book Didn't Say: Popular Myths and Misconceptions About the Bible,' by J. Stephen Lang. Page 14 (Kensington Publishing Corporation, 2003).
'Horns of Moses,' by Emil Hirsh and Max Schloessinger, *The Jewish Encyclopedia*.

Fit for a king

Histoire de secrets (History of Secrets): Marie-Louise O' Murphy.
'In the court of the Sun King's son,' by Frank McNally. *The Irish Times*, 13 April 2013.
'Boucher, Francois: Mademoiselle O Murphy (1751), The Independent's Great Art series,' by Tom Lubbock. *Independent*, 17 July 2008.
'Louisa O'Murphy: Louis XV's Irish mistress.' Published in *18th – 19th Century History*, Issue 1, January/February 2006, Volume 14.
historyireland.com.

Shock, horror

'A Man Who Loved Women: Titian, an art historian argues, painted women sexy, respectable and in charge of the situation,' by Garry Wills. *New York Times Books*, 1 March 1998.
'Pornography for the prude.' Uncredited. *Evening Standard*, January 2008.

Venus of Urbino

wikipedia.org/wiki/Venus_of_Urbino.
'Mark Twain Looks at Titian's Venus.' 2 July 2010.
artmodel.wordpress.com/2010/07/02/mark-twain-looks-at-titians-venu/.
"Phallic symbols' found hidden in famous Pre-Raphaelite painting 'Isabella' by John Everett Millais,' by Nick Clark. *Independent*, 10 September 2012.
'Tate Britain exhibition to uncover sexy, dangerous side of the Pre-Raphaelites,' by Mark Brown. *The Guardian*, 10 September 2012.

Art to die for

'FDR's Final Days.' Television Documentary, The History Channel, August, 2009.
wikipedia.org/wiki/Unfinished_portrait_of_Franklin_D._Roosevelt

Priceless tales

'Antiques Roadshow portrait revealed to be by Anthony Van Dyck,' BBC News, 29 December 2013.

'The £6million TV stand,' by Paul Harris. *Daily Mail*, 10 July 2013.

'7 Great Scandals In Art' *The Blot* magazine, 20 April 2015.

'Ben – the man who binned a Lowry ...' *Manchester Evening News*, 4 March 2010.

'I threw away Lowry sketches worth thousands of pounds,' by Ben Timperely, *The Guardian*, 10 April 2010.

The Golden Buddha:

'The Golden Buddha at Wat Traimit,' by Jeffrey Miller. *The Korean Times*, 2 June 2005.

wikipedia.org/wiki/Golden_Buddha_ (statue).

A law unto themselves

'Shoelace costs museum dear as vases are shattered,'Charlotte Higgins. *The Guardian*, 31 January 2006.

'Seven art blunders to rival Taiwanese boy who punched hole in £1m painting,' by David Hodari. *The Telegraph*, 25 August 2015.

'The Mona Lisa is stolen from the Louvre: The theft of the most famous painting in the world on August 21st, 1911, created a media sensation,' by Richard Cavendish. *History Today*, Volume 61, Issue 8, August 2011.

'100 Years Ago: The Mastermind Behind the Mona Lisa Heist,' by Jeff Nilsson. *The Saturday Evening Post*, 7 December 2013.

'Who stole the Mona Lisa?' by Simon Kuper. Financial Times, 5 August 2011.

wikipedia.org/wiki/Mona_Lisa.

'Salvador Dali Original Hangs in N.Y. Rogues' Gallery,' by Robert Tanner. *Los Angeles Times*, 10 May 1998.

'A Dali Vanishes From Rikers Island,' by Susan Saulny. *New York Times*, 2 March 2003.

'Art Too Tempting at Rikers; Plot to Steal a Dalí Was Far From a Masterpiece,' by Paul Von Zeilbauer. *New York Times*, 4 October 2003.

'Warden Sentenced for Stealing Dali Painting From Rikers Island Jail,' by Matthew T. Clarke. *Prison Legal News*, 15 July 2004.

Chapter 10

Carved in stone

'Pompeii's Graffiti and the Ancient Origins of Social Media,' by Adrienne Lafrance. *The Atlantic*, 29 March 2016.

'What can we learn from Roman graffiti?' Harry Mount. *The Telegraph*, 1 August 2013.

'An Introduction to Wall Inscriptions from Pompeii and Herculaneum' by Rex Wallace (Bolchazy-Carducci Inc. 2005).

pompeionline.net/pompeii/graffiti.htm.

pompeiana.org/Resources/Ancient/ Graffiti_from_Pompeii.htm.

Chapter 11

Eighteen hundred and froze to death

'Eighteen-hundred-and-froze-to-death: 1816, The Year Without a Summer,' by Shirley T. Wajda (Curator of History at the Michigan State University Museum). connecticuthistory.org.

'1816, the Year Without a Summer.' BBC Radio 4 Program, 21 April 2016.

'Summer of 1816: 'Eighteen Hundred and Froze to Death,' by Ann Marie Linnabery. *Niagara Gazette*, 4 Jun3 2016.

'Eighteen Hundred and Froze-to-death: A Legend of 1816,' by Ernest Vinton Brown (Junius Press, 1934).

wikipedia.org/wiki/Year_Without_a_ Summer.

In the drink

'What really happened in the London Beer Flood 200 years ago?' by Rory Tingle. *Independent*, 17 October 2014.

The Gentleman's magazine: and historical chronicle from July to December, 1814. Page 390, by Sylvanus Urban, Gentleman.

historychannel.com.au/this-day-in-history/london-beer-flood/.

'It's 202 years to the day since the London Beer Flood killed eight people,' by Georgia Diebelius. *Metro 108 News*, 17 October 2016.

thehistorypress.co.uk/articles/the-london-beer-flood/.

regrom.com/2017/01/18/regency-events-the-london-beer-flood-of-1814/.

Black death

'Molasses tank explosion injures 50 and kills 11.' Uncredited. *Boston Daily Globe*,

16 January 1919.

'12 killed when tank of molasses explodes; hugh (sic) sheets of steel, hurled through air, destroy structures on Boston waterfront.' Uncredited. *New York Times*, 16 January 1919.

'Nearly a century later, structural flaw in molasses tank revealed,' by Peter Schworm, *Boston Globe*, 14 January 2015.

'What we know about the Great Molasses Flood of 1919,' by Jaclyn Reiss. *Boston Globe*, 15 January 2017.

'Incredible physics behind the deadly 1919 Boston Molasses Flood,'by Jennifer Ouellette. *New Scientist*, 24 November 2016.

'A Sticky Tragedy: The Boston Molasses Disaster,' by Chuck Lyons. *History Today*, Volume 59, Issue 1. January 2009.

The Earth's venom

'Volcano destroys West Indian town, dead may number 25,000.' Uncredited. *New York Times*, 9 May 1902.

'The calamity in Martinique.' Uncredited. *New York Times*, 10 May 1902.

'Three minutes of horror when 30,000 perished,'by Robin McKie. *The Guardian*, 28 April 2002.

'Mount Pelée, Martinique 1902-2002,' by Christina Reed. *Geotimes*, May 2002. geotimes.org/may02/geophen.html.

'Volcanic eruption buries Caribbean city. 1902.' This Day in History. The History Channel.

'How One Man Survived the Mount Pelée Eruption that Wiped Out 30,000 People,' by Karl Fabricius. *Scribol Online Magazine*, 28 June 2011. scribol.com.

wikipedia.org/wiki/Mount_Pelée.

Dead in the water

'Remebering (sic) Sultana,' by Stephen Ambrose. *National Geographic*, 1 May 2001.

'Sultana: A Tragic Postscript to the Civil War,' by Jerry O. Potter. *American History Magazine*, August 1998.

'Dreadful disaster: Explosion of a Mississippi Steamer Fourteen Hundred Lives Supposed to be Lost.' Uncredited. *New York Times*, 29 April 1865.

'Loss of the Sultana and Reminiscences of Survivors,' by the Rev. Chester D. Berry (Lansing, Michigan, 1892).

wikipedia.org/wiki/Sultana_(steamboat).

Dancing with death

'Dancing death,' by John Waller. BBC Radio 4, 12 September 2008.

'What was the dancing plague of 1518?' by Evan Andrews. Ask History, The History Channel, 14 September 2014.

'Dancing Plague' and other odd afflictions explained,' by Jennifer Viegas, *Discovery News*, 1 August 2008.

oddlyhistorical.com/2014/10/03/dancing-plagues-mass-hysteria-middle-ages/.

Hanging in the balance

'The Man They Couldn't Hang,' by Geoffrey Scott. *Sydney Morning Herald*, 26 September 1953.

'Joseph Samuels and James Hardwicke hanging.' Uncredited. *Sydney Gazette*, 2 October 1803.

'The Australian People: An Encyclopedia of the Nation, Its People and Their Origins,' edited by James Jupp. Page 525 (Cambridge University Press, 2001).

'Mystery solved in time for Police Remembrance Day,' by Gemma Jones, *Daily Telegraph* (Sydney), 27 September 2007.

Projectiles on the brain

wikipedia.org/wiki/Gryazev-Shipunov_GSh-6-23.

'Phineas Gage: Neuroscience's Most Famous Patient,' by Steve Twomey. *Smithsonian* magazine, January 2010.

'Old Accident Points to Brain's Moral Center,' by Sandra Blakeslee. *New York Times*, 24 May 1994.

'Phineas Gage and the effect of an iron bar through the head on personality,' by Mo Costandi. *The Guardian*, 8 November 2010.

'Lessons of the brain: The Phineas Gage story,' by Ned Brown. *Harvard University Gazette*, 29 October 2015.

Breaking the fall

'Promising Lives Cut Short.' *International Ministries* Magazine On Location, Winter 2013.

'Infant survives leap in Dad's arms from fiery plane' Uncredited. *Chicago Tribune*, 1 February 1947.

'Picture power: Fire-escape drama.' BBC News, 30 September 2005.

'A mother and her daughter falling from a fire escape, 1975.' Photograph by Stanley Forman. Rare Historical Photos. rarehistoricalphotos.com/mother-daughter-falling-fire-escape-1975/.
'Falling babies.' Uncredited. *Time* magazine, 17 October 1938.

Don't lose your head
'Beside the Guillotine,' by Herman Winfield. *The Lodi Sentinel* (California), 30 August 1910.
wikipedia.org/wiki/Cult_of_Reason#cite_note-Schama778-15.
'M. de Chateaubrun, sauvé de la guillotine.' Uncredited. *La Marachine Normandie.* shenandoahdavis.canalblog.com/archives/2013/10/04/28148615.html.
'A Flight from Death,' by James Bralnard. *Jefferson County Journal*, 19 September 1912.

Skirting death
'Rash act was the result of a lovers quarrel' *The Bristol Magpie*, 16 May 1885.
'Skirt that turned into a parachute.' Uncredited. *Bristol Evening Post*, 4 December 2014.
'The Bristol Book of Days,' by D. G. Amphlett. 8 May (The History Press, 2011).
Clifton Suspension Bridge: Mysterious Britain. mysteriousbritain.co.uk/england/avon/hauntings/clifton-suspension-bridge.html.
brisray.com/bristol/bagorge1.htm.

Not quite dead, and buried
findagrave.com/cgi-bin/fg.cgi?page=gr&GRid=109705734.
'Buried Alive: The Terrifying History of Our Most Primal Fear,' by Jan Bondeson. Pages 259–261 (W.W. Norton & Company, 2001).
'A Fate Worse Than Death,' by Susan Adams. *Forbes Magazine*, 5 March 2001.
alchetron.com/Angelo-Hays-1707416-W.
The Birmingham Conservation Trust. 'A life-preserving coffin in doubtful cases of death', by Julia Webb, 3 May 2013.

Chapter 12
'Dictionary of Buckish Slang, University Wit and Pickpocket Eloquence,' Francis Grose (C. Chappel, Pall Mall, London, 1811).

'31 Adorable Slang Terms for Sex from the Last 600 Years,' by Arika Okrent. mentalfloss.com.
'How 'Netflix and chill' became code for casual sex,' by Oscar Ricket. *The Guardian*, 29 September 2015.

Businesswomen
'City of Sin: London and its Vices,' by Catharine Arnold (Simon & Schuster, 2010).
'London - The Wicked City: A Thousand Years of Prostitution and Vice,' by Fergus Linnane (Robson Books, 2007).
'Corpus Linguistics and 17th-Century Prostitution,' by Anthony McEnery, Helen Baker. Page 104-105 (Bloomsbury Academic, 2016).
wikipedia.org/wiki/Bawdy_House_Riots_of_1668.
'The Origin of Religions: An Open-Eyed Journey Through a Mystic World,' by B. K. Karkra. Page 125 (Authorhouse, 2012).
'La Maison de Madame Gourdan,' by Eugene Defrance (Societé de Mercure de France, 1908).
wikipedia.org/wiki/Marguerite_Gourdan.
'The Everleigh Club,' by Louise Kiernan. *Chicago Tribune*, 24 January 2016.
'The Golden Age of Chicago Prostitution,' by Melissa Lafsky. *Freakonomics* magazine, 1 August 2007.
'Everleigh Sisters: American Madams.' britannica.com/biography/Everleigh-sisters.
chicagology.com/notorious-chicago/everleigh/.

Working girls
'The Curious Case of Nashville's Frail Sisterhood,' by Angela Serratore. *Smithsonian* magazine, 8 July 2013.
'Dangerous Liaisons: Working Women and Sexual Justice in the American Civil War,' by E. Susan Barber and Charles F. Ritter. *European Journal of American Studies.* Volume 10, No. 1, 2015.
'Prostitution and the Civil War,' by Annika Jensen.
gettysburgcompiler.com/2016/03/28/prostitution-and-the-civil-war/.
wikipedia.org/wiki/Joseph_Hooker.
maggiemcneill.wordpress.com/2010/07/31/phryne/.

britannica.com/biography/Phryne. 'The Most Infamous Courtesan in Ancient Greece.' 31 August 2015.

ancienthistory.about.com.

'The Deipnosophists,' by Athenaeus. Book 13, Pages 589-599. Written 3rd cent. AD.

'An Introduction to Wall Inscriptions from Pompeii and Herculaneum' by Rex Wallace (Bolchazy-Carducci Inc. 2005).

'Theodora: the empress from the brothel,' by Stella Duffy. *The Guardian*, 10 June 2010.

'The Secret History of Procopius, tr. by Richard Atwater, Chapter 10 (Covici-Friede, New York, 1927).

Theodora: Encyclopedia of World Biography.

'Veronica Franco. Poems and Selected Letters,' edited and translated by Ann Rosalind Jones and Margaret F. Rosenthal (The University of Chicago Press, 1998).

dornsife.usc.edu/veronica-franco/biography/.

maggiemcneill.wordpress.com/2013/04/18/skittles/.

'10 of the Most Famous Prostitutes in History,' by Jennifer Wirth.

allday.com/10-of-the-most-famous-prostitutes-in-history-2180813134.html.

'Letters to the editor,' *The Times*, 16 July 1862.

Party animals

'Science and Technology in World History, Volume 3,' by David Deming. Page 60 (McFarland & Co., North Carolina, 2012).

'Pope Hosts Scandalous Ballet of Chestnuts.'

historychannel.com.au.

wikipedia.org/wiki/Cesare_Borgia

'Friction and Fantasy: Opening Pandora's Box,' by Ramon Pinon Jr. Pages 52-53 (Strategic Book Publishing, Texas, 2014).

Phillip Stubbes' Anatomy of Abuses in England in Shakespere's Youth, A.D. 1583 (N. Trubner, London, 1877-79).

'History of the Celts,' by Clayton N Donoghue. Pages 55-58 (Friesen Press, Canada, 2013).

'The Religion Of The Ancient Celts,' by J. A. MacCulloch. Chapter 18, Festivals, Bealtane (T.T. Clark, Edinburgh, 1911).

'Sex and booze figured in Egyptian rites,' by Alan Boyle. NBC News, 30 October 2006.

'Hatshepsut: From Queen to Pharaoh,' by

Metropolitan Museum of Art (New York N.Y.). Pages 182-183 (Yale University Press, 2006).

britannica.com/place/Dayr-al-Bahri.

'The Etruscan World,' edited by J MacIntosh Turfa. Pages 427-429 (Routledge, Oxfordshire, 2013).

mysteriousetruscans.com/theopompus/.

'The Hell Fire Caves,' by Katy Lewis. BBC Home, 9 September 2008.

'Hell Fire Club,' by Marjie Bloy, Ph.D., Senior Research Fellow, Victorian Web. victorianweb.org/history/pms/hellfire. html.

wikipedia.org/wiki/Francis_Dashwood,_11th_Baron_le_Despencer.

hellfirecaves.co.uk/?id=30.

Scarlet women

biography.com.

'The Poet and the Vampyre,' by Andrew McConnell Stott. Chapter 10 (Pegasus Books, 2014).

'The Art of the Seductress' by Arthur Berger. Page 70 (iUniverse, 2001).

wikipedia.org/wiki/Praskovya_Bruce.

'Catherine the Great and Potemkin: The Imperial Love Affair,' by Simon Sebag Montefiore. Chapter 11, Anna Protasova (Orion, 2010).

'The Divorcing Kid,' by Brenda Maddox, *New York Times*, 19 November 1995

'All for Love - The Life of Jane Digby.' 25 October 2007.

scandalouswoman.blogspot.ie/2007/10/all-for-love-life-of-jane-digby.html.

A *Scandalous Life: The Biography of Jane Digby* (Harper Press, June 2003).

'In Bed with the Romans,' by Paul Chrystal. Chapter 17 (Amberley Publishing, 2015).

'Matriarchal Marketing: The Emperor, The Empress, and The Army,' by Jenni Royce. *The Sunoikisis Journal*, Harvard, 27 April 2013.

Historia Augusta - The Life of Marcus Aurelius, Part 2. Author unknown. 4th century.

'Roman's palace of deparavity,' by Zoe Brennan. *Daily Mail*, 18 August 2006.

'Julia the Elder - The scandalous daughter of Rome's finest emperor,' by Max Paschall.

forumancientcoins.com/Articles/Julia_the_Elder.htm.

britannica.com/biography/Julia-daughter-of-Augustus.

'Marie of Romania, beloved and controversial Queen of Romania.' 18 January 2014. touristinromania.net.

'Marie of Edinburgh, Queen of Romania,' by Taylor. 10 February 2017. historyofroyalwomen.com.

wikipedia.org/wiki/Marie_of_Romania.

Random sex

'Women and the Glorious Qurãn,' Gunawan Adnan. Page 35 (Universitätsverlages Göttingen, 2004).

'Women in Pre-Islamic Arabia,' by Muslim Women's League, September 1995. mwlusa.org/topics/history/herstory.html.

'Film Studies. The A-Z of the Birth of Cinema,' by Phil De Semlyen. Empire Magazine, 4 December 2013.

'Le coucher de la mariée : pantomime en un acte.' Short film by E. Fromont, 1895. filmsite.org/sexinfilms1.html

'Harris's List of Covent Garden Ladies,' by Jack Harris. Publisher unknown. 1787. etymonline.com/index.php?term=merkin.

'A short and curly history of the merkin,' by Gareth Francis. The Guardian, 26 June 2003.

'A Complete History of the Lives and Robberies of the Most Notorious Highwaymen,' by Alexander Smith. (1714) (G. Routledge & Sons Ltd, 1926).

'Rousseau's Queer Bottom: Sexual Difference in the Confessions,' by Angela Hunter (University of Arkansas, 2007).

'Friends of Rousseau,' by Leo Damrosch. Humanities Magazine, August 2012, Vol. 33, No. 4.

'The Enlightenment: History, Documents, and Key Questions,' edited by William E. Burns. Page 101 (ABC-Clio, LLC, 2016). wikipedia.org/wiki/Jean-Jacques_Rousseau.

'The Animal-human Boundary: Historical Perspectives,' by Shelby Cullom Davis Center for Historical. Page 141 (University of Rochester Press, 2002).

'1642: Thomas Granger and the beasts he lay with.' 8 September 2008. executedtoday.com.

'In Bhutan, Phallus Worship Revives Among New Generation Of Religious Followers,' by Tara Limbu. Huffington Post, 3 March 2014.

'Drukpa Kunley,' by Kim Carson, May 2015: Tibetan Biographies. tibetan-biographies.wikischolars.columbia.edu/Drukpa+Kunley.

'India's Temples of Sex,' by Charukesi Ramadurai, BBC Travel, 7 October 2015.

'A Catalogue of Desire: The Erotic Sculptures of the Khajuraho Temples,' by Elanor Cunningham. theculturetrip.com.

wikipedia.org/wiki/List_of_children_of_Ramesses_II.

Maitresse-en-titre.

wikipedia.org/wiki/Maîtresse-en-titre.

'History's 12 Most Sex-Crazed Royals,' by Kar Shaw. Huffington Post, 29 November 2011.

britannica.com/topic/Mancini-sisters.

'Most outstanding sex records of all time.' Pravda, 16 October 2004.

'Herodotus, The Histories' edited by A.D. Godle. Ref: 1.199. Harvard University Press, 1920.

'The sex toys dating back 28,000 years,' by Victoria Woollaston. Daily Mail, 13 January 2015.

'Is this the world's oldest sex toy?' by Tom Phillips. Metro 109 News, 27 July 2010.

'Leather sex toy from 18th century discovered,' by Kate Pickles. Daily Mail, 15 April 2015.

'Lysistrata,' by Aristophanes. Written 5th century BC.

'The School of Venus, or the ladies delight.' Author unknown. Written 1680.